THE PEOPLE OF TIBET

A noble family of Lhasa tracing its descent for 1400 years

Seated on left, two small sons, who are Living Buddhas, with teacher behind and boy servants in front. Mother and brother's wife beside them

The
People of Tibet

Sir Charles Bell

MOTILAL BANARSIDASS PUBLISHERS
PRIVATE LIMITED • DELHI

First Indian Edition: Delhi, 1992
Reprint: Delhi, 1994, 2000

First Published: U.K., 1928

ISBN: 81-208-1049-x

Also available at:
MOTILAL BANARSIDASS
236, 9th Main III Block, Jayanagar, Bangalore 560 011
41 U.A. Bungalow Road, Jawahar Nagar, Delhi 110 007
8 Mahalaxmi Chamber, Warden Road, Mumbai 400 026
120 Royapettah High Road, Mylapore, Chennai 600 004
Sanas Plaza, 1302 Baji Rao Road, Pune 411 002
8 Camac Street, Calcutta 700 017
Ashok Rajpath, Patna 800 004
Chowk, Varanasi 221 001

Printed in India
BY JAINENDRA PRAKASH JAIN AT SHRI JAINENDRA PRESS,
A-45 NARAINA, PHASE-I, NEW DELHI 110 028
AND PUBLISHED BY NARENDRA PRAKASH JAIN FOR
MOTILAL BANARSIDASS PUBLISHERS PRIVATE LIMITED,
BUNGALOW ROAD, DELHI 110 007

TO

' THE YELLOW AND THE GREY

IN THE LAND OF SNOW '

THE CLERGY AND THE LAITY

OF TIBET

PREFACE

In an earlier volume [1] I have written about the history, and especially about the modern political position, of Tibet. The present book is an attempt to speak about the life of the people in their own homes.

The busy round of official duties does not allow much time for gathering knowledge about the social and domestic intimacies which form the well-springs of national life. But in Tibet we were at any rate fortunate in this that when, by one means and another, we had gained the friendship of the Tibetans, our official positions were no bar to friendly intercourse, as happens sometimes in other countries. On the contrary, they served as letters of introduction to this most exclusive of peoples. We had no wish to menace their independence, but rather to help them as far as conditions allowed. So we became friends.

I should not dream of attempting a complete study of Tibetan domestic life. A miscellany of facts, and occasional ideas to clothe those facts, are all that I can offer. But such as I have garnered during a residence of nearly twenty years, in conversation with my Tibetan acquaintances, I have obtained by speaking to them in their own language, not through interpreters. The latter both limit an inquirer's range, and lead, unconsciously, to many errors. I would fain hope that others also may continue to contribute from their store, so that in time the Western world may come to a fuller understanding of this remote but interesting people.

In order to keep this volume within moderate limits I

---

[1] *Tibet Past and Present.*

have had to exclude from it many aspects of Tibetan life. These I hope to deal with in a subsequent book or books. The religious life, indeed, in its highways and byways might well need a volume of its own.

Though the white man's life and customs were penetrating Sikkim, yet Lhasa and Tibet generally were, during the years of my residence, practically untouched. Shut off from the outer world by their immense mountain barriers, Tibet still presented a virgin field of inquiry. We could observe the real, inner life of the people, and that but little changed during the last thousand years. Now that the country is opening little by little, it will in course of time become increasingly difficult to separate the national ideas and customs from foreign importations.

The area of Tibet is large. Intercourse of one part with another is restricted, for the country is difficult and the means of travel are primitive. It follows that manners and customs vary in different districts and provinces. So a custom or interpretation need not be condemned as inaccurate because another sojourner has seen or heard it different elsewhere.

I write words as they are pronounced in Lhasa rather than after the complicated Tibetan spelling. One instance will suffice. The Tibetan name for Sikkim is pronounced *Den-jong* and I write it accordingly. The Tibetan spelling, transliterated in the usual style, is *Hbras-ljongs*. I feel sure that most readers will prefer the former.

The photographs are mainly my own. For permission to use others I am indebted to Mr. Macdonald, Mr. Martin, and Mr. Rosemeyer. To Mr. Tshering Phuntsog and Negi Amar Chand, and especially to the late Kazi Dausamdup of Gangtok, I am indebted for translations of

Tibetan and Bhutanese histories; to Mr. L. H. Dudley
Buxton, Reader in Physical Anthropology, Oxford, for
a sketch of the mountain masses of Tibet; to Miss M.
K. Grindrod for a careful index. And among my many
Tibetan friends who have aided me, the Tsen-drön, Ku-sho
Ne-tö, Ku-sho She-sur, and numerous others from the
Dalai Lama downwards, I must make especial mention
of Ku-sho Pa-lhe-se. Not only did he place his full and
intimate store of knowledge at my disposal during our
years in Tibet together, but he journeyed also from his
home in Lhasa to mine in Berkshire and checked the book
throughout, correcting errors.

NOTE

THE Tibetan words used in this book should be pronounced as in English, subject to the following limitations and exceptions:

a when ending a word or syllable as the *a* in *father*, e.g. *tsa-tsa*. Otherwise as *u* in *rub*, e.g. *Cham*, pronounced like the English word *chum*.

e when ending a word or syllable as *é* in French, e.g. *Rim-po-che*, *Dre-pung*. Otherwise as in English, e.g. *Den-sa*.

ö as *eu* in French *peu*.

u as *oo* in *root*.

ü as *u* in French *sur*.

ai as *eye*.

ny as the initial sound in *nuisance*.

ng and *ts* as in English. They are frequently used in Tibetan to begin words. Say *coming in*, eliminating the first four letters *comi*. Similarly, *weights*, eliminating *weigh*.

Hyphens have been freely inserted throughout the book to show where syllables end.

Amban denotes the high Chinese official stationed in outlying dependencies, or in regions claimed as such, e.g. in Lhasa or Sining.

Dzong. A fort, the head-quarters of a Tibetan district. In it reside the *Dzong-pön* or *Dzong-pöns* with their staff.

Dzong-pön, i.e. 'Governor of Fort'. The Tibetan official in charge of a district. In some districts one holds sole charge; in others two exercise joint control.

Kung. A hereditary title given to the father, or to one brother, of each Dalai Lama, corresponding somewhat to the title of *Duke* in England.

Ku-sho. Honorific form of address applied to the upper classes, especially to officials. Joined to *Cham*—or the higher form *Lha-cham*—it is applied to ladies also.

La = a mountain pass.

Chu = river.

Tso or *Nor* = lake. *Tso* is the Tibetan, *Nor* the Mongol word.

CONTENTS

CONTENTS

CONTENTS xiii

'Third Son Tamang'—Women's influence in government; chieftainesses and queens—Women in religion, signs of their inferiority,
blessed with tassel only, forbidden to enter Ta-lung Monastery, girl's in-
delicacy causes student to become a priest, Burmese women, women's
different outlook on religion—Religious services for women—Cases in
which women have shone in religion also—'The Thunderbolt Sow'—
Nunneries—Prophetesses.

LIST OF ILLUSTRATIONS

MAPS

I

GEOGRAPHICAL

THE people of Tibet do not call their country by this name. They call it *Pö*.[1] In early Arabian works it is termed *Tobbat, Tubbat, Tibat,* and other such variants. It is generally surmised by Western scholars that our word Tibet, with its variations, is derived from two Tibetan words *Tö Pö*[2] meaning Upper Tibet.

The country lies between India on the south and west, and China Proper on the east. To the north Chinese Turkistan and a narrow strip of the Chinese province, Kansu, separate it from Mongolia. The Tibetans and Mongols are of kindred race, of the same religion.

Tibet is the loftiest country in the world. More than three-fourths of its area lies over ten thousand feet above the level of the sea. Through large areas, especially in the north, plains and valleys range over sixteen thousand feet, higher than the summit of Mont Blanc, the highest mountain in Europe. These are ringed round by massive mountain ranges towering another four or five thousand feet into the turquoise Tibetan sky. And so it comes that, though its area is some eight hundred thousand square miles—more than fifteen times the size of England—its population is estimated at only three or four millions. You may ride for miles and miles on your sturdy Tibetan pony without passing a single human habitation.

It may well be imagined that these tumbled mountain masses of Central Asia, rising and falling, pressing in and spreading out, furnish the Tibetan with lands of various types. His mind's eye sees them in four classes, namely, *Tang* (Plain), *Gang* (Ridge), *Drok* (Pasture), and *Rong* (Valley).

Tang are the uncultivable plains and valleys lying

[1] བོད་   [2] སྟོད་བོད་

mostly at elevations higher than the loftiest mountain summits in Europe. Scoured by the wind, baked by the sun, and crackled by the frost, these desolate uplands have a rugged grandeur of their own, set as they are in the cold, clear air high above the haunts of men. Salt lakes abound. Mile upon mile is often covered with saline incrustation, making the ground so white in this rarefied atmosphere that travellers suffer as if from snow-blindness. Land of this type is chiefly found in the *Chang Tang*, the great plateaux in the north of Tibet, to be described presently.

Gang are the ridges like those round Gyangtse, as well as the cultivated plains which these ridges enclose. Eastern Tibet, too, is largely of the *gang* type.

Drok are the upland grazing-grounds. The country round Nag-chu-ka, north of Lhasa, is an example of *drok* land.

Rong are the valley areas, e.g. in the south where Tibet debouches into the Himalaya, and in eastern Tibet.

It will, of course, be understood that different classes of land are often combined in the same region. *Gang* may well give place to *drok* on one side, and to *rong* on the other.

An order of the Tibetan Government for transport from Lhasa to Gyangtse will specify *by the ridges*,[1] i.e. across the Kam-ba La and Ka-rö La; or *by the valleys*,[2] i.e. via Shigatse down the valleys of the Rong Chu, Tsangpo, and Nyang Chu.

European writers usually divide Tibet into three parts.

First, the Northern Plains (*Chang Tang*), extending from 80° to 92° east longitude and from 31° to 36° north latitude. These cover northern Tibet, a tangled mass of plains and valleys, lying at an elevation of sixteen thousand feet and upwards. It is too cold for crops, too cold for trees. On the fringes shepherds tend their flocks of yaks and sheep, living mainly on meat and milk products, for grain and vegetables are difficult to procure. Bands of

---

[1] *Gang-gyü.*   [2] *Rong-gyü.*

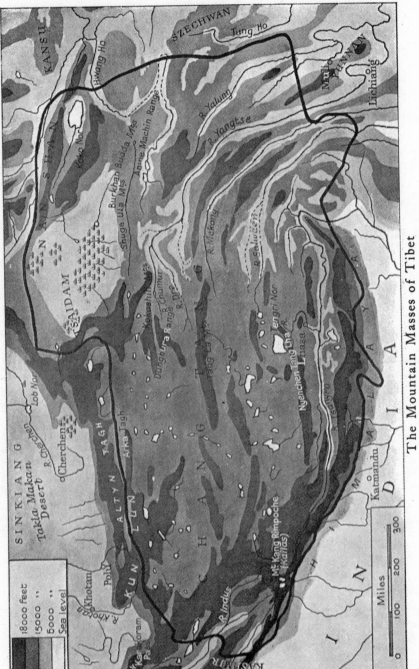

The Mountain Masses of Tibet

An approximate indication. Lakes are shown in white

brigands prey on unprotected travellers, especially in the inner reaches.

The Chang Tang is studded with lakes, but they have no outlets, and so their water is salt. Indeed, some of the lakes are known not as 'Lake' (*tso*), but as 'Salt Pit' (*tsa-ka*). Potash, borax, and soda are found in thick deposits round their shores. Hot springs sometimes gush forth in the vicinity, and are prized highly for the medicinal treatment which they afford. But hot springs abound throughout Tibet. The highest lakes in the world are found here. Many are over 15,000 feet above sea-level. Among these are the 'Sky Lake' (*Nam Tso*)—usually mapped under its Mongol name, Tengri Nor—on the fringe of the Chang Tang, with an area of 950 square miles.

The second territorial division is southern Tibet, containing the valley of the Tsang-po and its tributaries. It is usually called central Tibet because it contains the central (Ü) province with Lhasa the capital. The main route from the Chang Tang meets central Tibet near Tengri Nor and the great mountain range which Tibetans know as 'The Spirit of the Expanse of Great Fear' (*Nyenchen Tang Lha*).

Now we are among towns and villages. Here is Shigatse—the chief town in the Tsang province, which adjoins Ü on the west—here are Gyangtse, and Lhasa itself. To this central area converge trade routes from China and India, from Mongolia, Turkistan, and Siberia. Monasteries are dotted over the mountain sides and on the plains below; red-robed monks go from village to village, intoning prayers, collecting alms. The lower plains and valleys give crops of barley, mustard, and peas, with occasional wheat. And there are trees, but not many.

As the lakes of Tibet are the highest in the world, so the Tsang-po is perhaps the highest navigable river. For four hundred miles, at twelve thousand feet above sea-level, the light Tibetan coracles ply up and down its course. They are formed of yak-hide stretched on a frame of thorn scrub or willow.

To the south of this area are the wooded tracts where Tibet falls away into the Himalaya down valleys some ten thousand feet above the sea. This is usually classified as within this second territorial division, but buckwheat, maize, and other warmer crops flourish here; apricots and walnuts ripen; vegetables can be grown. Well-wooded, well-watered, it is a genial country of the true *rong* type, and merits a separate classification.

The last division is eastern Tibet. Here flow some of the largest rivers in Asia, including the Yangtse, which carries more water than any river in the world, excepting only the Amazon. The valleys in this area trend approximately north and south, and are deeply eroded. The average elevation of Tibet slopes downward from west to east. So it comes that the valleys here fall to an elevation of six thousand feet above sea-level, though the inhabitants live in the main at altitudes between nine and thirteen thousand feet. This is the most fertile part of Tibet. Agriculture does well; there are forests, plenty of water, good grazing. Mineral wealth—gold, silver, copper, iron, and lead—appears to be present, though hitherto undeveloped.

This area is known as Kam, the people as Kam-pa. Most of them are particularly fine specimens of humanity; hardy, too, and courageous. They do not, however, escape criticism at the hands of their countrymen, who charge them with fickleness. For the proverb says:

> Brother Kam-pa, though you think him trustworthy,
> Has not the long-tailed monkey's tail.

A long tail is the mark of steadiness. Of one who is steadfast in friendship or in other ways from year to year, men say, 'He has a long tail'.

Among the many states and provinces of Kam is the kingdom of Der-ge, whose subjects are the most skilled of all Tibetans in metal work; farther to the north-east the dreaded nomads of Go-lok, who live largely by brigandage. I have met them in other parts of Tibet, where they

Men and yaks clearing the road to the Chumbi Valley
under deep snow

Coracles on the Tsang-po

have come as peaceful traders. The people tolerate them as such, but keep a sharp eye on them, for the predatory instinct is deeply ingrained. In the extreme east is the province of Nya-rong, rich in minerals. The folk of Nya-rong, too, are turbulent and inclined to robbery. The chief border town between Tibet and China is Tachienlu, the trade depot where goods are exchanged between the two countries. It remains only to add that a large part of Kam is under nominal Chinese control. In southern Tibet much territory, e.g. Ladakh, Lahul, Sikkim, and Bhutan have been brought within the British-Indian orbit.

The lakes of the Northern Plains have been mentioned. But, except in eastern Tibet, there are frequent lakes throughout the country. The largest is Koko Nor on the north-eastern border, with an area of sixteen hundred square miles. Tengri Nor, already mentioned, is the largest in the interior, being only a hundred miles to the north-west of Lhasa. The Tibetan lakes tend to shrink continually, and their waters to become more saline.

In Sikkim there are now three races, Sikkimese, Lepchas, and Nepalese. The Lepchas are the earlier inhabitants of Sikkim who dwelt there before the first Tibetans arrived from eastern Tibet, and in their masterful way took over control of the country. These Tibetans, now long settled in Sikkim, may be called Sikkimese. The people of Tibet term them *Den-jong-pa*, i.e. people of *Den-jong*, the Tibetan name for Sikkim. Europeans and Indians style them Bhutias or Bhotiyas. This term is applied to all of Tibetan race, being derived from Bhot, the Indian name for Tibet.

The features of the Lepchas recall those of the southern branch of the Yellow Race. Their language is connected, though distantly, with Tibetan: according to their own tradition they came to Sikkim from the east. By nature children of the forest, they are versed in all forest lore. They know bird and beast, tree and shrub, flower, fruit, and fungus. Of the fungi they eat many varieties. Their character is gentle; they are easily taught.

Both Sikkimese and Lepchas are vastly outnumbered in Sikkim and Darjeeling by the Gurkhas of Nepal, many of whom have left their own overcrowded country to search for new homes where land is plentiful.

The rivers of Tibet are credited with strange performances. We are told in one of the most trustworthy of Tibetan histories[1] that a river was choked and flowed upwards for three days. A landslide, no doubt, but the Tibetan explanation is different. It was taken as an evil omen portending the fall of the reigning dynasty.

Though uncommon in Tibet, landslides are frequent in Sikkim. Here the old legend says that a river, having once upon a time been insulted, refused to pass on the water that it received. And so a flood enveloped the mountains and drowned all but a very few, who took refuge on a mountain that had lived a good life and thus was raised miraculously above the flood level. Even in prosaic modern times much damage is done by landslides in the Himalaya.

The rivers swell during the summer rains, adding to the toils and dangers of travel. During the nine months of dry weather a river will meander down its wide bed in a few narrow channels. But in July and August, and maybe in June and September, all will unite in one broad rushing flood. Another characteristic of Tibet is that streams frequently disappear into the ground.

A Tibetan place-name often gives you an indication as to the sort of place it is. Your destination is, maybe, *Pu-sum*.[2] *Pu* means the 'head of a valley', *sum* means *three*. You will find it, therefore, in the upper part of a valley with two other such valleys close by. With the name *Do-chen*,[3] we know that it lies in the lower part of a valley, which has broadened out. A pass called 'Black Pass' will certainly prove troublesome; one called 'The Vulture's Difficulty'[4] must be treated with especial care.

At the head of a valley near Lhasa is 'The Pass of the

---

[1] Tep-ter Ngön-po, vol. i, folio 25.　　　　[2] ཕུ་གསུམ་

[3] མདོ་ཆེན་, i.e. 'large lower part of valley'.　　　[4] གོད་ཁབ་ལ་ Gö-ka La.

Lepcha house in a forest in Sikkim

A Lepcha

In a Sikkim forest

A Gurkha boy in Sikkim

Iron Dagger' (Chak-pur La), so called because the ascent is steep and stony. The *iron* shows its stoniness, the upright *dagger*—used by priests for combating devils and driven into the ground—prepares one for an almost precipitous climb. But this once surmounted, the next on the road is 'The Saddle Pass' (Ga La). It is a grassy and gentle ascent.

The greater part of inhabited Tibet lies between altitudes of ten thousand and sixteen thousand feet. The rainfall is small, the Himalayan range cutting off most of the Indian monsoon. Tibetan tradition asserts that in times long past the rainfall and snowfall were heavier, and that cypress and other trees grew plentifully. Now, however, but little snow or rain falls between October and May.

The climate is thus dry and cold, and the air is marvellously clear, beyond the clearness of even the Swiss valleys. The sun is hot, but, when the sun sets, the temperature drops with surprising rapidity. When Colonel Kennedy and I were at Lhasa in 1921 the difference between the temperature in the sun by day and the temperature at night frequently amounted to over 80° Fahrenheit. During our year in Lhasa there was frost for eight months out of the twelve, then a short, hot summer with shade temperatures often exceeding 85°, the highest being 91°.

Tibet, in fact, is a very dry country, with consequent extremes of heat and cold. During the short summer there is considerable heat, but the nights are always cool. During the winter there is great cold, which is further intensified by the winds that rage during the latter half of the day. The dryness has the effect of raising the line of permanent snow. In Sikkim, south of the Himalaya, this finds its level round about seventeen thousand feet, but to the north, in Tibet, it is some two thousand feet higher.

You wake on a clear morning to a vision of yellow-brown rounded hills, and deep valleys, winding out into broad plains. The air is calm, the frost is keen, in the sky

not a cloud. It is indeed good to be alive. But by eleven
o'clock a wind rises. Two hours later it has deepened
into a gale, which sweeps unchecked across the wide,
treeless uplands of Tibet. As you ride across the plain,
your head bowed to the storm, you are frozen to the
marrow and begrimed with dust. Soon after sunset the
wind may abate, but sometimes continues to whistle
through half the night.

Thunderstorms are prevalent in Tibet during the rainy
season, especially in July and August. They are most
severe on the highlands of western Tibet and on the
Northern Plains.

It is worth noting that in Tibet, as elsewhere, the idea
prevails that a noise made on mountain peaks and passes
brings down rain. I was crossing the Lung-nak La, a
difficult pass in north Sikkim, during a season of excessive
rainfall. Some of my porters, on reaching the summit,
gave vent to shouts of triumph. 'The gods have conquered,' they cry, 'the devils are defeated.' Proper sentiments these, and in accordance with custom when crossing
a pass, but on this occasion the local headman restrains
them, saying, 'Do not make a noise, or rain will fall'.

There is a Tibetan work on geography,[1] written about
the middle of the nineteenth century, but it does not add
much to our knowledge of Tibet. It aims, indeed, at
being a geography of the whole world; but its statements
are often fanciful, especially when dealing with other
lands. Of Corsica, we read that 'The dogs of this country
are so large that people can ride on them'. Of Sicily, that
'There is a high mountain; from among its rocks a big
fire comes out. This goes to the ocean and returns to the
rocks. It does not burn grass or trees; but burns gold,
silver, copper and human beings. And there is a certain
kind of grass, which grows in no other place. If a man
eats it, he dies of laughter'. Tibetans like miraculous
interpretations; it is a trait deep down in their nature.

---

[1] *Dzam-ling Gye-she Me-long.* འཛམ་གླིང་རྒྱས་བཤད་མེ་ལོང་ །

II

HISTORICAL

'OUR account of the origin of Tibet,' said the Lord Chamberlain,[1] during my stay in Lhasa, 'is that it was formerly all under a sea or a lake caused by the flooding of the Tsang Chu.[2] The Buddha of that period cut through the Himalayan mountains away to the south-east and so the Tsang Chu flowed off, and Tibet rose above the water. Then the Lord of Mercy[3] took birth as a monkey at Tse-tang, and, living with a rock demoness, begat several children who played there. And so the place became known as Tse-tang, "the place of play", because the children played there.'

Thus in Tibet also, as in so many countries, we have the story of the Flood. Deep and narrow indeed are the gorges down which the Tsangpo flows through the Himalaya. They are even now so difficult of access that until recently they were entirely unexplored.

Western scholars are inclined to place the earlier home of the Tibetans on the north-eastern borders of the country in the vicinity of the lake known as Koko Nor. Philologically, the Tibetans belong to the same linguistic family as the Burmese. It would seem that the early Tibetans led an entirely pastoral life. The heavy-looking men with the rugged faces and the shambling gait, clad in fur caps and sheep-skins, who drive their sheep and yaks across the hills and plains, are probably the purest specimens of their race.

Legend relates that the earliest King of Tibet came from India about the first century B.C. During the reigns of his successors, as is believed, charcoal was burned, silver, copper, and iron were extracted from the ore, ploughs were made, the irrigation of fields introduced, and mining slightly developed. Coats of mail were brought into

---

[1] Chi-kyap Kem-po.   [2] The Tsangpo of the maps.   [3] *Chen-re-si.*

use. The religion of this period is that known as *Pön*, and appears to have been a form of nature worship. We know very little of Tibet during these early days, but the general picture is that of a virile race of nomads, from time to time over-running the territories of their neighbours.

It is to this legendary period that the great Tibetan saga or epic belongs. It tells of Ke-sar, the King of Ling, a country in Tibet or on the eastern border. The King of Hor, a neighbouring land, carried off Ke-sar's wife. A war ensued to recover the queen, in which Ke-sar was eventually victorious. The whole epic is full of tales of fighting and miraculous prowess. In his difficulties King Ke-sar is aided by a goddess,[1] his aunt, who helps him in his difficult undertakings, just as the Grecian and Trojan heroes are protected and guided by their gods and goddesses.

The epic is a long one, and is divided into three parts. There are no printed copies of it in Tibet, and but few manuscript copies. It is recited orally by both men and women, especially among the pastoral tribes. There are many who can recite it for days together without repeating themselves.

During the seventh century A.D. we come to the reign of a king who was one of the most famous, if not the most famous, in all the Tibetan annals. His name was Song-tsen Gam-po. He was at once a conqueror, a law-giver, and a religious reformer. His armies attacked neighbouring countries; they overran and conquered western China and Upper Burma.

During the reigns of the early kings Buddhism had penetrated gradually into Tibet; but it was not until the reign of King Song-tsen Gam-po that it gained a firm hold. He took to wife a daughter of the Emperor of China, as well as a princess from Nepal, and it seems to have been largely through the influence of these two queens that the king himself adopted Buddhism and

[1] A-ni Gung-men Gyal-mo.

established it in the country. Until that time Tibetan is said to have been purely an oral language, having no written characters. But in order that the Buddhist scriptures from India might be translated, it was necessary that writing should be evolved. The letters appear to have been based on the Indian alphabet as then used in Kashmir.[1] The king himself retired into seclusion for four years in order to learn reading and writing.[2]

Song-tsen Gam-po formulated a code of criminal law punishing murder, robbery, adultery, and other crimes. He inculcated the sixteen virtues:

(i) to have faith in 'The Chief Rare Ones' (*Kön-chok*);
(ii) to perform religious observances and to study;
(iii) to honour one's parents;
(iv) to respect the virtuous;
(v) to honour elders as well as those who are of high birth;
(vi) to pay heed to relatives and friends;
(vii) to be useful to one's own country;
(viii) to be honest;
(ix) to realize the proper use of food and wealth;
(x) to follow the example of those who are good;
(xi) to show gratitude to benefactors and to return their kindness;
(xii) to use correct weights and measures;
(xiii) to be free from jealousy and to be at harmony with all;
(xiv) not to listen to the words of women;
(xv) to be gentle in speech and acquire skill in conversation;
(xvi) to bear sufferings and distress with patience and meekness.

The form of Buddhism which was adopted was that which prevailed in the neighbouring country of Nepal, though China and Kashmir also, no doubt, contributed their influence. It was strongly mixed with nature worship, as religion always appears to have been in these

[1] Pu-tön Rim-po-che's Chö-jung, folio 111.   [2] Ibid.

mountainous lands. It is clear also that the Pön religion
had far too strong a hold over Tibet to be altogether
ousted by the new religion, even though the latter had the
powerful support of the king and his two queens.

The Buddhist missionaries introduced arts and customs
both from India and from China. The Tibetan people
learned how to make pottery, looms, and water-mills.
It is also averred that barley beer (*chang*), butter, and
cheese were then used in Tibet for the first time. The
king built the Potala palace at Lhasa, though on a much
smaller scale than at present. It was built as a fort: a plan
of it may still be seen on the wall in one of the entrances
to the modern Potala.

Song-tsen Gam-po's grandson introduced tea from
China, and this has become the national beverage of the
Tibetans, who drink from thirty to seventy cups of it
every day. In the years that followed, works on astro-
nomy, astrology, and medicine were translated from Sans-
krit and Chinese. Tibetan civilization and culture of the
present day are largely due both to China and India; to
the latter for the religious side, to the former in the main
for the material side. But we do not yet know enough to say
how far the Tibetans had a civilization of their own before
these Indian and Chinese influences impinged upon them.

Another of the great Tibetan kings was Ti-song De-
tsen, who, according to the Chinese histories conquered
much of western China and extended Tibetan rule over
India as far as the Bay of Bengal, which was known as
the Tibetan Sea. Ethnological and linguistic evidence
of this domination has been found.

During his reign the Tantrik Buddhist, Padma Sambhava, from Udyayana in north-western India, visited
Tibet, where he suppressed demons and founded the first
large monastery, the monastery at Sam-ye. In spite of
opposition among a section of the King's ministers,
Buddhism was now established on a much wider basis.
Padma Sambhava is also believed to have concealed a
number of sacred treasures. These were sometimes in the

nature of written prophecies, which his knowledge and prophetic power enabled him to lay up in places where each writing would be discovered, when people had become sufficiently enlightened to understand it.

This, the original Buddhism of Tibet, is known as the Red Hat sect. Padma Sambhava, often also known as Lo-pön Rim-po-che, 'The Precious Teacher', is its chief saint. His image may be seen in the place of honour on Tibetan altars as often as that of Gotama Buddha himself. It is a common saying in Tibet that the Lord Buddha himself would be helpless, unless the priesthood expounded his doctrines. By the middle of the eighth century A.D., when this teacher came to Tibet, the Buddha's doctrine had been greatly modified in India by Tantrik additions. It was this later phase of Buddhism that penetrated Tibet.

Ti-song De-tsen was followed by Mu-ni Tsem-po, who manifested the democratic spirit inherent in the Tibetan character by dividing the wealth of the country equally among all the people. The equality, however, soon vanished. It was done a second time with the same result. Yet again it was done for the third time, but it was found that the inequalities had become worse than ever, for the poor, being indolent during their time of ease, had lost the habit of working. After the third effort, the king's mother, who disapproved of these experiments, poisoned her son.

One of the foundations of Buddhism, as of Hinduism, is the law of Karma. To put the matter briefly, this ordains that as a man sows so shall he reap, both in this life and in future lives, for both Hinduism and Buddhism believe in the doctrine of reincarnation. How then can there be equal opportunities for all, since each must start where the deeds, good and bad, of their previous lives have placed them? And thus it was that the priesthood of Tibet explained the failure of the king's scheme.

The third and last of the great monarchs of Tibet was Ral-pa-chan. He, too, conquered the territories of his neighbours; he, too, promoted the cause of Buddhism, extending the priesthood and allotting land for their support. He appears, in fact, to have pushed the religion too vigorously, for when only forty-eight years old he was assassinated at the instigation of his brother Lang-dar-ma, who was at the head of the anti-Buddhist party.

The wars and the treaties between Tibet and China are recorded in the Chinese and Tibetan histories. An account of them was also engraved on two remarkable obelisks, which were erected at the time in Lhasa and remain to this day. One stands at the foot of the hill on which the great Potala palace is built. The other is just outside the main entrance of the temple. To the Tibetans such obelisks are known as *Do-ring*, i.e. 'Long Stone'. The same term is applied to three long slabs of stone. Two of these announce victories in war; the other—more recent though half obliterated—deals sorrowfully with an epidemic of small-pox.

Lang-dar-ma succeeded to the throne and did what he could to destroy the new faith. He himself was killed after a reign of only three years by a Buddhist priest, but the set-back to Buddhism continued for seventy years.[1]

The long line of Tibetan kings now came to an end. A period of civil war intervened. The country was split up into petty principalities, ruled by chiefs, the ruins of whose forts can still be seen on the mountain sides. When a chief died, his widow or daughter would sometimes succeed him and rule the little kingdom, and to this day are pointed out the forts in which these chieftainesses held sway. The position of women in Tibet has always been a good one.

Although Buddhism was officially suppressed by Lang-dar-ma, yet many Buddhist priests maintained religious services in their own homes with the approval of the laity around them. So when a forward movement commenced again some seventy years later, 'Ministers and priestly

[1] Tep-ter Ngön-po, vol. viii, folio 108.

Obelisk engraved with historical inscriptions below the Potala Palace

In the small house on each side is a stone slab announcing a victory

organizations arose in every place as if by magic',[1] as the chronicle informs us. Many Indian Pandits came to Tibet. The chief of these was Atisha from Bengal. They preached varying shades of doctrine and helped in the translation of Indian Buddhist works.

Later on, the native priesthood of Tibet developed in numbers and in strength. One of the most vigorous and picturesque of these was the poet-saint Mi-la Re-pa, i.e. 'Cotton-clad Mila'. He lived a life of extreme asceticism; clad in a single cotton robe he braved the Tibetan winters in caves among the high mountains. Intent on gaining Buddhahood before he died, he would not waste time by begging for food, but preferred to subsist for some years on the nettles which grew round his cave. So runs the story. His verses, often tinged with a humour of their own, are still read and heard with delight by Tibetans of all classes.

Towards the close of the thirteenth century the great Kublai Khan, the first Mongol Emperor of China, invited to his court the High Priest of the large Tibetan monastery of Sa-kya. The Hierarch converted the Emperor to Buddhism, and received in return the sovereignty of Tibet. Thus began in Tibet the rule of priest-kings. This first instalment of it, however, lasted for only seventy-five years, from 1270 to 1345. Invasions by Mongols and northern Tibetans continued, for Buddhism, with its softening influence forbidding the taking of life, had weakened the martial power of the nation.

Tibetan Buddhism, having been derived from the later and weaker phase of Indian Buddhism, neither the doctrines nor the priesthood satisfied the more ardent minds in the country. In 1358 there was born in north-eastern Tibet a man named Tsong-ka-pa, 'the Man from the Land of Onions'. He inaugurated a movement by which the priesthood were forbidden to marry or to drink wine. Monastic discipline was tightened up. He founded the large lamasery at Gan-den, twenty-seven miles east of

[1] Ibid., vol. iii, folio 46.

Lhasa. His disciples were known as the Yellow Hats, to distinguish them from the Red Hats of the existing priesthood. The sister foundations at Se-ra and Dre-pung, on the outskirts of Lhasa, were built by two other priests, who were thus linked with the great reformer as 'The Three Kings, Father and Sons'.

Tsong-ka-pa's successor was Gan-den Trup-pa. After the latter's death in 1474, his spirit was held to have passed into an infant born about the same time, and this child became his successor. He, too, died, and was rein-carnated in the same manner. His successor, Sö-nam Gya-tso, converted a large part of Mongolia to the faith. From the Mongol chieftain Altan Khan he received the title of Dalai Lama Vajradhara, 'The All-embracing Lama, the Holder of the Thunder-bolt'. Thus it was that the name Dalai Lama originated. From now onwards Buddhism increased steadily throughout Mongolia, and the title of Dalai Lama was held in turn by each head of the Yellow Church.

The fifth in the succession, i.e. the second after Sö-nam Gya-tso, was Lob-sang Gya-tso, who, through the assis-tance of the Oelöt Mongols, gained the sovereignty over the whole country. His reign lasted from 1641 to 1680. During his reign and the years that followed, the great Potala palace, which had been destroyed in previous wars, was rebuilt on its present lines. His chief minister, Sang-gye Gya-tso, established the administration of Tibet in general, and of Lhasa in particular, very much on its present lines. To the Lama and his Minister are due also the religious ceremonies which centre in Lhasa, and especially the festival of the 'Great Prayer' which draws worshippers each February from all parts of the country to the Holy City.

It was during the earlier years of the fifth Dalai Lama that the first Europeans entered Tibet. Some thirty years later, two entered Lhasa. The names of these were Johann Grueber, an Austrian Jesuit, and Albert d'Orville, a Bel-gian. From 1708 to 1745 a small settlement of Capuchin friars resided and preached in Lhasa. The mission was then abandoned, not from Tibetan opposition, but from lack of funds.

During the reign of the seventh Dalai Lama the Chinese were able to increase their influence in Tibet, and a subsequent invasion by the Gurkhas augmented it still further. Among the several petty kingdoms which occupied Nepal during the first half of the eighteenth century was one known as Gorkha, to the north-west of Katmandu. In 1760 the ruler of Gorkha succeeded in establishing his power throughout Nepal, and twelve years later these people—whom Europeans know as Gurkhas—captured Shigatse, the large town half a mile from Ta-shi Lhün-po. The Chinese Government dispatched an army composed partly of Chinese and partly of Tibetans, which drove out the Gurkhas, pursued them into Nepal, and overwhelmingly defeated them within a few miles of their capital. By this feat the Chinese influence over Tibet was for a time greatly strengthened. The British power had then become paramount in Bengal, and was growing throughout India, and so the Chinese took the precaution of closing Tibet to Europeans.

As but little space is available for this historical *résumé*, I must now pass on to the year 1904. Disputes had arisen between Tibet and the British-Indian Government. The latter were convinced that there was a danger of Russian influence being strongly established at Lhasa, and feared the consequent menace to India and to British interests in India. A British Mission was dispatched to Tibet under Colonel (now Sir Francis) Younghusband. The Tibetans refused to negotiate. The Mission eventually became an armed expedition and penetrated to Lhasa. The Dalai Lama fled, and the Tibetan Government left behind in the capital eventually concluded a treaty with the British representative, a treaty which, in conjunction with subsequent events, has led to a great expansion of British influence in Tibet.

The Chinese were, however, alarmed. They, too, invaded Tibet and penetrated to Lhasa. The Dalai Lama and his ministers fled during the night of their arrival, and succeeded in reaching India. Here he and his ministers were safe from their foes, received personal kindnesses, and were accorded the benevolent neutrality of the British Government. The British having been so recently their enemies, this kindly treatment caused a deep and favourable impression throughout Tibet. Moreover, the Chinese expedition was markedly less merciful than that of the British.

So when the outbreak of the Chinese Revolution in 1911 enabled the Tibetans to expel the Chinese from the greater part of Tibet, the Dalai Lama and his party returned to their country with feelings of friendliness towards the British and hostility towards the Chinese. Tibet—now at any rate—claims to be independent of China, and no longer sends a Mission to Peking.

III

SHEPHERDS AND HERDSMEN

THE men and women who graze the flocks and herds over the wide spaces of Tibet are, as I have said, probably the purest specimens of the race. So I will begin with them. They have herds of yaks and ponies, flocks of sheep and long-haired goats. Dogs they keep, especially mastiffs, cats too occasionally. To their own people they are known as *Drok-pa*.[1] Hardy, independent, cautious towards strangers, but hospitable withal, are these wandering folk with the far-away eyes. To many a weary traveller in the Tibetan wilds has the *drok-pa's* tent proved a welcome haven.

This tent is made of yak hair; the *drok-pa* and his family make it. In shape it is rectangular, often some twelve feet in length, but sometimes up to fifty feet. An aperture, about two feet in width along the middle of the roof, lets out the smoke, or some of it. Under this vent is a ridge-pole, supported by a pole at each end. The roof is stretched by cords, which are fastened to the sides and corners, pass over short poles some distance from the tent, and are then pegged to the ground. The lower edge of the tent is held down by iron pins or by horns of animals. Father Huc, the Lazarist missionary, who, with Father Gabet, visited Tibet and Lhasa in the middle of the nineteenth century, has aptly compared these tents to huge black spiders with long, thin legs, their bodies resting upon the ground. To keep off wind and snow a low wall of mud and stones, or of dry dung, is built round the tent.

In the centre, or near the entrance, is a large stove made of stones and mud. Dung is used as fuel, for the herdsmen usually live above the elevations at which trees can

[1] འབྲོག་པ་

grow. Along the walls, or stacked so as to form recesses, we shall find our friend's daily needs: cooking utensils, buckets and churns, rugs, saddles, and leather bags containing food. An ordinary tent affords a home to five or six persons, but many are larger.

The dress of both sexes and of all classes in Tibet consists of a very full gown (*chu-pa*), with a high collar and long sleeves. In the summer this is usually of the ordinary Tibetan cloth (*truk*) or of silk. A gown made of the cloth or serge, woven in Tibet, is far more durable than those of the machine-made foreign cloth. Though the wear be hard, it will last for five years. The winter gown is of sheepskin or of cloth lined with lambskin or wadded cotton. It is tied tightly round the waist—which among the Tibetans, it should be noted, is much broader than among our people—with a woollen or cotton band, and is puffed out above. In the capacious pocket thus formed are carried drinking cups and other odds and ends; perhaps even a small dog. The robe for laymen reaches to the knee, for priests and women to the ankle. Silk gowns often have collars of fur. In central and in parts of eastern Tibet the women wear aprons, woven in varied colours and often so broad that they nearly meet at the back.

Shirts are of cotton or silk; trousers—differing greatly in shape from the European garment—of silk or cloth.

The national boot is also of Tibetan cloth, felt, or leather of various colours, among which red is almost always included. It rises to the knee, with a slit behind the knee, and is tied with gay-coloured woollen garters, three or four feet long. The soles are usually of raw yakhide. There are no raised heels; toe and heel are on the same level.

The hats worn by men are of various kinds, but are usually fur-trimmed in winter. Most are of felt, but cloth hats are also common. One variety is somewhat in the style of a tam o'shanter. It is one of the old national hats of Tibet, is yellow in colour, and is known as *bok-do*.

Tibetans, high and low, may wear it; a villager going before one of gentle birth, a gentleman going into the town, visiting friends, &c. Such hats are made in various qualities. In central Tibet Homburg hats, imported from India, are growing in popularity.

The women wear ornate head-dresses, those of the upper classes being bedecked with pearls, turquoises, and corals on a wooden framework. The people of eastern and north-eastern Tibet go often bare-headed, indoors and out. But this custom is not followed by the inhabitants of central Tibet. When out of doors the man, as a rule, wears his hat, the woman her hat or her head-dress.

The dress of the priests differs from that of laymen. The gown is of maroon, its skirt is wide. Underneath are a shirt and waistcoat, both without sleeves. The upper parts of the boots are white. The head is shaved in nearly all cases. The caps are often peaked, and vary greatly in size and colour; the reformed sect wears yellow hats, the old sects wear red.

Let me describe a typical herdsman's home. Here and there inside the tent are pails of milk, cream, curds, and cream cheeses. There is a basket full of tea leaves which have been used once, but are being reserved for a second brew. On a small shrine a butter-lamp is burning in honour of the Great Name, for where will you find the meanest abode without its shrine? In the middle of the tent a cauldron is simmering over a fire of yak-dung.

Outside in the sun sits mother weaving clothes for the menfolk. Besides her husband she has two sons aged twelve and ten respectively, as well as two girls of eleven and seven. And a baby too. A couple of Tibetan mastiffs —large, black, long-haired dogs with heavy jaws and bloodshot eyes—are chained to pegs in the ground outside. They bark continuously when any stranger approaches, and, if he should come within reach, would unhesitatingly fly at his throat.

The *drok-pa* frequently shifts his grazing-ground to gain fresh grass for the herd. Those in Sikkim may leave their warm, moist valleys in the summer and seek the drier uplands of Tibet. Here they escape from the leeches which swarm unendingly in the wet lands below an elevation of ten thousand feet, and make the life of man and beast one long-drawn misery.

It was a cattle owner of this kind that I met during the month of July in the neighbourhood of the Chumbi Valley. He was looking after his herd of thirty *Siri* cattle, large, black, and powerful, a fine breed. From October to May he lived down in Sikkim with his wife, who, like himself, belonged to the Sikkimese branch of the Tibetan race. But in June he drove his cattle above the leech line and up across the passes into this cool, dry valley where the young grass thrived after the long rest of winter. His wife stayed behind to look after the Sikkim home, and so he had taken temporarily two wives of central Tibetan stock.

The people of the La-chen and La-chung Valleys in Upper Sikkim drive their herds higher and higher up these valleys as summer waxes hotter. Living in a wooded area, they build rough-timbered shelters at set stages along the streams, forming welcome additions to the tented encampments. At each stage they halt and graze their animals for a month or so on the way up, and again when autumn drives them down once more. In some parts of Tibet the shelters are formed of stone walls, over which a ridge-pole supports the tent roof. Or the walls may be of sods with a roof of yak-hair stretched above.

Shepherds, too, make small refuges for themselves eight or nine feet square and six or seven feet high. The walls will be of stone throughout, or of stone below with sun-dried bricks or simple slabs of earth above. Such will accommodate two shepherds. Their dwelling is open to the sky. Only if a prolonged stay is contemplated are a few rough-hewn planks laid across the top.

The grass on the Tibetan plains looks withered and useless, but the people believe in it. I was talking to a groom in the employ of a landowner as we were crossing an arid plain in the high borderland between Sikkim and

' The walls may be of sods with a roof of yak hair '

Northern nomads arriving at Lhasa

Tibet. I spoke of the luscious meadows down in the Chumbi Valley, where the plain widens out and the river gives generously of its overflow. 'Yes,' replied my companion, 'but this grass of the "Black South" [1] is more nourishing. The long grass near water is poor stuff, but from the short, dry tufts that grow on these mountains and plains comes the food that gives strength to our animals.'

One sometimes sees papers fastened to the yaks as they graze. They are inscribed with prayers, addressed to the guardian deity of the yak-owner. Every Tibetan has a guardian deity, not a mere vague idea to comfort fretful or wayward children, but a living personality to help and advise him throughout his earthly life.

On the grazing-grounds of the Sikkim-Tibetan frontier aconite is a much-dreaded scourge. I remember meeting a string of donkeys above Lam-teng in north Sikkim on their way to Tibet. One unfortunate among them lay on the roadway stricken sore with the poison which grows in pitiless profusion along this beautiful valley. The remedy adopted was severe, though of doubtful efficacy. It consisted in slitting off the tips of its ears and pricking its hind-quarters. I asked a man of the place how often such treatment effected a cure. 'It relieves them a little,' was all that he could say. Tibetan donkeys, mules, yaks and sheep, and those from the lowlands in Sikkim, die not infrequently from eating aconite, as there is but little in Tibet, and none in Lower Sikkim. But the home-bred flocks and herds know better than to touch it.

The people of the Chumbi Valley employ their own method of protecting a pony against aconite. Having burnt or boiled the leaves of the plant, a man will rub them over the pony's mouth and nostrils as well as a little inside his mouth. To emphasize the lesson he may add a grim warning in some such words as these: 'Your father died from eating this; your mother died from eating this.' The rubbing sets up irritation, so that the animal recognizes the aconite afterwards and does not eat it. One such

---

[1] The name of the district.

application is sufficient; it is unnecessary to do it afresh each year. Such treatment is applied to ponies, mules, donkeys, and yaks, but not to sheep or goats. It is used in those districts of central Tibet where aconite is found.

Once yearly the herdsman descends to lower levels to sell his products and to buy what he lacks. Especially during the early winter you will find him, a heavy-footed man with heavy, lumbering yaks plodding into Lhasa and the other large centres. He brings for sale wool, salt, soda for flavouring tea, and butter, as well as some sheep, yak and yak tails, these last for use in the Hindu temples of India and as fly-whisks for horses.

A couple of months suffices for his stay. He takes back with him barley, wheat, and tea, as well as a little of peas and woollen cloth. On his way home, before leaving the cropped lands he buys his stock of dried radishes and turnips. Of these he can take enough only for occasional use, perhaps two or three times a month, unless he be one of those that work near a cultivated tract. They are simple folk, these men of the flocks and herds.

The Pa-lha household own some twenty thousand sheep altogether, which are grazed in scattered grazing-grounds within fifty miles of Gyangtse. An ordinary grazing-ground may feed five hundred to a thousand sheep; if the grazing is very good, two thousand.

The shepherds employed by the family must produce one lamb yearly for every three sheep. Anything over this proportion they may keep for themselves, any deficiency they must make good. The wages of the shepherds and their assistants and the salt for the sheep are provided from the Pa-lha coffers. Lambs are seldom brought forth in the spring, but from September to November, so that the death-roll among them is heavy.

According to another form of tenure, the owner may specify a fixed amount of yak-hair, butter, and cheese to be produced each year. Any excess goes to the servants. One *sho* (about twopence-halfpenny) per sheep is also paid in return for the right of keeping the wool. A tenure

of this kind is called, 'No birth, no death', implying that
any increase in the flock belongs to the shepherd, and any
decrease must be made good by him. As to the rent paid
by the owner of the herd to the proprietor of the estate,
I have dealt with this elsewhere.[1]

The herdsmen drink but little milk from the goats or
the sheep, but make butter from both. This is used in
feeding their servants, and in paying the Government
revenue to the *dzongs*. The latter pass on some of this in
their prescribed payments to monasteries, who use it
chiefly in lamps burnt on the altars in the cause of religion.

The butter of sheep and goats is consumed by poor
people only. The gentry and the richer people generally
eat only the butter from the *dri* (female yak) and the cross
breed between yaks and ordinary cattle. The butter of the
ordinary cow is held as inferior to these two kinds, though
in the matter of milk all three are equally regarded. As
for the milk of sheep and goats, even poor people drink
but little of it.

Large landed proprietors have, after feudal fashion,
large staffs of servants. Many of these spin the wool and
weave it into cloth (*nam-bu*). This they do, most of all,
sitting round the fires during winter, when not only is it
cold out of doors, but the land itself is icebound and crops
cannot be tended. Much of this cloth is expended on
their servants' clothes. The balance is sold to traders,
or to neighbours who have not been able to weave enough
for themselves. And the surplus of unused wool finds a
ready sale.

During September you may see the women in the fields
cutting the weeds. They are to be stored for the cattle
against the winter days. Nothing edible can be wasted
here. But manure is plentiful, even after yak-dung has
been used as fuel. So the land is not impoverished by
this close cutting.

As you pass from the centres of cultivation up the
colder valleys to the heights where grazing alone is

[1] See p. 83.

possible, you see the crops of barley and peas becoming steadily shorter and thinner. You are on the fringe between the peasant and the grazier. One such tract is found at Re-ting, sixty miles north of Lhasa, and in the surrounding districts. The inhabitants are known as *Sa-ma-drok*, *literally*, ' Not cultivators, not graziers', i.e. a combination of the two. In this cold district cultivation alone is not sufficient to supply the needs of a household.

I was staying in the large Re-ting monastery, and one afternoon I walked up the mountain side behind the monastery with the 'Holder of the Keys',[1] the alert, kindly priest who had charge of the monastic property. We climbed to the top of a rock that juts out, and were rewarded with a good view both up and down the valley. Wisps of incense smoke rose from the farmers' houses below us. It was the time for the yaks and other cattle, for the sheep and goats, to come home. And so the incense went up as a prayer to the deities to bring them safely down the steep slopes.

'In the morning', said the Holder of the Keys, 'they *may* offer incense for the safety of their herds; in the evenings they *must* do so. For our people here are peasant-graziers, owners of herds as well as tillers of the soil. And there is no hope for the herds unless the divine assistance be invoked.'

Religion lies deep down in the hearts of the Tibetans, and not least among the shepherds, who spend their lives, in calm and storm, wandering over the wide, open spaces of the Tibetan hills. Even those nomad tribes that rob and raid, can often be controlled by religious influences. The herdsmen, too, will send their boys into the monasteries; others join the priesthood when full-grown. Of such a one, living in the eleventh century, we read that he became a priest, though he had been married. He rose to a commanding position as a teacher in the early Church, being followed by a band of over three thousand disciples.

[1] *Di-chang-nga* in Tibetan.

He was noted for the retentiveness of his memory and the accuracy of his mind.[1]

Tibetans sometimes divide their Church into two branches, those who, like this priest, influence others by their teaching; and those whose influence, unseen but none the less effective, proceeds from a life of religious devotion. And of this last the outward sign is often a stern asceticism.

The daily life of the herdsmen and shepherds does not vary much. They rise at cock-crow, an hour or so before dawn, and put on their clothes. Any washing or rinsing of the mouth is done perfunctorily, or not at all. They may mutter a few prayers or invocations. Some will take a vow to say a certain invocation so many times a day. It may be the brief, and universal, formula, 'Om Mani Padme Hum', or the lengthy supplication to 'The Deliverer', the goddess Dröl-ma, which takes fifteen minutes or so to recite. Having heard or read his prayers hundreds of times, perhaps thousands of times, our friend will have no difficulty in repeating it. He will, however, have little, if any, idea as to its meaning.

Tea having been made and drunk, the yaks are called down from the mountain side. Some of the women go to milk them; others stay at home to make the butter and cheese from the milk of the previous day, which is kept in leather bags. These bags, securely closed, are rolled backwards and forwards till the butter forms.

The buttermilk is boiled; the cheese (*chu-ra*) forms in it, and is drawn off with the help of a strainer. It is wrapped in a cloth, and, when partially dry, is pressed down with weights to squeeze out more of the moisture, and to shape it after the prescribed pattern. Later on, it is cut into cubes, through which a string made of yak-hair is passed. The cheese is then hung up to dry thoroughly. You may often see a mule driver take a cube from his robe on a long journey and cut off a lump for his sustenance on the road. After the cheese has been made,

1 Tep-ter Ngön-po, vol. v, folios 14 and 15.

the milk residue is given to calves and dogs. But some people also enjoy drinking it. The heavy work of the camp is done by the men. They hunt, pitch the tents and repair them, make ropes, belts, &c. They take the yaks and the sheep to pasture. In addition to the milking and butter-making the women grind the barley and do the general work round the tents. The children help them in this, and some go out with the sheep and goats, but not much with the yaks till they are twelve or thirteen years old.

Breakfast is taken an hour or two after sunrise. It may consist of tea, barley-flour, yak-beef or mutton, curds and cheese. Some will now take the cattle out to graze. These carry with them for their midday meal barley-flour and dried raw meat. Others will stay in and around the tents, making the butter and cheese, spinning and weaving wool, collecting yak-dung for fuel, &c.

Somewhat after midday there follows the second meal, which is much the same as breakfast. In the late afternoon the yaks and cow-yaks, with the other cattle, come home, are milked and put in their pens. The evening meal at sunset differs little, if at all, from its predecessors. Variety is neither expected, nor perhaps desired.

Our family then retire to rest. Or, maybe, sit up for a time singing or telling stories, perhaps legends of King Ke-sar, the Tibetan hero of pre-history days.

IV
THE PEASANTS

As you listen in the quick-growing Tibetan dawn to the deep notes of the herdsmen summoning the yaks down from the mountain slopes, and as you think of the day's march before you across the arid plain, you might be tempted to suppose that this is a land of yellow or slaty hills, with scanty grazing but practically no land for the plough. Yet it is not so. Descending to lower levels, you come to broad valleys and plains where more than three-quarters of the soil is regularly and closely cropped.

It may be that the plain—as at Gyangtse—is more than thirteen thousand feet above the level of the sea. Still, in ordinarily favourable years, the fields give good returns. The long, cold winter allows only one crop in the twelve months. And so the land gains the vigour that comes from a full rest each year. The peasants, too, spread large quantities of manure over it, and the irrigation channels bring down from the neighbouring hills fine particles of earth and manure, and deposit them on the fields. During the summer the river that flows across the Gyangtse plain is coloured a deep shade of brown by the earth and dung which it carries along, giving to the fields here and there as it passes by.

The truth is that Tibet does not lack land for cultivation, but lacks the men to till it. The population appears to be decreasing steadily owing to polyandry, to venereal diseases, and to the large number that live celibate lives in monasteries instead of rearing families. This process of reduction continues steadily, and the man-power that remains is to a great extent withdrawn from the cultivation of the soil. So a large amount of arable land lies fallow.

The need for men rather than for land is emphasized by the fact that a peasant is not allowed to quit his home without first obtaining the landlord's permission. If he wishes to go away, he must ask for leave, known in

Tibetan parlance as to 'petition for man-separation'.[1] He must also pay a large sum if the request is allowed, but such permission is not readily granted. If a substantial tenant goes away temporarily, even for a few months only, either he or his family is expected to inform the landlord, guaranteeing that they will be meanwhile responsible for the land and taxation. If a peasant, who has fled, is subsequently caught, he is liable to have to make good the rent for the years during which he was absent. He is also liable to be fined, beaten, or otherwise punished.

The chief crop in the Tibetan uplands is barley. Next to it come peas, wheat, and mustard; radishes and turnips are the favourite root-crops; potatoes are but sparsely cultivated, at any rate in central Tibet. Barley is the main cereal in Tibet and takes the place of wheat in England. Wheat is grown at the lower altitudes, mainly below 11,500 feet, but nowhere in such quantities as to oust barley from the premier position. The latter is of two kinds, white barley (*ne kar-mo*) and black barley (*ne-nak*). This last is also termed mottled barley, for the ears are not quite black. A mixed crop of barley and peas is a very frequent sight.

Buckwheat, both the sweet and the bitter, is fairly plentiful below 11,000 feet; it is consumed mainly by the poorer classes, and, like barley, can be used in the brewing of beer. It is a popular crop in Sikkim and Darjeeling, being grown and eaten by all the hill races, the Sikkimese, the Nepalese, and the Lepchas. I have seen buckwheat growing at an elevation of twelve thousand two hundred feet above sea-level on the mountains overhanging the Chumbi Valley, the wedge of Tibet that juts southward between Sikkim and Bhutan. In the interior of Tibet it is but little grown.

The mustard serves both as oil for lamps and for rubbing on the bodies of small children, especially those of the peasantry. The gentry use less oil on their children and wash them more. As for the shepherds, butter is

[1] *Mi-trö shu-wa.*

plentiful with them, and so they rub that on children and aged persons alike. Since it is cold on the grazing-grounds, this is done between ten and twelve in the fore-noon, the warmest time of the day. Those who are out with the flocks can find an upstanding rock that shelters from the wind.

Tibet is not well suited for the growing of green vegetables, and the Tibetan has no great liking for them. But the Chinese, being accustomed to vegetables in their own country, grow them as far as practicable. Round Lhasa and other towns may be seen several vegetable gardens set out by Chinese, and the products of these find their way into the Tibetan shops. When we spent eleven months in Lhasa—from November 1920 to October 1921—it was difficult to procure green food, especially during the winter. We made use of cabbages until they became too far decomposed to eat any longer, and then perforce abandoned green food until the advance of spring showed us some wild plants, which remotely resembled spinach, sprouting on the Lhasa plain.

In the lower parts of the country, more especially in eastern Tibet, fruit is freely grown, apricots, walnuts, pears, and peaches. The garden adjoining our house at Lhasa, being enclosed by a high wall, was a veritable sun-trap. In it were several apricot trees of a hardy type, and one tree with a crop of diminutive apples. The apricots and apples ripened after a fashion, though we found them lacking in flavour. But in the Lhasa shops we could buy dried apricots, brought in from the lowlands of Kong-po, two hundred miles away over the eastern hills, and these were very pleasant to the taste.

Maize, which is the staple food-crop in Nepal and Sikkim and generally in the eastern Himalaya, grows but little in Tibet. My friend, Ku-sho She-sur, managed to grow a little each year in Lhasa, but used the grain, ripened with such difficulty, as offerings on the altars of his private chapels. This was the highest altitude, eleven thousand eight hundred feet, at which I heard of maize ripening. At Chu-shur, on the banks of the Tsang-po, forty miles from Lhasa and two hundred feet lower, I found a little fully ripe under the wall of a villager's house.

In the lower parts of Bhutan and Sikkim we shall find many kinds of tropical crops and fruits, including even rice. The kind of rice most in favour with the Sikkimese is that known as *takmaru*. Its out-turn is less than that of other kinds, but it will grow at a higher elevation and is more nutritious. The people believe it to be beneficial in cases of diarrhoea, and to be a mild antidote against malarial fever. In Bhutan rice grows at an altitude of over eight thousand feet; in Sikkim and Darjeeling up to five thousand feet only. In the interior of Bhutan the climate is drier, and the sun consequently stronger. In Tibet itself rice is an expensive delicacy, the bulk of it being imported from Bhutan and Nepal over long and difficult tracks.

Geographically and historically, by race, religion, and language, Bhutan, Sikkim, and the district of Darjeeling are Tibetan, though politically they are now distinct, for they have been drawn into the British-Indian orbit. And in Sikkim and Darjeeling those of Tibetan race are greatly outnumbered by immigrants from Nepal.

Oranges flourish in Sikkim. They are grown by Sikkimese, but still more largely by the Lepchas. Small are these oranges, like tangerines, and of excellent flavour. Cultivators sell them by the tree, the price being at the rate of about six hundred oranges to the shilling. They ripen mainly between November and February, and are carried down the valley of the Teesta river and other avenues of trade by long strings of Nepalese porters, who flock every winter to Sikkim and Darjeeling for this and other purposes. Riding down the Teesta Valley you will see little heaps of oranges exposed for sale by the roadside. Higher up the valley are five or six in a heap, lower down only three or four. Each heap shows the number that you can purchase for a farthing.

Yams in Sikkim are both wild and cultivated. It is believed that wild yams can be eaten by invalids when the cultivated yams would disagree. One notices frequently in Tibet, Bhutan, and Sikkim that foods derived from wild plants are regarded as more digestible than those obtained from the cultivated varieties.

At Yum-tang in north Sikkim a fungus ripens during the summer. The people collect this and send half to the Maharaja as his share. It irritates the skin so greatly that their hands become raw from the picking.

It remains only to notice a weed named *yok-po*, like oats in appearance, which comes up profusely in Tibet unless the land is well ploughed, manured, and otherwise carefully tended. It is fed to ponies, mules, &c., and mixed with second-class grain by dishonest vendors to increase the weight, but it is not eaten by human beings. It comes up in large holdings, especially of landlords, for their tenants work these for them, and there is often insufficient manure to cover them efficiently. A small farmer will seldom have much of it, as his stock of manure is ample for his little holding, and he will naturally be keener in tending his own plot than in working the fields of his landlord.

In central Tibet land, which is very poor, lies fallow every second or third year. The best lands are cultivated with but little intermission. Fallow land should be ploughed yearly at least once lengthways and once across. Those who own sufficient cattle may plough four or five times during the year. The grass and weeds are thus worked into the ground.

An ordinary rotation of crops in central Tibet on inferior land would be:

1st year . . .	Barley
2nd ,, . . .	Fallow
3rd ,, . . .	Barley
4th ,, . . .	Peas
5th ,, . . .	Wheat

The barley crop in the third year is expected to be double

of that in the first, and is known as 'the borrowed'.[1] Letting the field lie fallow is, as it were, a loan, and the double crop obtained this year is the repayment of that loan.

Two crops are often grown together, barley and mustard being one of the most usual combinations. Peas are sown before barley and ripen a little earlier. Barley, wheat, and mustard are sown at the same time, and ripen at the same time.

In Tibet barley, wheat, peas, and mustard are reaped in September, whether they are sown between March and May or during the previous September. In the latter event the fields are ploughed five or six days after reaping the previous crop and are then often sown with peas, and with barley and mustard. The new crops appear above ground in April or May. As a rule it is in the less fertile fields that the seed is sown during September; the better lands receive their seed in the spring. The return on these better lands would no doubt be somewhat improved by an autumn sowing, but in their case it is not considered worth while to undertake the additional ploughings and other labour that a commencement during September involves.

In Sikkim and Darjeeling, grown as they are at altitudes of only three to six thousand feet above the sea, barley, wheat, and mustard are winter crops, for they must be reaped before the heat of the summer has had time to scorch them, or the torrential rain to rot them. Thus barley and wheat are sown in October or November, and reaped in March or April, while mustard is in the ground from September-October to January-February. Buckwheat in Sikkim is cultivated both as a summer and as a winter crop. It does not mind the heat and rain of summer.

The instruments of husbandry used in Tibet are simple and few. It will suffice to mention the plough (*shö*), harrow (*ri-bu*), rake (*ang-se*), spade (*kem* or *ja-ma*), hoe (*tok-tse*), sickle (*so-ra*), and pitchfork (*gya-se*). In some

---

[1] *Yar-ma* (གཡར་མ་) in Tibetan.

parts of the country flails are used for threshing. The hoe is somewhat smaller than that generally used in India or Nepal. The spade has a longish pole as a handle, without a cross-piece; the blade is pointed and somewhat smaller than that used in England. But it was interesting to find it in common use in Tibet, for I had not seen a spade of any kind used in agricultural operations in India.

The plough is roughly made. It is drawn by a pair of ordinary oxen, or by yaks; or else by *dzos*, the cross-breed between the two. Sometimes one will see a male and female *dzo* together drawing the plough. This calls forth the criticism of the Sikkimese, for in their country cows are not harnessed to the plough. In some parts of the country a single animal will do the work, but this, in central Tibet at any rate, is unusual. Ploughing is a hot occupation, especially for a warm-blooded people. And so the man who guides the team is often scantily clad even when facing the cold wind that sweeps across the plains in spring.

Sometimes the plough-yaks are decked out gaily for the work. One such pair I saw near the large Gan-den Monastery, some twenty-five miles from Lhasa. On their heads were red tufts of yak-hair, above these tufts of white sheep-wool, and on the top were inserted sprays of cocks' feathers. Strings of cowries, wound round the necks and on the nostrils of the yaks, added further to the colour scheme. The right horns carried tufts of yak-hair. Behind the plough a man came sowing, and this was noticeable, for sowing is ordinarily a woman's part.

Yaks, donkeys, ponies, &c., being plentiful, even in the vicinity of the fields, these are liberally fertilized with manure. This may be applied about a month before sowing, having been stored maybe in the village street. Human ordure is also used. Daily during the winter and spring one saw strings of donkeys carrying loads of this out of Lhasa. The privies in Tibet are closed up. From time to time they are opened and the contents sold to the villagers for manure at the rate of about one penny per hundred pounds. Down away in Sikkim and the district of Darjeeling, though inhabited to some extent by people of Tibetan race, such manure is not used. But here in the dry, cold uplands, laid by for awhile and mixed with earth and ashes, it is free from all offensive smell.

The dryness indeed is such that without organized schemes of irrigation the crops would have no chance. This has long been recognized. In a Tibetan history we read that Atisha, the Indian Buddhist teacher who visited Tibet eight hundred years ago, stopped at Töl, near Lhasa, and 'built a dam for the good of the people there'.[1] In Atisha's biography we read to the same effect.

The landlords work the systems of irrigation jointly in accordance—as the head of the Do-ring family informed me—with the various schemes contained in the archives of the *Dzongs* concerned. Any dispute between the land-lords is referred to the *Dzong-pön*; and, if the latter cannot settle it, to Lhasa. The labour required for constructing or repairing the irrigation channels is supplied by the tenants. The amount of work to be done by each tenant depends on the quantity of seed that he sows in his fields, not on the area of his land. No wages are paid.

In Sikkim also according to the prevalent custom tenants' rent is similarly fixed. In India, under British administration, the rent as a rule depends on the area of the land and the class of the soil as appraised by Government officers.

But man's work alone is not enough. If the rain fails, irrigation alone will not secure the crops. During our year in Lhasa there was a severe drought. The month was June; no rain, and practically no snow, had fallen for eight months. The farmers were all waiting anxiously. So the Divine Power was invoked to do what man could not do for himself.

A Tibetan friend, a land-owner, put it thus:
'It is vital to have rain in the fourth (May–June) month. Rain in the fifth and sixth months will not com-

[1] Tep-ter Ngön-po, vol. v, folio 8.

pensate for absence of rain in the fourth. Unless therefore a fair quantity of rain falls early in the fourth month, the high lamas hold the "Rain-Bringing Services".[1] They go to the sacred springs round Lhasa, those where the *Lu* [2] dwell. These are often situated near willow trees. Here they hold religious services on the appointed day from morning to evening, and feed the fishes in the pools by these springs with grain.

'If rain does not fall after such services have been prescribed, the Dalai Lama sends a message to the Council to inquire whether they were conducted properly. The Council then dispatches messengers to inquire in the various places, for the services are held not only by the monasteries in and near Lhasa, but far and near throughout the countryside, though especially by the "Three Seats", the large monastic corporations at Se-ra, Drepung, and Gan-den. Any monasteries found to have been lazy in conducting the services are liable to fine.'

These intercessions are, of course, carried on although there be no apparent prospect of rain. But my friend, whom I have quoted, was sceptical as to the prayers for rain from a sky that seemed set fair. His little yellow hat, like an under-sized tam o'shanter without a tassel, bobbed up and down on his head as, with a half-humorous sigh, he replied, 'I do not see much use in prayers for rain when the sky is clear. I hold with the view of Uncle Töm-pa.'

'And who was Uncle Töm-pa?'

'He was a clever man who lived in Tibet a long time ago. Though not much good at ordinary prophecies, he had studied the rain question and understood it. He refused to pray for rain, when there appeared no chance of it, but used to say that the proper time to hold these religious services was when the clouds were going from the south to the north. That is the time when rain is most

[1] *Cham-be* (ཆར་འབེབས་).

[2] Serpent spirits who live underground and have charge of water, trees, crops, flowers, and treasures.

likely to fall. So even in the present day people repeat the saying:

> When the southern clouds go northwards,
> Uncle Töm-pa prays for rain.' [1]

Still, the Rain-Bringing Services conducted by the priests are held to be of vital importance; it would be flying in the face of Providence to neglect them.

There is a tendency to deify men of this kind, so that I was not surprised to hear another Tibetan friend of mine express himself as follows:

'A-ku Töm-pa, though a layman, was regarded as an Incarnation of *Chen-re-si*, the patron deity of Tibet, and was sent to teach the Tibetans worldly wisdom and cleverness, for till then they were too simple and ignorant. They took even a jest to be the plain truth. They were like our simple drok-pas (herdsmen) are now, but even more so. In the Pem-po country he came across some children, who were playing on the edge of a pool. He brought a shower of hail on them to test their cleverness. They immediately covered their heads with baskets and plunged into the water, thus avoiding the hail-stones. So, thinking that as even the children have so much sense, these people must be well advanced, Töm-pa composed a couplet about them, of which the following is a rough translation:

> Clever are the Pem-po folk;
> Uncle Töm-pa need they not. [2]

'So he left them without instruction, with the result that they are now reputed to be one of the most stupid communities in the country.'

Every year a written proclamation is circulated by the Tibetan Government to all Dzong-pöns, i.e. officers in charge of districts. It is known as *tsa-tsik*, the 'Root Word', and in effect lays down general rules of conduct

---

[1] *Lho-trin chang-la chin-na,*
    A-ku Töm-pe cham-be.
[2] *Pem-po rik-pa-i jung ne la;*
    A-ku Töm-pa gö-che me.

for the observance of all. It contains one curious provision which runs as follows:

'During that portion of the summer in which there is scarcity of rain (i. e. May and June) no one is allowed to construct any building.'

The reason for this prohibition is that a person building a house makes offerings to the gods in order to prevent rain from falling, as thereby the house under construction will be injured. But by thus stopping the rain he is harming the cultivation of his neighbours. It is therefore forbidden to erect houses during these months, when rain is urgently needed and is apt to fail.

Careful farmers weed their fields twice or more, but there are many who weed no more than once. It is the women's work. In the lands above twelve thousand feet, September is pre-eminently the harvest month. In the Chumbi Valley, between ten and eleven thousand feet, barley is reaped in July and August, but here it is sown in March and April, a month earlier than in the neighbourhood of Lhasa. At Gyangtse (thirteen thousand one hundred feet) the barley is usually reaped during the middle of September.

During our year at Lhasa it was later there owing to the rainy season lasting longer, a fortunate event which gave good crops throughout the country. According to Tibetan interpretation, this extension of the rain was due to a rearrangement of the calendar. The Tibetan year is a lunar one, necessitating the insertion of an extra month every second year or so. This year's addition had been made during August, which was accordingly extended, and its rainfall automatically extended also.

Round Lhasa the peasants should not reap their crops until the Dalai Lama has given permission for operations to begin. Specimens of the ears are shown three times to His Holiness. On the 12th September, in this year of late crops, they had been shown once. On the morrow or the next day they were to be shown for the second time, and for the third and final time a day or two later. The harvesting then commenced in earnest.

Such restrictions seem to prevail elsewhere also. They are imposed with due regard to the state of the crops. I left the Re-ting Monastery, sixty miles north of Lhasa, on the 3rd September. The young officer, a member of the Sha-tra family, who accompanied me throughout, told me on our departure:

'Now that you have left Re-ting the monks will go to the Dalai Lama's pleasure park on the river bank for three days, pitching their tents there. Meanwhile the peasants will not be allowed to cut any crops. It is not permitted to use cutting instruments, at any rate on so large a scale, until the monks return to the monastery.' In point of fact, the crops could not have been ready for another eight or ten days.

By Europeans, and occasionally by Japanese also, Tibetans are often described as lazy. This, however, has not been my experience, though, when there is nothing to do, they can stay doing nothing for a long time without falling into boredom or peevishness. But, if work is to be done, there is no shirking.

I have frequently been at Gyangtse, staying by the fields, when the crops were reaped. The peasants and their households rose at one or two o'clock at night, partook of a little tea and barley flour, and went out immediately to their plots of land. They ate brief meals there at about seven in the morning, at noon, and at three or four in the afternoon. At seven in the evening they took their last meal, and then went home for a few hours' sleep, but some passed the nights in the fields to keep off thieves. They used every effort to gather in the crops before the hail or frost came. All worked their hardest, and while they worked, they sang. Often have I heard, between one and two o'clock at night, the tinkling of the bells round the donkeys' necks as the patient animals passed my little bungalow, bringing back from the fields their first loads of barley.

No eight-hour day here, but rather eighteen. And the donkeys too. What loads they carry! Like their human

Carrying the barley harvest in the Chumbi Valley

'The barley is dried in high, narrow stacks'

Household servants of a Ta-shi Lhün-po official

overlords, they work hard and long. Each household,
after getting in the crop, takes a day off and spends it in
feasting.

The air of Tibet is so dry that it is best to have a little
rain during the harvest. Otherwise, in the reaping, a good
deal of the grain falls out of the ears, and this has to be
picked up from the ground, entailing trouble and loss.

The mode of threshing varies in different localities and
on different farms. On the plateaux of Tibet and in the
broad valleys a common method is to spread out the
sheaves thickly over a large threshing-floor, and then to
drive a number of yaks from one end to the other. These
run across independently of each other, and at the other
end are driven back again. A number of people are employed, running to and fro, waving and calling, a laborious
occupation. The threshing-floor is an open enclosure near
the farm buildings. The floor is of clay, beaten to a satis-
factory hardness; a wall of the same material surrounds it.
In some parts of the country goats or ponies are driven
over it. The Sikkimese use a few cattle which go round
and round after the fashion prevalent in the plains of
India and throughout the Himalaya. In Tibet also this
latter procedure is sometimes adopted. It is admitted
to be a better system than that in which the yaks dash to
and fro.

In some parts of the country a flail is used. It is in two
pieces, jointed together by a wooden pin. The shorter
piece is held in the hand, the longer works freely on the
pin and beats out the grain.

In the Chumbi Valley the barley (*ne*) is dried in high
narrow stacks (*ne-pung*) raised off the ground. When
ready for threshing the heads are pulled off the stalks by
hand, gathered into a long heap and beaten with flails
(*kor-gyuk, li-ga*). Both men and women join in the work.
Then the grain and the heads are gathered up, placed in
sacks or baskets (*le-po, tse-po*), and carried to the winnow-
ing-ground.

Here they are placed in trays (*pe-kyap*), and waved in

the wind, which in Tibet seldom fails. This is repeated two or three times, after which they are put into a bamboo basket (*shi-me, kyö-ma*) which is shaken so that the grain drops to the ground through the interstices in the bottom of the basket. The grain is then brought into the house and kept in boxes or bags. Sometimes also it is winnowed on the flat roofs of the houses.

Another method of winnowing is by throwing up the grain and chaff with wooden rakes. The grain falls down on the heap, the chaff is scattered by the wind.

As there is plenty of water-power throughout the country, water-mills are in common use for grinding the grain. A small channel led off from a stream supplies the power. Usually each such mill has its own little house, but occasionally two are housed together. An ordinary rate of payment for the services of the mill is to give the owner one out of every twenty measures ground.

Ploughing is done by men, sowing as a rule by women; weeding, irrigating, reaping, threshing, and winnowing by both sexes. Milking and the making of butter are within the woman's province.

In Sikkim barley and wheat are grown only by the Sikkimese and the Lepchas. The fields are prepared in November by burning the weeds. The land is then ploughed and the clods broken up. After this the seed is sown. The crop is reaped in March and April; on the highest lands in May. The ears are cut off with a sickle or with two pieces of split bamboo used like scissors.

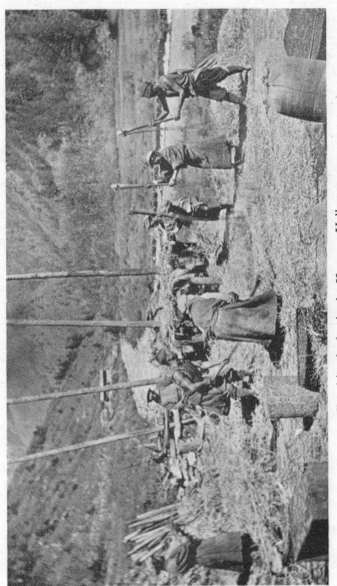

Threshing barley in the Kam-pu Valley

Winnowing barley at Ka-la

V

THE PEASANTS (*continued*)

HAILSTORMS in Tibet are sudden and overpowering. They do great damage to the crops. The Tibetan, however, is not content to take his chance, and, when the hail comes, to bewail his loss. He makes an effort to prevent it from coming.

To what then is hail due? The Tibetan calls it 'The War of the Elements', and ascribes it to fighting between Wind, Fire, and Water. Earth does not take part in this war. The other three bring the 'Eight Demons of the Country' [1] with them, and these throw the hail.

'When "The Precious Teacher" [2] came to Tibet,' as a Tibetan official informed me, 'he subdued the eight kinds of demons who bring the hail. They bowed their heads in submission, and he gave them the following orders: "You may harm only those who break their oaths, parents who maltreat their children and children who wrong their parents, landlords who oppress their tenants and tenants who disobey their landlords, people who maltreat animals and other evil-doers."'

There are in Tibet persons who are known as Ngak-pas. The Ngak-pa is hardly a priest, but rather a magician, one versed in charms that are contained in the religious books. Among other powers he is credited with that of stopping hail. There are, indeed, priests who can ward off hailstorms, but none are so efficient as the Ngak-pas. This is recognized even by the priests themselves. The Tibetan Government therefore employ two of these magicians to keep hail from falling on Lhasa and the surrounding plain. They give them small grants of land in part payment for their services.

[1] *Lha-sin De-gye.*

[2] *Lo-pön Rim-po-che*, the Tibetan name for Padma Sambhava, the Indian Tantrik teacher who was largely instrumental in converting Tibet to Buddhism.

So the farmer employs a Ngak-pa to ward off hail from his crops, paying him a small amount of grain each year. In Sikkim and in the Darjeeling district the usual contribution was eight pounds of grain per household, and this was paid not only by his co-religionists, the Sikkimese and Lepchas, but by the Hindus from Nepal also. So great was the belief in the Ngak-pa and the fear of angering him.

If the hail comes, the farmer withholds this payment. But should hail fall on the Dalai Lama's palace in Lhasa, known as the Potala, or on his country house near Lhasa, known as the Jewel Park,[1] or on the great Temple in Lhasa, known as the Tsuk La Kang, the two Ngak-pas responsible for Lhasa are punished. For, as a highly placed priest informed me, 'Hail is not allowed to fall on the Potala, on the Jewel Park, or on the Tsuk La Kang.' When I was in Lhasa, hail fell on these three sacred buildings. To atone for their inability or neglect the Ngak-pas had to plant a number of willow trees, a useful punishment no doubt where trees are scanty, as on the Lhasa plain.

The methods by which the Ngak-pas and others seek to stop the hail would need a long description, and can be more conveniently set forth when dealing with the religion of the people, as I hope to do in a subsequent volume. Let it suffice here merely to add that hail is believed to fall chiefly in countries in which the inhabitants are quarrelsome, or in which many illegitimate children are born.

Floods, at any rate in the interior of Tibet, are not one of the main adversities with which the peasant has to cope. He is in this respect better off than the Indian cultivator Still, the larger rivers do cause considerable damage by their overflow. Embankments are occasionally set up along the bank of a river, and supported by training works, rough but strong. Such may be seen by the Kyi Chu near Lhasa, and especially outside the walls of the Jewel Park, which is in considerable danger during the rainy season.

[1] Nor-pu Ling-ka.

For floods, however, as for hail, human inadequacy is recognized.

Several hundred years ago there lived in Tibet a priest named Tang-drong Gyal-po. He is credited with the construction of the suspension bridges, remains of which may be seen in various parts of the country. It is therefore believed that he had power over water. During the rainy season, from July to September, the Pem-bo Chu and the Kyi Chu are broader rivers than the Thames in London, and swirl rapidly down well-cultivated valleys. At their junction floods are common, almost inevitable. So here a large *chö-ten* [1] has been erected, and in it are kept images of Tang-drong Gyal-po in order to keep the water under control. In the Jewel Park are kept a thousand images of the saint for the same purpose.

Great is the fame of Tang-drong Gyal-po. He was of powerful build. His face showed his strength of character, and seemed to shine with a brilliance of its own. He lived to a great age. It was an easy matter for him to change the forms of material objects, such as turning a porcelain cup of tea into the shape of a dumpling without disturbing the tea inside it.

'Even now his Incarnation lives', says Ku-sho Pa-lhe-se, 'in the monastery above the bank of the Tsangpo on the Lhasa–Gyangtse road. He has not the power over water that Tang-drong Gyal-po had. For these are lesser days. Doubt has crept in; there is no longer the old faith. And so our holy men have not the power that they had.'

When in Lhasa I was talking with Ku-sho Sur-kang, a Tibetan official, about Am-do, a country inhabited by Tibetans on the Chinese border. The conversation came round to the *do-rings* in Lhasa, the obelisks with historical inscriptions on them.[2] He said:

'Up to some fifteen years ago, the people of Am-do, who are simple folk with great faith in the religion, used

---

[1] *Chö-tens* are masonry structures of varying sizes and somewhat varying shapes. They contain relics of saints, offerings to aid deceased relatives in their next life, &c. They are extremely common throughout Tibet. [2] See p. 14.

to take imprints in ink from the obelisk near the Temple
in Lhasa. There are rivers in their country which eat
into the fields on their banks. They used to put up stone
revetment walls, but the rivers cut into these also. So,
to prevent this erosion, they took to placing copies of one
of the inscriptions from this *do-ring* among the stones,
believing that such had the power of turning the river
aside.

'They did not take copies from the obelisk below the
Potala; the one by the Temple, being as it were in the
presence of the Cho,[1] was held to have more power.

'During recent years these copies are not taken. Possibly the Tibetan Council[2] forbids the practice on account of the hostility now prevailing between China and
Tibet.'

Hailstorms and floods are indeed devastating, but their
attacks are limited. Of all the enemies that the husbandman has to fear the most terrible is frost. A brief spell of
this is sufficient to kill the crops throughout the whole
countryside. And so during the latter half of August the
farmer who lives on higher, colder lands prays for the
cloudy nights that keep the frost away. And that the
divine assistance may not be wanting the Government
sends parties of monks from the 'College of Victorious
Heaven' in the Potala to the different *dzongs* in central
Tibet. These carry earthenware jars, known both as
'earth taste jars' and as 'frost prevention jars', which are
placed on the tops of high mountains, being buried or
half-buried in the ground. In each jar is a little barley,
a small piece of silk, and a fragment of gold and silver.
Before they start out the monks have already conducted
a preparatory service, lasting for some days, in their own
college.

For this service and for the jars the people pay nothing.
They merely lend to these preventers of frost mattresses,

---

[1] The image of the Buddha in the Temple, the holiest image in Tibet.

[2] *Ka-sha.* In charge, subject to the control of the Dalai Lama and certain
other influences, of the detailed administration of Tibet.

Chö-tens at the entrance to Lhasa

carpet rugs, firewood, &c., and provide them with transport for their baggage from place to place.

When I was in the Chumbi Valley in July 1915, swarms of locusts passed up every day for about a fortnight. They were carried along by the south wind that prevails throughout the year except during the winter months. One of my orderlies, Ne-tuk Lepcha, some forty-five years old, told me that he remembered two previous visitations of this kind.

'One such happened,' said he, 'when I was nine years old, destroying a large proportion of the maize, marwa,[1] and rice crops in Sikkim. Again, when I was twenty years old, swarms passed over the land. The marwa was just ripening and they worked their will on it. The maize on the higher lands was also injured, for this was not yet ripe. These locusts travel farther and farther north, and eventually die on the passes. The last time they came I saw them lying dead in heaps on the Si-po La (between Gyau-gang and Kam-pa Dzong). Locusts are believed to be the reincarnations of *yi-das*.'

Yi-das are a class of beings who dwell in the lowest of the six worlds, excepting hell alone. They have large bodies, but mouths and throats so small that they can only swallow a crumb at a time. Thus are they tormented with perpetual hunger and thirst, because in their lives on earth they were covetous, gluttonous, uncharitable. Then when the evil karma has been sufficiently worked out, the return to earth may be as a locust, a creature whose hunger is never satisfied. The punishment fits the crime.

Rats sometimes do considerable damage. It was the practice, when I was touring, for the landlords and other local notables to bring small presents of fruit, eggs, &c. This afforded an opportunity for inquiring about recent events, including *inter alia* the condition of the crops. On one of my visits to a place in Lower Sikkim, some four thousand seven hundred feet only above sea-level,

[1] A millet grown largely in Sikkim and used in the brewing of beer.

I inquired accordingly about the growing rice. The local magnate replied:

'It is good so far, but it is not reaped yet, and the rats may attack it.'

'But why should the rats attack it this year?'

'Because the *Pom-tsi* (known to the Gurkhas as *Lepcha phal*) has fruited abundantly this year; it grows on the tops of the hills round here. The rats usually come for it and then come down the hills for the rice. They work their way down the hillsides till they reach the main river in the valley.'

'Where do they go then?' I asked.

'They are carried away by the river.'

'But why do they go into the river, when it means certain death to them?'

'It is their custom; they always do so,' my friend replied, as he recalled to my mind the habits of the lemmings and the ballad of Bishop Hatto.

Apart from the preventive measures, human or divine, adopted against particular dangers, general prayers for the crops are sometimes conducted by the villagers themselves. When Colonel Kennedy and I were returning to Lhasa from the north, we came upon a service of this kind. It was in progress at a village called Ya-tsa near Lhün-trup Dzong.

The villagers walked in single file. Their course apparently lay round the village boundaries. One in front carried the banner of the god of the district; each of those following carried a volume of the Buddhist scriptures. Some carried banners and drums as used in monasteries. Behind them all came the headman of the village, mounted on a pony.

The object of this procession was to ward off frost and hail. It was in fact a service of prayer for the crops which were to be reaped not many days later. Tibet being a country where great importance is attached to omens, good and bad, my companions did not fail to point out that the meeting with this religious procession was a good omen for our party.

The cultivating communities are careful to preserve grazing-grounds for their stock. I inquired somewhat closely regarding those in the Chumbi Valley, an area in which cultivation being comparatively close, the necessary reservation is all the more rigorously observed. This valley area, known to the people themselves as Tro-mo, the 'Wheat District', is divided into Upper and Lower. Upper Tro-mo had twenty-one grazing divisions; Lower Tro-mo had eight.

The possession of these divisions was settled by the throwing of dice, the highest throw gaining the first choice. In Upper Tro-mo the grazing-stations were changed twice (making three stations) for each summer. All the herds were moved on the same day from one station to another. The dice, too, were thrown three times each year. At the first throwing a yak calf was sacrificed to the local deity, and the effigy of the deity was set up there.

The winter quarters were retained for three years. Each station accommodated sixty or seventy head of cattle, and for each a small rent was paid to the communal fund, which is administered by the people themselves. There is much that is democratic in the Tibetan scheme of government. For yaks owned by outsiders the grazing fee was fivepence a year; for ponies, mules, and donkeys somewhat more. But they did not realize from the Bhutanese, as the latter were physically strong and lawless, and the people of Tro-mo feared them greatly.

The houses of the peasantry are, as a rule, solid and substantial by comparison with the lightly built structures of the Indian cultivators. The walls are usually of stone or sun-dried bricks, these latter being fairly durable in the dry Tibetan air. Occasionally, as at Pa-ri, they are of clods of earth. Here, for the sake of warmth, the floors are sunk a couple of feet or so below the level of the ground.

The houses on the Tibetan uplands are built round a courtyard. They are two, and sometimes three, stories in height. Verandahs, opening on this yard, often run round the first and second floors. The ground floor is mainly occupied by cattle, ponies, &c., whose body-heat no doubt helps to keep the rooms above them warm. Granaries and store-rooms may also be found on the ground floor. In the cold, dry climate of the Tibetan plateau meat can be kept good for three or four years, and grain for two or three hundred years.

Flat roofs of beaten earth are the rule throughout the interior of the country, but in the Chumbi Valley, Bhutan, Sikkim, and other rainy parts they are laid on a gentle slope. Where pine trees grow, as they usually do, the roofs are constructed of pine shingles, which split easily into lengths of five or six feet. These are kept in position by heavy stones. No nails are used. In fact, you may see castles in Bhutan, accommodating over five hundred persons, complete with halls and chapels, galleries and apartments, but without a bolt or a nail in them anywhere. Dovetailing is an art which is thoroughly understood. In districts of this type the ordinary houses closely resemble Swiss chalets. They stand out on the mountain sides or in the bays of the deep valleys, seeking to catch the rays of the sun before it disappears, all too rapidly, across the overhanging ridges. It is only at the lowest altitudes, such as people of Tibetan race seldom inhabit, that the roofs are of thatch.

The inmates of the house do not live on the ground floor, but occupy the upper story. The staircase in central Tibet is usually of stone steps. A wooden ladder is sometimes found; it is more common in the houses of the rich. Those districts, such as Kong-po, Tak-po, parts of eastern Tibet, the Chumbi Valley, Bhutan, and Sikkim, which are favoured with plenty of trees, sometimes set up wooden ladders. But more often these prefer a log of wood. On one side of it are notches, cut just wide enough to rest half the foot when going up sideways, but worn round and slippery by constant use. In case of an attack the inmates can draw this up and so defend themselves with greater ease and efficiency.

'A wooden ladder is sometimes found'
Staircase at house entrance

Procession of villagers in prayer for the crops at Ya-tsa

The furniture of such a well-to-do farmer may consist of a few small tables of the Tibetan type, and mattresses (*böl-den*) stuffed with wool or straw and bound in cloth. On such the inmates sit; two, laid side by side, form a bed. The roofs are supported by a number of wooden pillars a few yards apart from each other. These are carved and sometimes painted. Along the walls of the room may be heavy wooden chests. One of the rooms will be converted into a chapel with an altar, images, and other religious accessories.

The flat roof is useful in various ways. You will find a line or two of prayer flags stretched across parts of it. These are short streamers of muslin with invocations to the gods printed on them, joined by a cord. There is sure to be an earthen receptacle for burning aromatic twigs as an incense offering. Where it grows, juniper is used.

At dawn the housewife goes on the roof and sets the incense burning, provided that it be between the second day and the middle of the month. Not much incense, however, is burnt on the first day, for the Tibetan saying runs, 'Worship not the gods on the first day of the month.' It is as though they were absent then. And seldom is it burnt during the last half of the month. It is felt by many that the devils are in greater power during this period, though they would not say so, for that would be a word spoken against 'The Three Chief Rare Ones'. So people say that the gods *prefer* incense during the first half of the month, and that it is *unfitting* (*mi-rung-wa*) to offer it during the second half.

From the roof of the neighbouring monastery will be heard the large conch shell or gong summoning the monks to the service of religion, a call to be repeated during the forenoon, at midday, and perhaps in the afternoon. Thus the new-born day is dedicated.

Barley may be stacked on the roof to be dried before threshing. Green grass, too, is dried there, the 'mud grass' from the marshes as well as other kinds. For the winter needs of the cattle must be considered. I have often also found a supply of firewood kept on the roof, branches perhaps of willow and cedar, because good firewood is scarce. On one such roof I found earthen pots placed upside down to dry in the sunshine. If this be done from time to time, their lives are lengthened. Near to these were a few onion plants in boxes.

On my way from Re-ting to Lhasa during September I stayed in several farm-houses. One such was at Gya-trong Dong in the Pem-po Valley. Below the window of my room was the sheep-yard; four or five hundred sheep were penned in it every night, packed close together. It was deep in black slime, for we had had heavy rain and the weather was warm. In due course this would be placed on the fields to their great benefit. But for us meanwhile it was extremely malodorous, like living on a manure heap.

My host was well-to-do. I was accommodated in the chapel, containing a bookcase with some thirty sacred books, three dozen images, large and small, bowls of holy water, a large temple drum, and other religious objects. When I stayed in farm-houses my host usually lodged me in the chapel, as being the cleanest and best kept room in the house. The sacred fire burned on the altar; one was careful to see that no mishap occurred to it.

The floor of my room would be covered with woollen blankets, and over these would be laid Tibetan rugs and large pieces of felt. Thus the floor coverings were two-fold or threefold, soft but full of the ever-plentiful Tibetan dust. Walls and ceilings were covered with cotton cloths and Chinese brocades.

During the afternoon I went on the roof. In the street outside children were dancing, whirling round and round as Tibetan actors do in plays. Tibetan children love doing this. On a terrace below us an old man was regaling some of the women of the house with amusing recollections as he ate his meal: all were laughing joyously.

One sees many ruined houses in Tibet. By some these are ascribed to the Mongol invasions which occurred so frequently during bygone days; by others to epidemics of small-pox which came with even greater frequency. No doubt both have contributed to the ruins. And a further contributory cause is the relentless decline in the population, due in great measure to the large numbers of monks and nuns vowed to celibate lives.

The domestic animals most in evidence on a Tibetan farm are yaks and other cattle, ponies, donkeys, and dogs; in a lesser degree, pigs. These last are kept mainly by the Chinese.

Dogs are, of course, required for watch and ward. They are often chained on the roofs, and, as you ride by, they dart forward and bark vociferously two or three feet above your head. They are of the size of a Newfoundland with long black hair, strongly built and unappeasably ferocious.

Many peasants keep ponies, using them for riding as well as for transport, since, rich and poor, all ride. Donkeys cost but little to buy or keep, and do much work. I have bought a good one, eighteen months old, for the equivalent of eighteen shillings.

In a well-known Tibetan play the kings of India, Persia, Turkestan, and Tibet send envoys to the Chinese Court, each seeking the Emperor's daughter as bride for his king. In one of the tests set to the envoys a hundred mares are kept in one place, a hundred foals in another, and the task is to identify the offspring of each mother. When the Tibetan envoy succeeded in this, the Chinese Emperor waved the matter aside, remarking, 'The test is not a fair one, for Tibet is the land of horses.'

The yak should be called *ya*, for the final *k* is not pronounced. The word is applied only to the ox. The cow is named *dri*. Ordinary oxen are crossed with the *dri*; the male offspring are termed *dzo*, and the female *dzo-mo*. The *dzo* are more docile than yaks, and the *dzo-mo* are better milkers than the *dri*.

The yak, with its cross-breeds, is the most useful of all animals to the people of Tibet. As a meat food it is consumed more largely than any other except perhaps mutton. Ordinary beef is regarded as inferior; chicken, fish, and eggs are seldom eaten. Yak-beef is used both fresh and frozen, both cooked and raw.

The hair is used for making tents and blankets, as well as ropes, which seem never to break, never to wear out. The hide furnishes trunks and bags; furnishes also the coracles, on which the Tibetan relies almost entirely for navigating his rivers. One man can carry the coracle, oars and all, but the handy little craft will carry eight or nine persons, or heavy logs of timber, for days together in the swirling floods of summer. And, finally, yak-tails form one of the chief articles of export from Tibet to other countries, to be used, especially when white, in temples or as fly-whisks.

It is perhaps natural that the stay-at-home Tibetan will sometimes express surprise that other nations should be able to exist without the indispensable yak.

VI

THE PEASANTS (*continued*)

In some of the Tibetan books are to be found instructions enjoining that the peasantry should be treated with justice and moderation. Among these is a history of Bhutan entitled the Lho-i Chö-jung, the best history dealing with this country. Towards the end is a chapter dealing with the duties of the Deb Raja [1] and the State officers under him.

> As the King conducts himself, so do the subjects behave;
> Therefore teach the Kings to live holy lives on this earth. [2]

Officers are enjoined to observe fairness towards the peasants. We are told:

If any tenant has any gold, turquoises, bronze vessels, ponies, cattle, images of the gods or other objects, persons in authority must not acquire these by an unfair barter or forced exchange.

Again:

No priest may take property in exchange for charmed strips of cloth or silk. All such dealings must be fair and according to the local rates and value of the article purchased.

Compulsion is forbidden. Neither salt nor butter may be forced on the tenant as a part or the whole of the price paid to him. Nor may wool be forced on tenants in order that they may be compelled to weave it.

And once more:

No officials or priests may send out alms-begging parties. These practices must cease henceforth. Such demands only may be realized as are due from the tenantry to the State.

The *tsa-tsik*,[3] too, ordains that the peasantry be treated with justice.

The dzong-pöns are to treat the subjects under them impartially and not to favour any one and not to give the subjects unnecessary trouble.

---

[1] *De-si Chan-dzö.*   [2] Lho-i Chö-jung, folio 105.   [3] See p. 38.

And again:

The dzong-pöns, the landlords, and the managers of monastic estates, are all forbidden to take by force the children or servants of the tenants into their own service.

The Tibetans and Bhutanese expect to find admirable sentiments of this kind in their books and governmental notifications. But they are not seriously sanguine that standards of such excellence will be attained in everyday life. For the golden age has passed long ago; it is the iron age that holds us in its grip to-day. And so, even if they are acquainted with this volume, they are not greatly disappointed. For facts are facts, and stubborn minds remain stubborn still.

In the winter of 1910 I went to Bhutan—Captain (now Lieutenant-Colonel) Kennedy accompanying me—to make a treaty with the authorities of that country, by which they placed their foreign relations under British guidance. We were received everywhere by Bhutanese officials. Among my orderlies was Ne-tuk Lepcha, whom I have referred to above. Now Ne-tuk was a man with a presence, physically strong, decided in speech, one of the kind that leads others. In Bhutan was much fertile land, and for this immigrants of a good stamp were desired.

So a Bhutanese dzong-pön had a talk with Ne-tuk, asking him to bring settlers from Sikkim to Bhutan. He promised to make him the headman of a village, exempting him from taxes as is usual in such cases.

But Ne-tuk demurred. 'I prefer to stay in Sikkim,' said he. 'You have no law in your country.'

'No, I will treat you well,' said the dzong-pön. 'A man like you, who knows how to control others, is just the type we want. Our soil here is virgin soil, and produces crops such as you will never get in Sikkim. You yourself shall pay no rent. It is a great opportunity for you.'

'I know exactly how it will be,' replied Ne-tuk. 'For the first three or four years, while we are clearing the land of the forest and undergrowth, you will treat us very well.

When we have spent money and labour on our holdings and worked them into good condition, so that we are tied to them, then you will begin. Our rents will be made heavy, but that is only a part of it. Your soldiers, your bailiffs, your private servants will come touring through my village. We shall have to feed them and their ponies, and not an anna [1] of payment will they make. If a villager has a good pony or a good cow, it will be taken away on one pretext or another. You have no law in your land. I prefer to remain in Sikkim.'

'Besides,' added Ne-tuk to me afterwards, as he recounted the incident, 'what about the spirits in my village? Will they not be angry if I leave? A friend of mine went to Bhutan against all the advice of his neighbours. Within a year or two his father died, his mother died, his wife and all his children. The whole family was exterminated.'

It is only fair to the late Maharaja of Bhutan to add that he lessened, as far as one man could do, the lawlessness inherent in this hardy but primitive people.

The rents paid by the peasants, as well as those paid by the herdsmen, will be dealt with together later on, when writing about the landed proprietors. And those taken by the State from the landlords will be discussed at the same time, that the taxation of the land may be studied as a whole. [2]

In the Chumbi and Kam-pu Valleys, and probably elsewhere in Tibet also, there is a custom of mortgaging land for a term of years in return for a loan. Both principal and interest are repaid by the mortgage, so that on the expiry of the term the owner receives back his land free of encumbrance. This is known as the 'period of years' (*lo-tü*). [3]

In the other type of mortgage the borrower gives the land for a term of years, but in this case the use of the land pays the interest only, and not the principal of the loan. When the period expires, if the lessor cannot repay the

---

[1] An Indian coin worth about a penny.
[2] See Chapter VIII and Appendix II.
[3] ལོ་དུས

principal, the lessee keeps the land. This species of mort-gage is known as *te-ma* or *mik-te*.

A common kind of sub-letting is that in which the sub-tenant pays a fixed sum yearly. In another recognized form the lessor and lessee share the produce equally. The lessor pays the rent; the lessee provides the seed and the labour. This is known as 'declaring the half' (*che-she*). In yet another kind of sub-letting so much is paid yearly for the land, either in cash or grain. It, too, is for a term of years.

All these forms of mortgage and sub-tenancy are found in Nepal also. Apart from them a landed proprietor may let out the whole of an estate to another, involving a full contract, inventory, and so forth.

In those districts in which the good land is all occupied the people are chary of allowing outsiders to buy in. The Chumbi Valley was a case in point. Divided as it is into two parts, Upper Tro-mo and Lower Tro-mo, with separate rural councils, the restrictions on selling were such that not even a man of the lower valley might buy land in the upper, or vice versa. In the adjoining Kam-pu Valley, where land was plentiful, they were ready to admit Tibetans from other districts.

On the initiative of a former Chinese Amban[1] the Tibetan Government created an Agricultural Department.[2] This was no doubt merely a small and simple affair, but it was able to bring a large amount of pasture land under the plough. The farmers profited, the food supply was increased, and the Government obtained additional revenue, which was sorely needed. The rentals for these holdings were fixed yearly amounts, but they were paid in grain, not in money. In Nepal the same kind of tenancy or sub-tenancy is known as *kuth*.

Slavery is not common in those parts of Tibet which I have visited. In Bhutan there was a good deal, but the slaves were often treated better than paid servants, for their masters felt that the latter, as they received wages,

[1] China's Representative in Lhasa.   [2] *So-nam Le-kung* in Tibetan.

Village headman in the Chumbi Valley
A member of the rural council

Houses in Ga-ling village, Chumbi Valley

could be made to do more work. The slaves were allowed to move about freely, for, when they were not at work, they had but to attend a roll-call in the morning and in the evening. Yet they did not run away very much. Like other men in Bhutan the slaves were privileged to carry swords.

The people of Tro-mo are exceptionally prosperous. Half the entire trade between Tibet and India passed down this narrow valley, known to Europeans as the Chumbi Valley. And the Tro-mo-was have a practical monopoly of this trade. As their prosperity grew, they took to employing as servants large numbers of men and women from the interior of Tibet. These drove the mules that carried the articles of commerce, and performed household tasks. To the Tro-mo-was, or many of them, fell the pleasanter duty of supervising the work and drawing the profits. To the servants were paid wages at least twice as high as they received in their own districts and provinces. The Tro-mo-was accounted the people from the Tsang province to be the best servants, hardy, industrious, and unsophisticated. The Lhasa men, they used to say, were fonder of talking than of working; the Kam-pas (eastern Tibetans), irritable and quarrelsome.

The neighbouring valley of Kam-pu does not share in the prosperity of the Tro-mo-was. They do not hold the latter's golden key. It is agriculture alone on which they must subsist; trade advantages are not for them. During the British-Indian campaign against the Tibetans in 1888 they had to supply free transport, as the custom is, to the Tibetan troops, and this impoverished them. They borrowed largely from the Bhutanese cattle-owners, who graze their yaks in the Kam-pu Valley, from a Bhutanese agent, known as Druk Lo-tsa-wa, and from their own landlord, Ku-sho Lho-ling. The rate of interest doubled a debt in three years, and so the burden was a heavy one. To the Tro-mo-was they owed also a little; this was paid by cutting grass for them during the winter.

For the villages situated where cold or lack of sunshine

prevents the crops from ripening, existence is hard, though to the Tibetan himself it is nothing out of the common. Such a one is 'Frozen Water' (Chu-kya) on the Pa-ri plain at the foot of Cho-mo Lha-ri, a snow mountain towering nine thousand feet above it. The villages subsist by means of their sheep, yaks, and *dri*. They have also a few fields of barley, which never ripens. So they sell the straw, with its unripe grain, to the traders passing through to India and back again. The traders give this to their ponies and mules; it is greatly prized as fodder and commands a high price.

Though his lot may be a hard one according to our standards, the Tibetan does not waste much time in repining. He prefers to sing. Men and women sing as they return from work in the fields. Teams of labourers sing as they carry heavy logs down the streets. In one such refrain the three carrying the fore part of the log chanted,

Whose the jewel?

while the three behind gave reply,

Pull it please.[1]

We lunched one day in Lhasa at the house of Ku-sho Ne-tö. He had invited us to celebrate his promotion to the rank of De-pön, a military rank corresponding more or less to that of colonel. The roof of a neighbouring house was under repair. As they rammed down the earth to make the roof watertight, the workers sang, both men and women:

Without is seen the wall;
Be there no change without!
Within are kept the gems;
Be there no change within!

Which being interpreted is, 'Let the protecting wall

---

[1] In Tibetan,

'Su-i ma-ni? (སུའི་མ་ནི་)

Drem-pa shu.' (འདྲེན་པ་ཤུ་)

remain as it is and not fall down. Let the residents and the property in the house remain uninjured and intact.'

Cheerfulness is one of the dominant Tibetan characteristics. The poor have, as a rule, their full share of it, and it often takes the form of song and dance. The theatrical troupes that tour in Tibet, especially at certain seasons of the year, are mainly recruited from the tillers of the soil. When the tour is finished, they return to work in their fields. Meanwhile they have seen a bit of the world outside their villages and have enjoyed it, for the Tibetan loves travelling. He has the instincts of the nomad and his life as a husbandman is humdrum.

Let me describe a typical day in the life of a peasant, and take as an example one who lives in the Chumbi Valley. Here he enjoys a somewhat milder climate than those who force their subsistence from the bleak uplands of the interior.

He rises before dawn, dons his clothes, washes but little if at all, and mutters a few prayers such as he may know. As a rule older men are more devout than younger ones. Some will take a vow to repeat the sacred formula 'Om Ma-ni Pe-me [1] Hum' so many times; perhaps three hundred, perhaps five hundred times a day. These repetitions will be worked through partly when rising, and partly when retiring to rest. Or he may utter a short prayer for long life and for freedom from illness and accident. During the day, if any one sees a pathetic sight, e.g. some animal or bird being killed, he will repeat, 'Om Ma-ni Pe-me Hum.'

Then our peasant goes out to his fields, or to the woods to collect fuel. It is now a little after dawn. But before going out he drinks tea, taking some of his stock left from overnight, a brew of tea made thick and strong, and mixing it with boiling water.

During the forenoon, probably between nine and ten, the women of the house bring breakfast to the fields. If the field is near the house and the workers there are but

---

[1] Often written *padme*, but in central Tibet pronounced *pe-me*.

few, breakfast is brought ready cooked. But if a long distance off or the workers many, the women come to the field at about seven o'clock and cook the food in a corner of it. For this repast there may be tea, barley-meal, or buckwheat bread, and some turnips or radishes. Or perhaps, instead of these vegetables some cheese which is sprinkled on the bread. This cheese has been kept in a closed jar for not less than six or seven months, and perhaps even for two or three years. It has thoroughly rotted and gives out a powerful odour.

Breakfast lasts from twenty minutes to half an hour. Work is then resumed. The women stay in the fields and break the large clods with the backs of the hoes, sow the seed, and help in most of the other work, except the ploughing.

At about two o'clock comes the heavy meal of the day. And now there may be barley, wheat, or rice (for the rice lands of Sikkim and Bhutan are comparatively close), meat with turnips, radishes or potatoes, tea and beer, or distilled liquor. This meal may last for three-quarters of an hour or so. But in many parts breakfast and lunch are replaced by a single meal. This comes usually at about eleven in the forenoon. The party then knock off work for an hour, and may refresh themselves with barley-gruel, barley-flour, and a little meat.

Then work till dusk. The women again join in, but of course leave early to go and do the necessary housework, for Saturday Long-Life would be justly incensed if the cows were not milked and the fire unlit.

Supper follows. A possible menu will include gruel, bones well covered with meat, some dried leaves of turnips or radishes, tea, and perhaps more beer. And those who have done the ploughing will receive a little extra meat to recoup them for their heavy toil.

The meal finished, if the season be winter and the household of the province of Tsang, where the climate is cold and sheep are plentiful, the women will work a little on the raw wool while the men do odd jobs about the house. A large peat fire is lit, spreading much grime and dirt, but with it all a cheerful warmth.

In the warmer lands round Lhasa there are fewer sheep, and so the household soon retire to sleep. They are not addicted to peat fires. Mustard oil is used for lighting everywhere.

But during the lengthening days of summer, when agricultural operations are in full swing, whether his home be in Tsang or Ü, Saturday and his family do not sit for long after their meal. Soon they remove their clothes, wrap themselves up in blankets, and lie down to sleep on the hard little Tibetan mattresses. These are stuffed with barley straw instead of cotton.

So ends the summer day.

VII
THE NOBILITY

As befits a country still in the feudal stage, the nobles of Tibet exercise great power and influence. With the priests they share the higher posts in the administration; like the monasteries, they own large landed estates. And over their tenantry they exercise magisterial powers, the extent of which varies in some measure with the distance of the estate from Lhasa. It will certainly include the power of putting in the stocks, of fine, flogging, and short periods of imprisonment; it may even comprise all forms of punishment short of death itself.

The nobility are a class apart. There is in many respects a great gulf fixed between them and ordinary folk who bow down low before them and use a different vocabulary in addressing them. Speaking of those in like circumstances to himself the peasant says, *Yong-ki-re*: 'He will come.' But of a petty landlord he will say, *Pe-ki-re*, and of a nobleman, *Chhip-gyu-nang-ki-re*. His own pony is *ta*, his landowner's must be styled *chhik-pa*. But with it all there is mutual fellowship. Master and mistress, man and maid, will all join in the song during an entertainment in the house or grounds. In Lhasa one would often meet a party returning from their picnic in a *ling-ka*. Husband, wife, and servants all walked together. In one case a stream had to be crossed: one of the maidservants carried first the mistress and then the master across on her back. The servants, at any rate of the nobility, appeared to take a genuine pride in the past traditions and present standing of the House. But if his landlord be unduly oppressive, the patient peasant will comfort himself with the old proverb,

> E'en the lion, king of beasts,
> By a clever hare was slain.[1]

[1] Ri-ta gyal-po seng-ge yang   རི་དགས་རྒྱལ་པོ་སེང་གེ་ཡང་ །
Ri-pong lom-den chik-ki se.   རི་བོང་བློ་ལྡན་གཅིག་གིས་བསད་ ॥

The Tibetan nobleman traces his descent to one of three sources. It may be that an ancestor was ennobled for good work done for the country. Take the case of the noble family of Pa-lha. The founder was a Bhutanese priest from the Pa-cho Lha-kang Monastery, near Tra-shi Chö-dzong in western Bhutan. He, along with others, was driven out of Bhutan in the seventeenth century during the warfare which established the power of the first Dharma Raja in that country. Coming to Lhasa, he abandoned the priesthood and entered the service of the Government. So successful was he in his work that he finally gained a place on the Supreme Council. This body, composed of one priest and either three or four laymen, has, under the Dalai Lama or Regent, the highest share in the administration of the country. The Government presented him with the estate of Pen-jor Lhün-po, containing a hundred and thirty farms, and lying one day's journey from Gyangtse. He took the name of Pa-lha from his old monastery Pa-cho Lha-kang, according to the system of contracting words, which is common in Tibet. He died leaving a daughter, but no son.

This daughter married a son of the house of Nu-ma, which claims descent from Ga-wo, the famous minister of the still more famous king, Song-tsen Gam-po, who ruled Tibet over twelve hundred years ago. Young Nu-ma entered his wife's family and carried on the Pa-lha line, according to the usual practice in Tibet when male issue fails. Their descendants were men of ability, who served the State in the highest posts, and in doing so, consolidated and increased the family property.

One of the ablest Tibetans of recent years was Sha-tra, the Chief Minister, who died in 1919. Himself a member of the Shang-ka family, his wife was a Sha-tra, and he thus joined this celebrated family, who have served Tibet for the last two or three hundred years in the highest positions, somewhat on the same lines as the Cecils have done in England. His younger brother was married to his wife's sister: formerly, indeed, the Minister had both as his wives.

The family in which a Dalai Lama or a Tashi Lama takes rebirth is *ipso facto* ennobled and receives a large estate from the Government. Some of the leading Lhasan nobles are descended from the brothers of previous Dalai Lamas. Sam-trup Po-trang traces his descent from the brother of the seventh Dalai Lama, who lived two hundred years ago; Pün-kang from the brother of the tenth. The house of Lha-lu owe their vast estates to the marriage which united two families, in one of which had been found the eighth, in the other the twelfth Dalai Lama. Each family was but that of a peasant, when the Incarnation of the Buddha was found in it.

As long as a Dalai Lama lives, his family is known as 'The New Patrimony' (*Yap-shi Sar-pa*). When he dies, they take the new name by which they will henceforth be enrolled in the ranks of the nobility.

The remaining section of the aristocracy is the oldest and smallest of all. These are· they who trace their ancestry right back to the early monarchs, who ruled Tibet several centuries before the Norman conquest of England. The house of Lha-gya-ri claim an unbroken male descent from the king 'Clear Light' (Ö-sel); the House of Ra-ka-shar a similar descent from the king known as 'The Bird'. Both 'Clear Light' and 'The Bird' ruled before the seventh century when Song-tsen Gam-po held sway and extended his conquests into China and elsewhere. These rulers are known as the 'Religious Kings' (*Chö-gyal*), and so it happens that the heads of the Lha-gya-ri and Ra-ka-shar families are even now greeted by their tenants with obeisances accorded only to lamas. They are in fact looked on as lamas. They do indeed marry, but so did the Religious Kings. When a head of either family dies, a tomb is made and encased in silver, just as those of the Dalai Lamas are encased in gold.

Some members of the nobility hold special titles, such as *Kung*, *Dza-sa*, &c. *Kung* is the rank given to the father of each Dalai Lama, together with the grant of land. From him these descend to one of his sons, not necessarily to the eldest, but to whichever may be agreed on in the family. The *Kungs* have the highest rank among all laymen, but not, as a rule, much power unless they can push their way up through the regular official line. The father or brother of a reigning Dalai Lama was formerly prohibited from holding any official post, though he might hold a post in the Dalai Lama's household. This rule, however, has been changed during recent years; for one of the Dalai Lama's nephews, the Kung, is Chief Minister of Tibet, while another nephew is Commander-in-Chief of the army.

Dza-sas may be appointed from either priests or laymen. The title is given to certain eminent persons or for eminent services rendered. It descends from father to son. They have not much power, but they—as also the *Kungs*—are entitled to attend meetings of the National Assembly.

Te-chi. This title ranks equally with that of *Dza-sa.* It is held by laymen only.

There is a tendency, though by no means a universal one, for the features of the older nobility to evolve into a type different from those of the ordinary Tibetan. Among the Sikkimese, i.e. those of Tibetan stock living in Sikkim, a long face is held to be an attribute of noble birth. They say, 'His face is long; it is the face of a nobleman.' [1] You will frequently hear in Sikkim that the faces of the masses have been flattened by the carrying of loads through many generations.

The usual Tibetan dress, clothes, hats, and boots, have been discussed briefly above.[2] The gentry combine the different kinds of national attire with Chinese dress. They frequently wear Chinese velvet boots reaching half-way from the ankle to the knee, shorter than the Tibetan boots but still warm.

The wool used in the clothes of the upper classes in

---

[1] *Dong ring-po duk,*
Pön dong-po be.
[2] See p. 20.

Lhasa is taken mainly from the sheep of central Tibet. Their wool is softer than that from the Northern Plains, which is not regarded as fit for making the gowns of gentlefolk. But it is rated as better than the wool from the Mongolian sheep.

Waist-bands of silk are often worn. One in my possession is of green silk with a clasp of white jade. It must be worn only with clothes of Chinese, not Tibetan, make, for it is out of tune with the latter. Dress is strictly regulated in Tibet. Nothing used to surprise the people of that country more when they visited Darjeeling than to see the Governor of Bengal wearing the same kind of clothes, hats, and boots as ordinary everyday Englishmen.

The fashions, being strict, do not change except now and then. Certainly now and then, for the demon of unrest has stirred the ladies of Lhasa, the fashionable set; to make a slight change during the last few years in the shape of their head-dress.

Dress plays an important part in the life of the Tibetans, of the men as well as the women. They do not dress only in sombre suits of black or grey or brown. In cloaks and waist-bands, hats and boots, gay colours—all colours —are for them. Wool and cotton, silk and brocade, each has its uses. The material as well as the fashioning of his costumes is as bright and as costly as that of his wife and her lady friends. When one attends a Tibetan festival on the Lhasa plain in the vivid Tibetan sunshine, it is indeed a brilliant spectacle, for the varied hues glint in the strong light and the holiday spirit pervades all.

Some of the noble families own dresses of great age, which are of such surpassing quality that they have gained national celebrity. Probably the most famous of all is that in the possession of the Pa-lha family, one in the Sha-tra household ranking second. This Pa-lha dress was taken —perhaps stolen—from one of the store-rooms of a Chinese emperor, several hundred years ago. So famous

indeed is it that the Tibetans have a popular verse about
it, which may be thus translated:

> On the green sward shines one rainbow;
> Two upon the stream, and on the
> Noble robes in Pa-lha's mansion
> Three bright rainbows shine together.[1]

The dress is worn but rarely. There are sports and
games during the concluding days of the 'Great Prayer'
(Mön-lam Chem-po) festival in the first Tibetan month,
which are presided over by two Masters of Ceremonies
(Ya-sö, lit. 'The Highest Worshippers'). When it is the
turn of the Pa-lha family to supply one of the Ya-sö, their
representative may occasionally wear the celebrated dress.
The most valuable portions of it are the gown and the
hat, the latter being of black fox-skin.

A black fox-skin is valued very highly in Tibet and
may cost in Chinese or Tibetan currency the equivalent
of a hundred and fifty pounds. One skin suffices to make
two caps. Such a cap is worn on exceptional occasions
only. These skins come to Lhasa through Kansu.

The houses of the nobility are imposing edifices,
usually built—at any rate in central Tibet—around a
rectangular courtyard. A solid, wooden gate affords in-
gress. On three sides are stables and storehouses; on the
fourth, opposite the gate, is the mansion itself, one or two
stories higher than the other three sides, and sometimes
as much as five stories in height. A building on this plan
offers the greatest protection against the blustering gales of
the Tibetan tablelands, and groups the entire household,
family, servants, and cattle, within its patriarchal embrace.

[1] The Tibetan runs as follows:

> Ja chik pang-la suk-song;
> Ja nyi chu-la suk-song;
> Ja sum Bang-gye-shar-kyi
> Nam-sa yar-la suk-song.

Each line contains three trochees (–∪–∪–∪). It is not possible to translate
into English within these limits, as Tibetan is a highly condensed language.
Bang-gye-shar is the name of the Lhasan house of the Pa-lha family. The
name means 'The Full and Victorious House that faces the East'.

We shall probably find on the entrance gate a painting faded with age. Frequently this is of the swastika (卐), emblem of durability. Or it may be the well-known picture, 'Mongol leading tiger'. This painting, which bears witness to the physical strength of some Mongols, brings good luck when put on the doors of houses, for it increases the power and prosperity of the inmates. Such signs are portrayed on the doors of all classes.

The floors may be of substantial wooden planks, roughly smoothed over. And often they are of small stones, mixed with sand and earth and ground into small pieces. The whole is then rammed down hard and polished with oil.

The walls are constructed of flat stones bound together with mud. In the smaller buildings, and especially in the upper layers, the stones are replaced by sun-dried bricks. The roof is flat and is formed like the earth floor, but is not polished. Windows are plentiful, but there is no glass, except in very few cases. Its place is taken by waxcloth or other similar material. Strong wooden shutters protect this from rough usage. On the roof we shall find a stand in which incense is burnt.

Every Tibetan, even the poorest, keeps a few images of the Buddha, deities, saints, &c., in his home. Not only the gentry and the merchants, but shopkeepers and peasants have 'religion-rooms' (chö-kang) in their houses. Even the poorest peasant has such a room. It may be only eight or nine feet square, the length of the short Tibetan beam, thus requiring no pillar in the centre. In this room Tuesday Purpose-Fulfilled keeps his religious books. These he may read in the mornings, for nearly all Tibetans can read a little, though not many can write. He has a few images modelled from clay, and a wooden altar inherited through many generations and black with age.

Modern Tibet, especially near the borders of Sikkim, shows the first glimmering of Western influence by permitting a photograph of the Dalai Lama on the altar to

'Mongol leading tiger'

Such robes and boots are often worn by Tibetans of the upper grades

Tibetan painting

serve as an image of His Holiness, receiving its own meed of reverence and worship. Seven little bowls of holy water on the front of the altar are essential, as well as a lamp or two. The wick of this floats in butter instead of oil, for cattle are plentiful in Tibet, but oil is scarce. Such lamps are burnt as sacrificial offerings in time of need, and especially when sickness or death opens the flood-gates of prayer.

Religious pictures, painted or embroidered on silk or paper, somewhat after the manner of kakemonos in Japan, hang on walls and pillars. And a bookcase with a few of the sacred volumes will find a place if the means of the householder can afford it. But whether in a bookcase or in a chest, some books there must be, for the Law unites with the Priesthood and the Buddha himself to form the supreme Buddhist Triad, 'The Three Chief Rare Ones'.

In his religion-room the farmer, poor or rich, keeps also his better clothes, the ornaments of his women, and other valuable goods. These are stored in chests or cupboards arranged round the walls.

One or two of the chapels in the houses of wealthy people may be a *gön-kang*, which British travellers often describe as a sort of Chamber of Horrors, from the fearsome masks that line the walls, and the stuffed wild yak that may hang from the ceiling. In sober truth, however, the *gön-kang*, as its name implies, is the room reserved chiefly for the Gön-pos, or Guardian Deities of the Faith, with especial reference to that one under whose protection the family rests.

A Tibetan landowner, of good position though not in the highest rank, explained his arrangement to me thus:

'The ordinary *ku-tra* (squire) employs a monk always to pray for him and his household, including his animals. horses, cattle, sheep, donkeys, pigs, &c. This monk prays regularly every day in the morning, midday, and evening; perhaps for an hour or so at each of these three times. If there is any special need, e.g. much sickness in the household or on the estate, his prayers will be extended.

'Such monk is changed every three years, when he returns to his monastery, after making over charge of his duties to the monk sent by the monastery to take his place. The nobility, e.g. Lhalu, Shatra, &c., will employ two monks permanently. My estate, Ne-tö, is near the Tse-chen Monastery, in the Gyangtse jurisdiction. Tse-chen supplies me with my monk.

'I pay my monk 60 *ke* of barley a year, each *ke* being worth ten *tang-kas*.[1] I give him also three measures of tea daily; and a lunch three or four times a month, especially on the three holy days of each month, i.e. the 8th, 15th, and last day. His meat, butter, &c., he can buy by selling part of the barley that I give him, half of which suffices him.'

' Do you give him tea of as good quality as you drink yourself?'

'Well, not quite, but not greatly inferior, and the same applies to his other food. For, if I give him inferior food, he will be depressed. And when he is depressed, the god he is worshipping will be depressed also. We Tibetans have a saying, "Gods, devils, and men are alike in actions and thoughts",[2] i.e. the same things will anger them and the same things will please them, and they will act accordingly.

'I have three or four chapels in my house at Ne-tö; the largest contains images of Sa-kya Tup-pa (Gotama Buddha), King Love, Chen-re-si, and Dröl-ma. In the smaller chapels are kept the lesser deities, one of these smaller chapels being the Gön-kang in which the image of my Gön-po is kept with other fierce deities. Such is the regular practice in Tibetan houses.'

'Which of the Gön-pos is yours?'

After thinking a little, 'Oh, well, I don't know which

---

[1] A *tang-ka* was at the time worth fourpence.

[2] Lha dre mi sum chö-nang chik.　ཀླུ་འདྲེ་མི་གསུམ་སྤྱོད་སྣང་གཅིག །

of them he is; there are such a lot of them; but in any case he gets his worship regularly.'

'Do you have other services besides these regular ones every day?'

'Yes, whenever there is any great sickness about or any special danger or calamity, some monks come in and read a part of the Kan-gyur. I have the complete Kan-gyur in a hundred and twelve volumes in my large chapel. If, for instance, I am ill and the medicine I am taking is not doing me any good, the reading of a suitable part of the Kan-gyur will make that same medicine effectual. Yes [seeing perhaps a flicker of doubt pass over my face], there is no doubt whatever of that. Or, if one of us has some special work to undertake, or something out of the common is likely to happen, a part of the Kan-gyur will be read. I do not tell the monks what the special event is, but merely that there is a special event in which we wish to be successful, and they then read whatever is necessary.

'And once every year I have the whole Kan-gyur read through, to give prosperity to us all, human beings and animals included, and to ward off sickness and other ills. For this special service thirty-five to forty monks come, and it takes them about ten days.'

It should be stated here that the Kan-gyur—the Buddhist Scripture of Tibet—or other work to be read, is divided among the monks called to read it. Each takes his own appointed portion and reads it aloud, but in a low voice. All sit together. It is thus possible to read through the whole in the space of ten days or so. A row of monks, shorn and bare-headed, in their robes of dull red, seated in some room or verandah, each head bowed over its appointed portion of the sacred book as it intones in a quiet, far-away voice, this is a common sight in Tibet.

Not all Tibetans take so casual an interest in their guardian deity as my light-hearted friend. A nobleman of old family knew well under whose protection he rested. He said, 'It is usual for a nobleman and a squire, as well as for a few of the richer traders and farmers, to keep a *Gön-kang* in addition to a *Lha-kang* (chapel) in his house. In the *Gön-kang* among other images are those of the *Gön-po* and his attendants. There are five or six *Gön-pos* from among whom the choice is usually made. Of these the '*Six-armed Gön-po*' is perhaps the one most commonly worshipped. Another kind has four arms, another has two arms. The six-armed one is popularly regarded as being exceptionally powerful.

'I worship the six-armed *Gön-po*, because my ancestors have always worshipped this one. In the first instance a lama settles by astrology which *Gön-po* a family should worship. Not only of these but of all gods and goddesses, one's worship is inherited from one's ancestors.'

In 1898 a new Tibetan palace was built for the Ruler of Sikkim. The first step was to exorcise the site, a ceremony which was performed by two Lamas, one from Sikkim, the other from eastern Tibet. The date of this exorcism is entered in the History of Sikkim. It was the third day of the eighth month of the Earth Dog year.

A little later the foundation-stone was laid in accordance with English custom, for Sikkim was then coming under the administration of Mr. White, a British official. In all Tibetan lands omens are anxiously observed. The historian, therefore, does not conceal his pleasure when he records that on this day 'a shower in sunshine and a rainbow spanning the mountains made the ceremony as auspicious as could be desired. And of course such an important event was concluded by a great feast to the workmen.'

Before a house is commenced on a new site, a Lama should always be consulted as to whether the land is good or bad; in other words, whether it is the resort of devils or not. Of course if devils have already been seen or heard, no further inquiry is needed, but there are few who have the power so to see or hear them. If the Lama passes the site as sound, the builder can go forward. Should devils be located, it is for the Lama to drive them away by exorcism or other religious services. When a house is completed, whether of a nobleman or a peasant, it must be consecrated before being used or within a short time afterwards. The priest who consecrates it should be one of deep learning.

In order to give a clearer definition to these general remarks let me set out briefly the arrangement of the rooms in the Pa-lha mansion at Drong-tse, some thirteen miles from Gyangtse down the broad valley of the river Nyang. Being in the quiet depths of the country, it escaped the British Expedition to Lhasa in 1904. It escaped also the far more devastating Chinese attacks in 1911, when the great Lhasa houses of the Sam-trup Po-trang, Ra-ka-shar, and Pa-lha families were completely demolished, and many others looted and partially destroyed.

The house at Drong-tse is built round a quadrangular courtyard. The side opposite the entrance rises to four stories above the ground. Formerly there were seven floors, but two were taken off, being found unsafe. On the topmost floor the members of the family live during the summer months, going one story down in the winter for the sake of warmth. Their sitting-rooms, bedrooms, and kitchen are here. There is a schoolroom also, to which come both the sons of the house and those of the retainers and the tenantry, but the Pa-lha boys have their own special seats. A small praying-room, where the family priests read prayers, though poorly furnished, is heated with braziers of yak-dung, the common fuel of high Tibet, where wood is scarce and coal practically unknown. Thus warmed, the family gather in it often during the cold mornings and evenings of the long Tibetan winter. All the sitting-rooms have altars and images in them, for, from prince to peasant, their religion is part and parcel of the life of the Tibetan people.

On the floor below are found the room for the two stewards, in which they do their work and pass the day. On the walls hang bows and arrows kept ready for the archery which delights the heart of Tibetan man and maid,

held as it is under the blue Tibetan sky and accompanied
by wine and song. On the floor are three or four of the
low Tibetan tables with teacups on them drawing attention to the national beverage. Beyond are two *Gön-
kangs*. Here, too, is the largest chapel in the house. It is
known as the Kan-gyur chapel, for it enshrines a complete
copy of the Buddhist canonical books, one hundred and
eight volumes in all. In the floor is a large trap-door
through which is poured grain into the storeroom below.
A kitchen for the servants, a storeroom, and a large reception room, used for important entertainments, complete
the tale of rooms on this story. It was on this floor that
my wife and I were lodged when on a three days' visit to
Drong-tse in 1915. For our room we were given a large
chapel, part of it being partitioned for our use. Behind
the partition a monk could be heard off and on from five
o'clock in the morning intoning the services for the Pa-lha
household.

At the New Year the more influential retainers and
tenants come to offer ceremonial scarves to the head of the
house. If a member of the house is present, he receives the
scarves; if not, these are laid on the table in front of his
empty seat.

On the floor below we are among the rooms for servants
and for storage. An apartment used for housing wool runs
along one side. From end to end of the other side runs
a long room for housing grain. Part of the latter, however,
is taken up by two open verandahs, separated by a partition wall and facing the courtyard. These spaces are used
by persons of rank somewhat lower than that of the master
of the house for watching the entertainments that from
time to time take place in the courtyard. Convention
requires that those of highest rank shall sit in the highest
seats, though thereby they lose the better view of the
spectacle. The nobility are accommodated with seats in
the gallery, the common folk are relegated to the stalls.

Rugs, tables, &c., filled a lumber-room; in another
bread was kept; in yet another was stored barley to be used

for making beer (*chang*). I had often heard that Tibetans laid in a large part of their meat supply once yearly, in October, and here I witnessed the proof of this. For in a large room joints of yak-beef and mutton were hanging from the ceiling. The meat had been killed for nine months—October to July—but was free from offensive smell. A bedroom for the priests and various servants' apartments found place on this floor.

On the first story are two rooms for brewing beer, a large room in which meat, barley-flour, oil, and such-like are stored together. Along the other sides we find rooms used for peas, barley, and other grain.

After the Tibetan custom a strong wooden ladder with steep, narrow steps leads to the courtyard below. At the top of the ladder, in a recess on each side of it, stands a praying-wheel, as high as a man and of ample girth. Thousands upon thousands of incantations and prayers are printed and pressed together within these great cylinders. At the foot of each sits an old dame, who makes it to revolve, and in so doing sets upwards this mass of prayer and offering for the benefit of the world at large and the Pa-lha household in particular. Of the two old women the son of the house remarks, 'They are past other work,' implying that merit is being gained without much cost. A great many other barrel-shaped praying-wheels are on this floor, overlooking the courtyard, but they are smaller.

Round the courtyard, under the projecting verandahs of the floor above, are stables. At the back of these are rooms for storing hay. The main stables are outside the house and courtyard but close to them. Barley stored in the granaries keeps good for at least a hundred years, and probably for much longer.

Of course Tibetan mansions are not all on the same pattern. That of Lha-lu, on the outskirts of Lhasa, is of a design somewhat different from the building just described. But a wall surrounds the house and checks the ferocity of the winter gales.

Though the family has vast estates, and though the

head of the family held the proud title of *kung*, the highest among the secular titles, yet things were not happy in the house of Lha-lu, when Colonel Kennedy and I visited it in 1921. The two *kungs*, father and son, had died recently and none of the family were living in it. It was given over to servants, and had a general air of desolation. The mother and the wife of the elder *kung*—the younger died when sixteen years old—were both living elsewhere in Lhasa. They could not bear to live in Lha-lu after their bereavements, and had even asked the Dalai Lama to take all their estates from them. But His Holiness had refused to do this.

Large portions of the house were rebuilt a few years ago, and to this fact Pa-lhe-se attributes the family misfortunes. He recalls the Tibetan saying:

> If a house be rebuilt,
> Then the pillar will fall.

And this in plain language means that a member of the family will die.

In four or five of the rooms small parties of monks were reading aloud from books of prayer. In a large hall down below fifteen or twenty were singing chants from memory, their bodies swaying from side to side as they sang. By these services it was hoped to render more easy the passage of the deceased through the Buddhist Purgatory, and to ensure them rebirths in good positions when they return to earth.

Notwithstanding their personal troubles, the household insisted on according to us the full measure of Tibetan hospitality. The room in which we were offered the usual tea, cakes, and fruit was, as so often happens, a chapel and sitting-room combined. But it was unusual in that it faced towards the north. Tibetans usually arrange that their best rooms shall catch as much sunlight as possible.

One of the many rooms contained a large gilt model of a *chö-ten*. These are conical masonry structures, derived from the *stupas* of Indian Buddhism, and often contain relics of saints, images, or other dedicated objects. From

Lha-lu Mansion. Reckoned by the Chinese as one of the five beauties of Lhasa

one end to the other the mountains and valleys and plains of Tibet are dotted with *chö-tens*. An inquiry about this model elicits the reply that it was set up, when the elder *kung* died, to ward off further misfortune, but alas! fell short of its purpose. Such models have other uses also, for when a Tibetan has a severe illness, he fears that it may recur in the same month of the next year, the illness being caused by one of the many kinds of devils which harass the inhabitants of this country. So, to prevent this, a *chö-ten* containing sacred images may be set up. This kind of devil is known as *Si*, and this kind of *chö-ten* as *Si-dok*,[1] i.e. 'The Reversing of the *Si* devil'.

Another room, a large one, has whitewashed walls. Photographs, mostly of Chinese worthies, are hung high up all round the walls, which otherwise are bare. A particularly cheerless room this, and we can think no better of it even when we are gravely informed that it is the 'English room', being furnished, it is believed, in the English style. I cannot help wondering what lonesome Indian bungalow is responsible for this travesty.

One small room, about ten feet by five, with a floor of solid well-fitted planking, is shown as the apartment in which the head of the house slept and prayed during each winter. His bed lies across the window of the room, which is cheerful with Chinese frescoes of a frivolous order.

The sacred pictures (*tang-ka*) in a chapel are on Chinese silk of exceptionally fine quality. And in almost all the rooms we see valuable old pieces of china and cloisonné, three or four such pieces in each room. Pictures on secular subjects adorn many of the walls; these are all frescoes painted by Chinese. Paintings on religious subjects, somewhat after the style of Japanese *kakemonos*, are all by Tibetan artists.

The verandah of a little house in the adjoining park reveals a box containing a pair of guinea-pigs. An in-

[1] སྲི་བཟློག

quiry as to whence they came brings the reply, amid laughter, that they belong to the Dalai Lama, who receives so many presents of animals that his subjects have to help him in looking after them.

Lha-lu is regarded by the Chinese as one of the five beauties of Lhasa. And so it is. But, when we came, it was unhappy, desolate.

Apart from the chapels with their altars, images, and other religious paraphernalia, there is not much furniture in a Tibetan house. Along the inside wall of the living-room may be wooden chests, holding clothes and other possessions. One or two small mattresses (*böl-den*) serve as seats during the day, and for bed at night. They are overlaid with gay-patterned rugs, usually of Tibetan, but occasionally of Chinese, manufacture. The colouring of these is from vegetable indigo and the numerous dyes obtainable in Tibet and the Himalaya. By these seats are placed the Tibetan tables. These can be folded up, the fronts and sides being tucked underneath. They are elaborately carved with designs of dragons, lotuses, gems, and such-like auspicious and pleasing objects. On the tables are the inevitable teacups. We may find also a few strong, stiff wooden chairs after the Chinese pattern, and a rough wooden table or two to accompany these.

Round the house is the *ling-ka*, which takes the place of a garden and park. It is carpeted with grass, and a wall of stone or sun-dried brick, which may be anything between four and twelve feet high, surrounds it. Inside are trees, mostly willow, sometimes poplar, and occasionally walnut, apricot, &c. These are planted at short intervals, and are often little more than shrubs, for tree-growth is slow at twelve thousand feet above the sea.

A feature of the *ling-ka* is the 'Pleasure House' (*tro-kang*). This is often of one story only, the roof being supported by strong uprights of poplar with scantlings of poplar or willow supporting the flat mud roof. The walls may be of stone, as are those of the main house, or of stone in the lower courses and sun-dried brick in the upper. A

' A feature of the *ling-ka* is the Pleasure House '

At Kung-tang, a few miles from Lhasa

verandah helps to keep out rain and snow, and adds to the
amenities in summer. In the verandah of one pleasure
house which I visited, charms were hung to keep off illness and frost. Hither the great man and his family may
retire during the summer months, to enjoy the greenery
and the quiet, while outside all is wind and dust. And if,
as often happens, he has a short archery course, it will
serve to pass the peaceful afternoons, and afford him an
opportunity for entertaining his friends and neighbours to
the accompaniment of wine and song, dancing and
gambling. Host and guest, manservant and maidservant,
whoever can play or sing, all join in together.

The fairest parks that I have seen are those near Lhasa.
One such, with its pleasure house, stands out in my
memory. Situated in the broad valley, a few miles above
Lhasa, the park of the Pün-kang family is beautiful beyond
the ordinary. Inside the pleasure-house is an enchanting
Chinese picture on some half a dozen panels. The colouring is pure and rich, the features are likelike. It is painted
on the inside of the glass which seems to frame the
picture.

This park is set with a variety of trees, including a
walnut, which is entirely innocent of fruit, for—poor
thing—with the large trees all round, it sees but little of
the sun, so much needed in this cold climate. The coun-
trywoman, who acts as a caretaker, explains that, if the
tree were pierced, it would exude a white juice, and then
walnuts would grow. But this would injure the serpent
spirits, of whom there are two in this park, one in each of
the corners nearest the tree. And this of course is un-
thinkable.

Sunk in the ground, square in shape and several feet
across, is a stone-built, open-air bath. It is fed by open
drains, likewise of stone. Near by is a solid stone plinth,
which formerly carried a wooden summer-house.

A large slab of stone supported on vertical slabs is for
the convenience of the lady of the house, who deposits
her odds and ends on it when she lingers in her charming

little garden. Once a week Pün-kang himself spends the
day here away from the glare and dust of Lhasa.

When leading a rural existence the feudal conditions of
Tibet assure to the large landowner a pre-eminent position. In spite of this—or perhaps because of it—he is
attracted by town life as a rule. 'We like Lhasa best of
all,' said one, 'and after Lhasa, Shigatse or Gyangtse.
Large towns are more pleasant than the country, for the
food is better and there is more to do and see. Monks
who are sincerely devoted to religion, prefer secluded
places, but we laymen prefer the towns.'

VIII

THE NOBILITY (*continued*)

TIBET is a poor country. Huge areas are sterile; other tracts give but scanty herbage. Even those lands which produce crops give no large outturn in this cold climate. Minerals have not yet been discovered in paying quantities.

Yet by comparison with their fellow subjects the nobles of Tibet are wealthy. On the Pa-lha estates are at least 1,400 farms, as well as thirteen grazing-grounds, each supporting fifteen to twenty families of graziers. To the Government Pa-lha pays revenue on some estates and holds others revenue free, but of his payments to the Government and of his receipts from the tenantry a small amount only is in coin. A larger share is taken and passed on in grain, mainly barley; but the chief item in both rent and revenue is that of service rendered without pay. And this last duty falls on the farmer and his family; the shepherd does not render unpaid service, unless he be of the peasant-grazier type, owning land in addition to his flock.

An average farmer on these estates pays his rent in labour, grain, and cash, as well as a little in oddments, i.e. wool, butter, yak-hair ropes, &c. His household may number five or six persons. His rental, including the market value of this unpaid labour, may average three to four pounds a year.

An average grazing-ground pays in kind, thus:

	£
(i) Butter worth about	12
(ii) Cheeses; hard and cubical, but nutritious and enduring, worth about	1
Total . .	13

Unpaid service does not have to be rendered.

To the Tibetan Government the family pays yearly

£150 in cash and 9,999 measures (*ke* [1]) of grain. And the tenantry's supply of laden animals and porters goes mainly to the Government, who issue requisitions in favour of officials and other persons travelling on Government business.

There are occasionally extra taxes, the chief of which are:

(i) *Yong-dön*. A grain tax, to be paid when any great event, such as a war, takes place.

(ii) *Shap-ten Lem-bü*. Last taken when the present Dalai Lama assumed his powers.

In addition to the above taxes the family is bound to supply two members to work as Government officials on nominal salaries. For each one short of this number a tax of about eight pounds a year, known as the 'Self Substitute', has to be paid.

Summing up the financial position of the Pa-lha landed estates one may say that the family receives yearly about five thousand pounds and pays two thousand two hundred to the Government on its landed property. But it will be understood that a thousand pounds in Tibet is worth far more than a thousand pounds in England, for prices and wages are much lower. And a Tibetan household, whether of noble or peasant, is almost self-contained, so that it needs not to buy greatly from outside. Moreover, the majority increase their income by trade. A love of buying and selling lies deep down in the hearts of the men and women of this land. And in other directions also the income is capable of increase. [2]

Riding one day during March 1921 up the valley of the Kyi Chu near Lhasa with a Tibetan companion, himself a landed proprietor, our talk drifted to the great landlords of Tibet. The greatest of all he estimated to be Sha-tra, Lha-lu, Ra-ka-shar, and Sam-trup Po-trang.

---

[1] A *ke*, i.e. 'a score'—so named because it comprises twenty *tre*—is a measure which holds about thirty-three lb. of barley or peas, and seventeen lb. of barley-flour.

[2] Fuller detail as to the management of landed property is given in the two Appendixes.

In the Lha-lu estates are forty or fifty head farmers who collect the dues from the others. Similarly among the herdsmen are fifty or sixty chiefs. From each head farmer Lha-lu receives on the average fifteen hundred measures (*ke*) of grain, mostly barley, in addition to consignments of butter, cheese, woollen cloth and some cash, worth in all some three hundred pounds. Each chief among the herdsmen brings butter, cheese, yak-hair and yak-tails worth perhaps sixty pounds. His incomings will thus amount to about twenty thousand pounds yearly.

'And, of course,' adds my informant, 'his tenants supply him with ponies, yaks, &c., for riding and transport when he needs them, and he does not pay wages to his servants, for these are his tenants. Yet the family is in debt, for as the saying runs, "To hold the land of the king is even worse than to take the property of the priest". Of course, there are many of us who have small estates, but that is in lieu of pay for the service which we render to the Government, and there is no great harm in that.'

'How did the family fall into debt?' I ask.

'Because there have been several deaths in it, and their funeral expenses have been high. When the last *Kung* died they set jewels in the head-dress of the great Buddha (*Cho*), which is in the Temple in Lhasa. These jewels were worth a thousand *do-tse* (about six thousand pounds). Such gifts and other expenses have indeed thrown them into debt. But what does that matter! They will give the *Kung* a better rebirth, and will serve to draw him up to a higher stage of existence, perhaps into the Gods' World (*lha-yül*), until the time comes for him to be reborn again in this human world. If he must go to Hell meanwhile, they will shorten the time there.

"To pay for their munificence the Lha-lu family has borrowed from the Ecclesiastical Treasury (*Tse Chan-dzö*) and the Secular Treasury (*Lab-rang Chan-dzö*), as well as from the three great monasteries Se-ra, Dre-pung, and Gan-den. It owes large sums also to merchants of Tibet, Nepal, and Ladakh for goods supplied. After a year or two these charge interest on money thus owing. As for the three monasteries, they lend large sums on interest. Many officials are indebted to them as well as to the Tibetan, Ladakhi, and Nepalese merchants in Lhasa.

'In spite of its debts, the Lha-lu family gave gifts to Se-ra, Dre-pung, and Gan-den during the recent Prayer Festival at the rate of one *trang-ka* for each of the twenty-one thousand monks then in residence, in order to bring good rebirths. No doubt they are heavily in debt already, but their rent-roll is large, and they feel the need of securing good rebirths for the heads of the family at any cost.'

Some of the younger generation among the Tibetan gentry, e.g. those who have themselves seen, or in other ways come to understand, conditions in India, hold that the landed proprietors ought to pay more land revenue to the State. They feel that some of the nobility, e.g. Sam-trup Po-trang, hold far too much land and give to the State too little service in return for it. *Per contra* that the late Prime Minister, Lön-chen Sho-kang, who happened to own but a small estate and whose salary in cash, as of all Government officials, was trifling in amount, was but poorly remunerated for his heavy work and high responsibility. Sho-kang himself, as was the case with most of the elder officials, belonged to the old school, and so did not desire any change.

However, the new idea was taking root, for the need of additional Government revenue is imperative, and the field of selection is, under the present system, closely restricted. Other ideas will inevitably follow. For when young Tibetans travel abroad to Europe, they can hardly fail to contrast the condition of the tenantry in their feudal country with those living in the advanced communities of the West.

The Tibetan landlord can have his tenant beaten as severely as he wills, short of killing him. He may put his neck in the heavy cangue, his feet in iron fetters. But there are limits. The *tsa-tsik* enjoins a measure of moderation. If any of the landlords', the order runs, 'or managers of the monastic estates punish their tenants by life imprisonment or mutilation of the person, the Dzong-pön must submit a detailed report immediately to the Government and he is warned against failing to report such matters.'

In actual practice proprietors of great estates may even inflict punishments such as these, provided that they first obtain permission from the Government in Lhasa. In mutilating, the hand may be severed at the wrist, or the leg at the knee. Or, in rare cases, the lower half of the nose may be cut off. Or both eyes may be put out, for then the hardened offender will at last be unable to pillage the countryside or commit other heinous crimes.

When Western education spreads through Tibet, it will open many eyes and incite the manual workers to claim far greater rights. And that is one reason why it was important to commence by educating the children of the upper classes. This commencement was made on my return from Lhasa, in 1921, when the Tibetan Government opened a school at Gyangtse for this purpose. To this school, at the request of the Tibetans themselves, an English head master was appointed.

The great landowners often own small pieces of land, scattered here and there, in addition to their main estates. A typical example of this is the little hamlet of Sa-lu in the Nyang Valley south of Gyangtse. It belongs to the Pa-lha family, a member of which explains that an official who serves the State with exceptional merit sometimes receives as a reward a little grant of land in the district where the good work was done. Thus small holdings accumulate.

The laws of inheritance would appear to vary to some extent in different parts of the country. Rockhill, whose experience lay in eastern Tibet, recorded that 'Property is inherited by the sons or brothers of the deceased. The daughters or wife get nothing'.[1]

But this is not the rule in central Tibet at any rate.

[1] Rockhill, *Notes on the Ethnology of Tibet*, p. 683.

When the father dies, the sons remain in joint possession, unless the common mess frets them beyond all endurance. In the latter event that son (not necessarily the eldest), who is regarded as the best or most intelligent, is retained for carrying on the family. He receives the larger share of the family property, especially of the land. The other sons may become monks, or marry into other families and carry on those families. Such is the practice in all households from the nobles to the peasants. Where there are sons, daughters receive no portion of the land. But in any case they are given a small share of the movable property—perhaps one-tenth or so—when they marry.

If, however, a father dies leaving a daughter, but no son, this daughter inherits the property. When she marries, she adopts her husband into her family. She does not take his name; he takes hers. And in such case she is entitled to the deciding voice in the management of the property. There have been innumerable instances of such adoption among the high families of Lhasa. As a general rule—at any rate in central Tibet and in Bhutan—a daughter succeeds in preference to a nephew, either brother's or sister's son.

Among the peasantry of the Chumbi Valley, if a man is likely to die leaving no son or daughter, he may call his relations together and adopt one. Should he not do so, the village headman can make over the house and land of the deceased to whomsoever he thinks fit, this successor being liable for the yearly taxes attached to the property. The object herein is no doubt the maintenance of the tax roll.

In countries where land is plentiful but labourers are diminishing, the tax roll must always be an object of especial solicitude. And so we find in Bhutan also that rules have been made to prevent the evasion of the labour taxes, for these, as we know, fill the largest item on the roll. Says the Lho-hi-Chö-jung, quoting the laws enacted by successive rulers of Bhutan:

The son succeeds to the property. If there be only a daughter, she succeeds. Two estates or holdings must not be combined into one with the result of rendering only one quota of service. In the case of an aged couple, who have neither children nor servants, let them render such service as they can conveniently perform. On the decease of the old ones, let the nearest in flesh and bone succeed them, and let the estate be maintained. . . .

An evil custom has arisen by which two or three holdings are combined under one owner. Thus it comes that the dry tax (grain or money) alone is paid, while the labour tax is evaded. This custom is injurious to all. In such cases, if a family has sons and daughters, they should each be made to maintain separate holdings, and to pay the taxes due from each.

Should it happen that a family, that has one of these combined holdings, is short of workers, it should be compelled to transfer a portion to any individuals that it may select from a large neighbouring family. By these means the number of real workers will be kept at the full.

The sure guiding principle should be this, that, if any one hold a property and yet pay no tax, he must be forced to render such as he is able to do, having regard also to the amount of cultivation held by him.[1]

Regarding the property left behind by those who have lived for religion, the law enacts as follows:

When a religious person dies possessed of substantial property, the lay relatives who succeed him, or the laymen who supported him, or the disciples who attended him, should out of love and regard devote his effects towards religious purposes.

Some of the sons in noble families join the priestly ranks, some of the daughters enter nunneries. It has always been so. In a history of Bhutan we read that a member of the royal family of La-dakh was brought to Bhutan when a young child, entered the priesthood, and rose to be Chief Abbot of the Bhutanese Hierarchy.[2] Of another we are told that 'he was descended from a very old and noble line', tracing back his ancestry to one who served the Buddhist religion during the reign of Ti-song De-tsen nearly twelve hundred years ago.[3] Nowadays only a few among the scions of the nobility become monks, for

1 Lho-hi Chö-jung, folio 112.   2 Ibid., folio 83.
3 Tep-ter Ngön-po, vol. iii, folio 129.

the fare is hard and scanty, and the whole mode of life too simple and severe for those accustomed to luxurious homes. Of course, if one is found to be a *Trül-ku*, i.e. an incarnation of a deity or saint, he receives special treatment even during boyhood. Of such incarnations there are several among the aristocratic families; in that of Ra-ka-shar, two have been born. These two young boys are treated with exceptional deference. By even their father and mother each is addressed as Sir! (*Ku-sho*), for are they not saints who have attained the rank of Buddhahood? But, though they have escaped from the wheel of rebirths, they have of their own free will entered the human world again, to bring the whole human and animal kingdom—all who are 'mind-possessors' (*sem-chen*)—to the knowledge of the truth, to the way of salvation.

Let me say somewhat more on different members of these ancient houses. It may serve to illustrate their own outlook and their position among their fellow subjects in Tibet.

Perhaps the greatest of all in the public service has been the line of Sha-tra. And the greatest of that line was 'Regent' Sha-tra, who was the only layman to hold the post of Regent during the minority of a Dalai Lama. Like so many others, this great man was not born into the family, but came into it by marriage. Such infusions of new blood, not always from the highest families, have no doubt checked the enervating influences of wealth and privilege. And as an ally in the fight the Tibetan nomadic instinct has played its part, sending rich as well as poor to gain strength and self-reliance by pushing their way across the inhospitable uplands of this cold, invigorating country.

A member of the Sha-tra family, who lived some four generations ago, was born during an eclipse. It was therefore foretold that he would rise high. He attained the rank of a Minister of State (*Ka-lön* or *Shap-pe*), and was known as Minister 'Black Darkness'. (*Mün-pa Nak-po*). He was credited with the power of telling from the faces of people whether they were endowed with the gift of good fortune or not. Tibetans firmly believe that some persons are by nature lucky all their lives, others the reverse. Luck can, of course, be increased by the appropriate use of auspicious days, but, if the man be a 'dry luck' (*so-de kam-po*) man, nothing will prosper of itself. Good fortune is a possession inherent in you, just as birth or brains.

Another family with which my wife as well as myself was brought into contact was the family of Do-ring. The head of the house had been dismissed from the service of the Government many years previously on the charge of being concerned in a conspiracy against the Dalai Lama. At the same time he was degraded in rank, and his best estate, the one near Lhasa, was confiscated.

We met this middle-aged couple and their son, aged fifteen, at Gyangtse in 1915. They have a country seat three miles away and came to see us in the staging bungalow. They had not been away from their beloved Lhasa for over twenty years, and had come here only in order to be near their son, who, with another Tibetan officer and fifty Tibetan soldiers, was undergoing a course of training under the British military officer at Gyangtse.

The parents were lamenting his military career, but had had no voice in the matter. 'For untold generations,' said Do-ring Ku-sho, 'we of the Do-ring house have always served the Government in a civil capacity. It is a blow to us that our son, our only son, has been made a military officer.' His wife also deplored the fact. I said what was possible, and in view of the generally peaceful condition of Tibet asked her not to be anxious.

'But I am very anxious,' she replied. And when I left the room presently for a few minutes, they both besought my wife to urge me to write to the Dalai Lama that their son might be transferred to civil employ. Incidentally it may be noted what a change this was from the time twelve short years before, when the same Dalai Lama refused even to receive a letter from the Viceroy of India, returning it unopened. The boy's parents were afraid that he might be sent to fight the Chinese troops in eastern Tibet. They remembered, too, that Buddhism forbids the taking of life. Every Tibetan remembers this, and it makes his work as a soldier much more difficult for him.

Both the husband and wife had the air and natural good manners of those accustomed to move in the highest social circles. Her refined face was like ivory, due to the fact that Tibetan ladies go out of the house but little in winter, and preserve their complexions as far as possible from the cold and rough winds, which batter their poorer country-women.

This boy of fifteen had received the high rank of *Te-chi* and so ranked above his father. And the rank was rigorously observed. For when we visited the son at Gyangtse, the father met us outside the house and conducted us ceremoniously into his son's presence.

But, with all their troubles, the house of Do-ring holds one privilege that is unique. In the great monastery of Se-ra, three miles to the north across the Lhasa plain, is kept the Sacred Dagger (*Pur-pa*) which flew there miraculously from India hundreds of years ago. A *pur-pa* is used in the main for killing devils, and plays a large part in the ritual of Tibetan Buddhism. But this *pur-pa* from Se-ra is the holiest of all.

The Tibetan official year ends in February. On one day shortly before its close this dagger is taken out of the monastery. On this day alone in the year is it seen. In February 1921 Colonel Kennedy and I were fortunate enough to see it in the Do-ring house in Lhasa. In the early morning it was taken to the Dalai Lama, who presented it with a ceremonial scarf (*ka-ta*), then to the Prime Minister at the Potala, who also presented a scarf, and was blessed by the dagger being laid on his head. And so with the few other officials to whom it is shown.

To no private house is it brought save to that of Do-ring. His most distinguished ancestor, known, on account of his great learning, as Do-ring Pandita, was Regent of Tibet for a few months, and his son, at that time a young man of twenty-two, was a Minister of State. Do-ring Pandita helped the monastery, which was then in difficulties. This unique honour was conferred, and has been continued ever since.

The dagger was brought inside the Do-ring house, carried with all reverence, and wrapped thickly in luxurious silks of different colours. Unless wrapped up, it will, report says, fly away. I could see but two or three inches of the tip, through the meshes of the fine silk that covered this portion.

The Pa-lha household, too, have suffered misfortune. The late *Lha-cham*,[1] having befriended Sarat Chandra Das, the Bengali explorer, during his secret journey to Lhasa, was fined heavily in jewellery and other property, while the Drong-tse estate, the best in the family's possession, was burdened with a severe tax. During the British Expedition to Tibet in 1904 the Pa-lha house near Gyangtse, being occupied by Tibetan troops, was captured and destroyed by our soldiers. And the fighting at Lhasa in 1912 between the Chinese and Tibetans witnessed the burning of their Lhasa mansion known as Bang-gye-shar. This is a typical Lhasa house with the living-rooms of the head of the family over the front entrance. A small balcony accompanies the central room, whose fragile windows are guarded by heavy shutters when not in use.

Throughout the greater part of Tibet there are families of noble stock. In the Tsang province eight or nine stand above the others. Eastern Tibet has its chiefs, styled *Gyalpo*, *De-ba*, &c. La-dakh has the remnant of a royal line, and Sikkim, till recently a part of Tibet, has its ruler descended from an eastern Tibetan chief. When the latter took up his kingdom in Sikkim the ceremony of enthronement was performed by one of the leading priests in Tibet 'according to the religious rites, with appropriate blessings

[1] The lady of the house in one of the leading families.

for the perpetual continuation of his line'.[1] But the Tibetan
aristocracy outside the central province, being as it were
localized, has not quite the wide influence of the families
from Lhasa, who are employed in multifarious posts, gaining experience and influence from one end of the country
to the other.

[1] History of Sikkim, p. 42. A history compiled by the late Maharaja and
Maharani of Sikkim in 1908. Not published.

Bang-gye-shar Mansion, Lhasa

IX

THE NOBILITY (*continued*)

Most of the noble families are rich, but not all. Some have lost their wealth long ago, but as long as the un-broken male descent continues, they cannot lose their social position (*rik*).[1] A family may have a good *rik*, though poor and without a high official position. And, having it, the sons and daughters will eat, drink, and marry with the most exalted in the land. The family of Pe-lhün is such a one. Throughout Tibet none have a better *rik* than Ra-ka-shar and Lha-gyal-ri, descendants of the early Tibetan kings.

How do Tibetan gentlemen spend their days? They wake about dawn and their servants bring them a cup of tea every ten or fifteen minutes until they get up—prob-ably between six and eight o'clock, according to the time of year. They may thus drink eight or ten cups before rising. They do not read in bed, but may think about what they will do during the day.

Let me describe a typical day in the life of M., a Tibe-tan acquaintance of mine, who was working as an official in the Chumbi Valley. M. was married, but his children had all died long before.

He would rise soon after dawn. After putting on his clothes—for Tibetans sleep naked—he washed his hands and face with a soaped towel, and brushed his teeth. He then offered prayers for half an hour or so. For these he had a large drum which he struck with a curved stick, as well as the small skull-drum, known as *damaru*, a small pair of cymbals, a bell, and some paste in a bowl. This last, made of barley-flour and water, was conical in shape, a propitiatory offering to spirits, good and bad. At the conclusion of the prayers a servant came in and threw

[1] རིགས་

away the offering on the roof or other clean place, where the birds would eat it.

M. would then sit down, drinking tea and talking to members of his household. Tea was drunk at brief intervals throughout the day. It is usual to gulp it rather than to sip it. Those who rise very early may take two or three cups of soup.

Breakfast came between eight and nine. It consisted of barley-gruel, barley-flour, mutton or yak-beef, either dry or fresh, two or three kinds of vegetables, and of course tea, but no alcoholic liquor. After breakfast official business, if any. If none, an hour's stroll outside with a couple of servants. Then he would come back to the house and spend the rest of the morning gambling with acquaintances, who had been summoned for the purpose. Dominoes and dice were favourite forms of gambling.

Between two and three o'clock in the afternoon the heavy meal of the day was taken. M., being exceptionally addicted to good living, would have four or five courses in the Chinese style; rice or vermicelli with soup, dried fish and vegetables, pork, mutton, yak-beef, &c. Liquor distilled from barley as well as tea. The meal lasted for an hour or more. These Chinese meals are expensive; those who are economical take ordinary Tibetan food.

After a dinner of this kind a Tibetan takes no other regular meal, but if it be a cold winter's evening, one or two large cupfuls of soup do not come amiss. In the Tsang province of central Tibet people of all classes drink soup more largely than in U, Lhasa's own province.

In the summer M. might then spend the time till dusk in archery. Instead of sharp points the arrows had square heads fitted on them, perforated with holes through which the wind whistled as they flew through the air. Girls served barley-beer (*chang*) to the host and guests. One guest played a kind of violin (*ho-chin*), another a kind of banjo, the girls and some of the guests sang, and there was general jollification.

When darkness stopped the archery, M. went indoors

and spent the time chatting and drinking both tea and barley-spirit till eight or nine, his usual bed-time. Sometimes he would have an evening entertainment, summoning girls and men to dance for his guests and himself, and this might continue till midnight. For refreshment on such occasions it is usual to have two or three kinds of meat, perhaps boiled, fried, and raw, as well as soup. At an ordinary party of this kind M. provided two or three men and two or three girls, whom he rewarded at the end of the evening with the equivalent of one or two shillings each. Those of his servants who could do so would also join in the singing and dancing.

M. was accounted a jovial man, fond of entertaining and gambling. When the poorer classes discussed him, some would say, 'He is a fine fellow', but the greater part would grumble that 'his entertainments give a lot of trouble to the people'. His successor lived quietly and entertained but little. In most kinds of gambling, however, he was very proficient, more so than M., and people disliked playing with him, because they usually lost. He was regarded as somewhat of a miser. Noticing his thin, careworn face, the people used to say that he was too fond of thinking how he might take down those whom he accounted high and haughty.

It must not be thought that all Tibetan officials spend their leisure in gambling. Some read religious books, or histories or tales. Some take their dinner at dusk. After dinner stories may be told, the servants coming in to hear these. And the work for the following day may be planned. Many of the wealthier classes nowadays light their houses with lamps burning kerosene oil. During recent years there is a tendency for these to take a heavier meal in the evening and to sit up till about ten o'clock, instead of, as before, retiring at eight or nine. Foreign customs, in fact, are beginning to creep in.

The conversation in official households will often be about official business or gossip about the doings of the neighbours. During each day our friend will drink from thirty to sixty cups of tea, the cups being somewhat small, like those used by English ladies for their afternoon tea-parties.

Such are the ordinary meals of the Tibetan gentry. But they are fond of feasts, appealing as these do to their love of hospitality, of company and show.

It was a pleasant autumn day in early September when my wife, Mr. Macdonald, Ku-sho Pa-lhe-se, and I rode across the Gyangtse plain to have lunch with the head of the House of Do-ring and his charming family, in their ancestral home, 'The Four Joys'. The first known ancestor of the Do-rings was the incarnation of one of the religious ministers (chö-lön) of the great teacher (Padma Sambhava), who foretold that this minister would be reborn in a salty, sandy plain where there would be four kinds of happiness: that of the fish to the north, the birds to the east, the human beings to the south, and the wild animals to the west.

The first head of the house to attain wealth and fame, Do-ring Pandita, received as a grant of land from the Tibetan Government this estate, Gap-shi. Its name means 'The Four Joys', and its situation bears out the prophecy. To the north is the river with the fish, in the east the birds cluster, to the south stretches the whole plain of Gyangtse with its fertile crops for the sustenance of the human kind, and to the west rise the hills, the home of the wild sheep (burrhel) and gazelle.

On the way out Pa-lhe-se rode a grey pony belonging to the Pa-lha Ken-chen, the head of the Pa-lha family. This pony was reputed to be forty-two years old, one year younger than he was. The owner told me that he had bought it about thirty years previously. During all these thirty years he never knew it to be ill or off work. Whatever this stallion's age, it was strongly built and active, pulling the whole way. Pa-lhe-se held that it was 'not very uncommon to find a pony in Tibet thirty years old, though not one in ten thousand reaches the age of forty'. The pony had spent nearly all its life in Lhasa. It died two years later.

Our host's wife and his son were at the repast, as well

as his two daughters aged nine and five respectively. The
Pa-lha Ken-chen was also a guest.

We first had some preliminary refreshment of tea and
little cakes. These we took at small tables. Before eating,
each takes a few drops of tea out of his cup with the third
finger of the right hand, and with the thumb and same
finger flicks it upwards as an offering to the gods. The
third finger is used as being the cleanest, for it is said
that babies are born with it in their nostrils. The first
course was served to us at small tables in a separate
room.

We then adjourned to another room and sat on cushions,
Tibetan-wise, at a round table. Lunch is no doubt an
inadequate term for this feast, which consisted of forty-
two dishes arranged in sixteen courses. We sat down at
a quarter to one, but did not win through till three o'clock.
Each course was brought in and put on the centre of the
table and usually helped by Pa-lhe-se, our host's sight
being dim. The dishes were of silver with silver lids, and
from them Pa-lhe-se took a little with a spoon and put on
each of our plates, and then we did out best with chop-
sticks. Nobody commenced eating till all had been helped.
The hors-d'œuvres of the feast itself consisted of various
small plates of nuts, chillies, &c., but the preliminary tea
and cakes, mentioned above, came first of all. After the
hors-d'œuvres came bowls of macaroni, one full bowl being
given to each person. Perhaps a list of the dishes, in the
order in which they appeared, may be of interest. They
were as follows:

Chinese macaroni, chui-tsa (a Chinese vegetable),
sheep's kidneys, Chinese sea-slugs, fish with vinegar,
chillies in mustard oil, chang-be (a Chinese vegetable),
fermented pulse done in Chinese style, another Chinese
vegetable, radishes, carrots, yak's tongue, roast mutton,
sheep's liver, sheep's ribs, shrimps, a Chinese vegetable,
Chinese nuts, crystallized sugar, raisins, dates, almonds,
shark's fins, Chinese peas, brinjals (an Indian vegetable),
roast meat with sea-slugs, pastry puffs containing meat,

peas, shrimps with a Chinese vegetable called wosun,
stewed mutton, fish, peas with sugar, bamboo roots, pears,
young shoots of the pea plant sweetened, pastry puffs containing sweets, fish, seaweed, fried mutton, fishes' abdomens, Chinese cabbage, and—a long last—a bowlful of rice.

Some of the above dishes are credited with special
merits of their own. Sea-slugs increase the strength of the
body, seaweed removes hoarseness, fishes' abdomens are
beneficial for bowel complaints, crystallized sugar and
raisins relieve colds and coughs, while bamboo roots are
good for the voice. As regards the fishes' abdomens,
a gelatinous substance, it was explained to us, that not
only did they relieve bowel complaints, but they were also
useful when one swallowed a hair, as they took th hair
down with them.

The son and two girls, even the little five-year-old, ate
heartily of almost all the dishes, but Ku-sho Do-ring's
wife took very little. The Tibetans generally ate half or
more than half of their helpings at each course, and must
have made enormous meals. Most drank nothing; one or
two drank a little tea, but nothing else.

After the feast was finished we went over our host's
carpet factory, which turns out some of the best carpets
in Tibet. The atmosphere of the factory, as indeed of the
whole house, is feudal. The carpets are made in the
verandah of one of the courtyards. There is no machinery;
all is done by hand. On one broad verandah sat the women
spinning the thread. As they worked, they sang a song
in praise of the House of Do-ring, the refrain of which ran
somewhat as follows: 'This is the great and noble house,
full of jewels and of all things precious. Here we work
and wish no greater happiness.' As the master of the house
looks on with his kindly smile, many tongues are thrust
out in greeting.

The manager (*Chang-dzö*) of the property is evidently
as proud of the family name as is Do-ring himself. A
shrewd but good-natured man, he is equally at home in
the daily details of management and in the ancient history

and prophecies that tell of the family fortunes. After we have seen the carpet factory, the manager takes us round part of the grounds. We see the park carpeted every-where with blooms of purple iris, and the ample barns, which are built of stone and house great quantities of straw. We see, too, an enormous threshing-floor of beaten clay, across which, when the time comes, the yaks will be driven helter-skelter to and fro to stamp the grain out of the ears.

We return to the house for cups of tea and more cakes. As we sit round the table, servants bring, uncooked, the remains of the large joints from which out meat dishes have been provided. We are able thus to see what good meat it was.

Tea finished, we hasten home in the growing darkness. Our host and hostess with their children and servants form a charming picture on the doorstep of 'The Four Joys', and it is with reluctance that we decline their hospit-able solicitations to stay on a little longer. Night falls fast in Tibet, and our way home lies along narrow paths across the countless irrigation channels which intersect the Gyangtse plain in all directions. Before leaving I give, in accordance with Tibetan custom, presents of money to the manager and other servants.

Sometimes, before the guests depart, the waiting-maids sing a song of good wishes.

> The signs without are eight. These welfare show:
>   So may your welfare be!
> Within the growth of happiness is shown;
>   May you be happy too!
>
> Welfare is ever welfare;
> Happiness is ever happiness;
> In neither is there change.
>
> Welfare is on the right;
> Happiness is on the left;
> And there shall be no change.

Some of us attended also a feast of similarly generous

proportions given by Pa-lha Ken-chen, the head of the Pa-lha family. The meal was served in one of the chapels. At the farther end of the room was the altar with various images, including those of three gods of long life, and a copy of the sacred books known as *Bum*, some sixteen volumes altogether. Tibetans and British, there were twelve of us altogether, and we sat on Tibetan cushions at two tables.

When the repast was at length concluded, a theatrical performance took place in the courtyard representing events in the life of the Buddha during one of his previous incarnations as a king in India.

I have mentioned that at our lunch with the Do-rings both host and guests drank very little. But at some entertainments there is heavy drinking.

As a general rule liquor should be offered at least three times to each guest, who, if he does not want to drink much, may take a sip only the first and second time, but should drink the whole cupful at the third offering. It should here be explained that, whether tea or wine or whatever you drink, as soon as you drink any of it, even a mere sip, your cup is immediately refilled. If a guest does not wish to drink anything at all, he takes a drop or two out of the cup with the third finger of the right hand, and with the thumb and third finger flicks it upwards, as already described.

Before guests of high rank a cup of jade or old china should be set; for those of ordinary position cups of new china will suffice. If the guests wish to drink a great deal, bowls of larger size, each bowl containing three or four cupfuls, are provided. Such bowls are almost always of silver, but those who are poor may use bowls of other metals silvered over to look as much like silver as possible.

The charge is frequently made against Tibetans that they do not wash from the cradle to the grave. But those who make these charges base them perhaps on travels pushed through outlying tracts, and have, maybe, not been brought into touch with the more cultured classes of

Tibetan nobleman with wife and children seated
Servants standing behind

Yak-hide bag containing mustard oil, which the landlord uses in
the payment of wages

the people. The gentry, in Lhasa at any rate, have long been accustomed to wash their hands and faces every morning with soap and water, and to brush their teeth at the same time.

M. was in charge of both the civil and the military administration of the Chumbi Valley. He held the rank of *De-pön*. His private servants were as follows:

Three Sim-pöns. These brought the De-pön his tea and other food, looked after his clothes, dressed him, and swept out his rooms. They accompanied him when he rode out. They were mounted, and each carried a gun.

Two maidservants. These brought the tea and other food to the De-pön's wife. On them also lay the duty of plaiting the De-pön's hair, for it is considered that women plait better than men.

One boy, aged ten or eleven, who attended on the wife.

One cook (ma-chen) with *two assistants (tap-yok)* who make up the fire and help the cook in various ways.

One groom (chip-pön), who is mounted when accompanying the De-pön. He too has *one assistant*, but the latter is not mounted except on long marches.

One tailor. He makes clothes for the *De-pön*, his wife, and the servants.

A professional gambler completed the establishment. It was his duty to join in games of gambling, when the number of guests fell short, e.g. to make a fourth at dominoes (*ba*), and so on. If his winnings or losings were heavy, his master took the one or assumed responsibility for the other.

No doubt in his own home M. had many other servants, for the number of these in a Tibetan household is large. Multifarious are their duties. Employment is found for all, even during the long winter months, when the frozen fields claim undisturbed rest.

Like many Tibetans of the upper classes, the *De-pön* kept a pony and a mule, the former for himself, the latter for his wife. For his servants the villagers had to supply ponies free of charge. A petty village official, called *Gu-re-ra*, i.e. 'He who waits by turns', had always to be in attendance on the premises, in order to fetch ponies or do whatever else was needed. The villagers would often address the *De-pön* as 'The Great Man' (*Mi Chem-po*), and his wife as 'The Real Person' (*Ku-ngö*).

M. had under him a *Ru-pön*, a few non-commissioned officers, and a nominal strength of three hundred soldiers. But of these only eighty or ninety were retained. The remainder received leave to go and live at their homes, giving the *De-pön* presents for the privilege of doing so. He also drew—and kept for himself—the salaries of the absent ones, so far as these were paid in money. Soldiers, however, received most of their pay in land, not much in money. Chinese military officers in Tibet made in this way large profits out of their own establishments.

Tibetan officials have one main living-room, which is dining-room, drawing-room, and office combined. The clerks are called in, and the official dictates his letters to them. His wife will often be present and advise him on Government business.

For the education of his children the Tibetan gentleman of position arranges for his own tutor, who keeps a small school for him. Here his own sons and daughters receive their early education, and in this they are joined by the children of his retainers and of the peasants living near. His own children sit, of course, on special seats apart, but all are in the same room. So the classes must in some measure gain an understanding of each other.

What does his son learn? Well, after the alphabet, a little arithmetic. He will read a simple book on spelling (*chi-pa tak-yik*) when he is ten to twelve years old. Then he tackles a more difficult book (*Sum-tak*) on the same subject. Now he commences, first on a slate and afterwards on paper, to write letters in the different phrasings suitable for the different classes, ranks, and occupations. When sixteen or seventeen years old, he must struggle with the *Nyeng-nga*, a book with hidden meanings, which will tax his ingenuity and put the finishing touch to his reading.

Many of the landed classes, and most scions of the nobility, enter the service of the Government, as lay-officials (*trung-kor*). In the Tibetan Government's service are two lists, one of the above officers, the other of ecclesiastics (*tse-trung*) who take part in the ordinary civil administration. Each list contains a hundred and seventy-five names. He who enters on the secular side must first pass an apprenticeship in the Finance Office (*Tsi-kang*), where he will receive lessons in accounts and further instruction in general correspondence. This completes his education.

When he is grown up, a Tibetan gentleman will probably read histories, biographies (*nam-tar*). and plays from time to time, one of the most popular being the history compiled by the fifth Dalai Lama. Occasionally he may read law books. And among the general favourites are books of moral precepts.

Let me conclude this chapter with a brief biography of a member of the Pa-lha household up to the time when he became one of the chief officers of the State.

Till the age of thirteen he lived at home and did not attend any school. Then, his father being a De-pön at Shigatse, he joined his mother at Lhasa and attended the Yül-ka-gang school till he was seventeen. He learnt reading, writing, and arithmetic. At this school there were about thirty boys of whom eight were sons of gentlemen and the remainder of the lower classes. There was a teacher and an assistant teacher. Next, he entered the Finance Office (*Tsi-kang*) at Lhasa. Here, where the secular officials of the Government are trained, he was taught the routine of Government business, especially the keeping of accounts. Here, too, he had to learn the art of official correspondence, embodying the compliments prescribed separately for each class and grade, and often preferring allusions, allegories, and proverbs to bare, blunt facts.

When he was twenty years old, he received his first employment in the public service. He was placed in the sixth grade, the lowest but one, and was made Dzong-pön of White Crystal Fort (She-ka Dzong), which stands a few days' journey south-west of Shigatse, and contains Mount Everest in its jurisdiction. He held this post for three years, but never went himself to She-ka. He governed his district, as often happens in such cases, through a deputy, important matters being referred to him at Lhasa by letter. There were, of course, no postal arrangements, such as we understand them. The letters were carried free of cost by villagers, who received only their food and the loan of a pony for every fifteen t. twenty miles of the journey. In this way the young governor received letters from She-ka every two or three days, and was able to continue living in his Lhasa home. Meanwhile he married. The choice of the parents fell on one of the daughters in the Nam-se-ling family.

No salary is attached to the post of Dzong-pön. At She-ka Dzong it is probable that Pa-lha Ku-sho earned some two hundred pounds yearly, half from the estate attached to the Dzong-pön's post and half from fines. Officials, however, look upon their family estates as part of their salary, because they hold these on condition that one, or in some cases two, members of the family serve the Government.

When Pa-lha was only eighteen years old, his father and his mother were banished to Chong-gye, a place three or four days' journey south of Lhasa, for having helped Sarat Chandra Das, the Bengali explorer, on his secret journey to Lhasa. They were kept there for seven years. Their son lived on in their town house at Lhasa.

The Tibetan Government do not visit the sins of the fathers upon the children, so far as the official careers of the latter are concerned. When only twenty-three, the young man was appointed as a judge—of the kind known as *Sher-pang*—a post which he held for ten years. As a *Sher-pang* he enjoyed the fifth rank, and had a colleague who was also a layman and of similar rank. These two judges work in Lhasa, where they decide both civil and criminal cases of considerable importance.

At the age of thirty-three he was appointed a 'Grain Paymaster' (*Dru Po-pön*) in the province of Tsang, a post ranked in the fourth grade. For this work his headquarters were at Gyangtse. He visited Shigatse from time to time and deputed a subórdinate to Ting-ri on the Nepal-Tibet frontier. An ecclesiastical colleague (*tse-trung*) was associated with him in the work. Their duties were to advance barley, wheat, and peas to the agriculturists of the districts in which they worked. The rate of interest charged in such cases is 10 per cent., the grain being lent before sowing-time, and payment being made, also in grain, after the harvest. Such rate compares very favourably with that taken by the Indian money-lenders in Sikkim, which frequently ranges from 70 to 80 per cent., and is sometimes even more. As a rule the Tibetan cultivators pay the interest but not the principal. The grain so received is stored in Government granaries throughout the country. In Gyangtse it is stored in the chief monastery (*Pal-kor Chö-de*), in the dzong, and in four or five houses in the town. Drongtse accommodates a large supply; other places according to their capacities. In times of war the Paymasters issue rations to the soldiers from these accumulated stores. During the war between the Chinese and Tibetans in 1912 such rations were issued.

In June 1913 Ku-sho Pa-lha was appointed one of the three Financial Secretaries (Tsi-pön). These occupy positions of great importance in the Government of Tibet. He attended the Finance Office daily in accordance with the rules which the Dalai Lama had recently laid down, prescribing daily attendance from nine to twelve o'clock. The Tsi-pöns, however, usually stayed in office till four or five o'clock. At the Tsi-kang, as at other high offices, the Government provides lunch at noon. In accordance with Tibetan practice the work is done jointly by the three secretaries. It is not divided.

After three years in Lhasa he was deputed as a general assistant to the Ka-lön Lama, the head of the administration in eastern Tibet. Although working there, he retained his title of Tsi-pön and the emoluments attaching to the Tsi-pön's post. He suffered from gout and rheumatism, as do many who go from Lhasa to the eastern districts. Difficulty in breathing also attacked him. This Tibetans ascribe to the blood rising from the lower part of the body to the neck and shoulders. And so he died at the early age of forty-nine, when there were hopes that he might soon be promoted to the high position of a member of the Supreme Council.

Pa-lha Tsi-pön had three sons and one daughter, but two of the sons died in 1910 of small-pox, the most dreaded of all diseases in Tibet. His eldest son, when nineteen, married a daughter of the Sha-tra family. She is a year younger than he is, and a lady of exceptional intelligence and charm.

The Secretary's daughter was a nun in her own private nunnery at Rin-chen-ling—near her Drong-tse home. In this nunnery she lived in comfort. Her principal chapel there included the usual altar running from one side of the room to the other. On this were the seven bowls of holy water, and the lamps, known as 'sacred fire' (chö-me), whose wicks are fed with butter instead of oil. Here, too, were images of the Buddha, of deities and saints, sacrificial offerings of butter and grain, drums to be used in the services, and the other paraphernalia of worship. Above these were her bookcases, affording room for thirty or forty volumes of the scriptures. At one end of the altar was the nun's seat, severe in its simplicity; by it the low Tibetan table. On the walls and pillars religious pictures (tang-ka) diffused an air of holiness and peace.

X

THE TRADERS

TIBETAN society falls mainly into two classes; the landed
gentry on the one side, the peasantry and shepherds on the
other. The trading community stand between the two,
forming a middle class with middle-class aims, but they
have so far little power. There is no strong middle class.

The check on the upper classes rests with the priests
from the Dalai Lama downwards. Many of these are self-
made men, and some of them are capable, strong-willed,
dominating. But their aims are not those of the middle
class, as we understand the term in Europe and America.
The traders, however, though lacking influence at present, leave their country in greater numbers each year and
go farther afield. Accordingly the wealth of the mercantile
community can hardly fail to increase. Meanwhile the
Tibetan Government is expanding its sphere of operations and needs an expanding revenue. It may well be,
therefore, that those who have the money will grow in
power and influence.

The chief products of Tibet exported to other countries
are wool, yak-tails, hides, the soft under-wool of the shawl-
wool goat, borax, salt, musk, and medicinal herbs. To
these must be added ponies and mules. Food grains are
not exported. Any surplus of these that may accrue during
a year of plenty is stored in the granaries, large and small,
that are to be found up and down the country.

Among the above items wool predominates. Throughout inhabited Tibet, be it valley, or plain, or mountain
slope, you will see flocks of sheep. When snow covers a
plain or valley, the sheep browse on the hill-sides above,
where the unfailing wind has swept the snow away. Does
the advance of summer dry the mountain pastures beyond
the endurance of even a Tibetan sheep? Then he and his
fellows can descend to the watered plain or valley below.

Of the yak-tails, which are exported in large quantities to and through India, some find places in Hindu temples. The hair of others is made into fly-whisks, a possession useful to those who ride in tropical countries. Many are exported to Germany.

The short downy growth beneath the coarse outer hair of the Tibetan goat is greatly valued for its soft silky texture. It is woven into the well-known *pashmina* shawls, which are popular in India, being light and very soft.

Salt is found in many parts of Tibet on the banks of rivers and lakes. The former type may be seen in the salt wells along large rivers, e.g. the Mekong[1] in eastern Tibet. The latter is plentiful round the large lakes on the plateaux, forming often a white band along the banks down to the water's edge. It is from these high uplands, especially from the lakes in northern Tibet, that the bulk of the salt is drawn.

Musk is a secretion in a small deer, which is found in most parts of the country and especially in Po, Kong-po, and other districts bordering the Himalaya. It forms as a pouch near the hinder parts of the male. Commanding, as it does, a high price, it is exported in large quantities, mainly at present to India, the trade to China being barred by both Tibetans and Chinese.

Many kinds of herbs with medicinal qualities are collected in various parts of Tibet, and are in great request both in China and India. And the horns of a species of deer are much sought by Chinese doctors, who manufacture from them a medicine which is believed to impart vigour to the body and lustre to the face.

Gold is found in places in the uplands of the Northern Plains and in numerous river-beds. On the face of a mountain in the Tak-po province, east of Lhasa, is a mine, which is believed to promise well. But there is an old-established objection to mining on religious grounds. 'If minerals be taken out of the ground', says the ordinary

[1] See *Travels in Eastern Tibet*, by Eric Teichman, pp. 190, 191 (Cambridge University Press).

Musk deer in the Jewel Park, near Lhasa

Silversmith in Lhasa engraving a charm-box

Wealthy merchant of eastern Tibet with servants

He wears a double necklace of corals and onyx. Scabbard of servant on
right holds three corals, as is usual in eastern Tibet

Tibetan, 'the fertility of the soil will be weakened.' Many think that minerals were put into the ground by the 'Precious Teacher', Padma Sambhava, when he brought Buddhist teaching from India, and that, if they are removed, rain will cease and the crops will be ruined.

The religious objection is intensified by an economic one. When a mine is found, the local peasants and others are expected to work it without pay. This work being for the Government, the system of *ula* (unpaid labour) is held to apply. So the villagers have every incentive to conceal the existence of mineral wealth, and will sometimes turn out and attack those who try to exploit the mine.

Other minerals found are silver, copper, coal, iron, lead, sulphur, and saltpetre. It is possible that Tibet is rich, perhaps very rich, in minerals. But nothing definite can be said, until the ground has been prospected scientifically and with some approach to thoroughness. Hitherto but little has been done. And it seems best that scientific exploration should proceed but slowly, so that the Tibetan Government may be able to cope with it and prevent the country from being overrun by foreign adventurers. Meanwhile the religious objection appears to be weakening, and, if a mine is good, wages can of course be paid.

The manufactures of Tibet are but few. They will be discussed in a separate chapter. It may suffice to say here that the people produce the ordinary needs of life in a primitive fashion. The Tibetan household, whether of nobleman or peasant, produces nearly all its own requirements, garnering its grain, weaving its clothes. It needs only to buy salt, perhaps some meat, and a few other things. The long, cold winter calls a halt to agricultural operations and encourages weaving and other indoor pursuits.

In trade transactions Tibetans, in common with many other Asiatic nations, conduct their bargaining through dumb signs. Holding the other's hand inside the long, capacious Tibetan sleeve, the unit is stated thus, *Do di*, i.e. '*Do-tse* these'. Three fingers being gripped three

Do-tse are indicated. The seller continues *Tso di*, i.e. 'Tens these', and grips two fingers. Then *Pu di*, i.e. '*Sangs* these', and four are gripped. The meaning of the whole is three *Do-tse* and twenty-four *Sangs*, for the tens refer to *Sangs*. A *Sang* is worth at present about one shilling and sixpence, a *Do-tse* three pounds fifteen shillings. The buyer makes his offer in the same manner. For six you take three fingers and turn them over, thus doubling the figure. For seven you take five fingers and then two. Similarly eight is four doubled, nine is five plus four.

Not in the petty purchases of the market-place, but in the larger trade dealings, the seller invokes a blessing on the buyer, a blessing which will be shared by both. Suppose a pony be sold. Resting his hand on the pony's shoulder, the seller may say, 'May you have good fortune, may the pony live long, may you escape sickness. And may our trade dealings with each other grow to hundreds and from hundreds to thousands.' In the case of a pony or mule that is especially prized, the purchaser or his servant may give it a pinch of barley-flour mixed with butter. This is done before the vendor's invocation, and sets in train causes which work good not only for the pony but for all in the household.

The simple country folk, before paying away the purchase money, will often wipe it on their money-bags to prevent the good luck that is in the coins from going away with them.

Lhasa and Shigatse are the chief centres of trade in central Tibet; Cham-do, Jye-kun-do, Der-ge, and Ta-chienlu (Ta-tsen-do) are important centres in eastern Tibet.

As befits a people who are naturally endowed with trading instincts, Tibet is well equipped with trade-routes. These go to India on the south and west, to China on the east, and to Mongolia on the north. I will take them in this order, enumerating briefly the more important lines. And first it should be made clear that the term trade-route does not connote a well-made road. The track is sometimes of the roughest, but the animal that carries the load, agile and enduring, does not ask for much.

Taking Lhasa as the centre, one of the routes to India is that which runs west and north through the length of southern Tibet to Leh, the capital of Ladakh. Another goes westward to Almora, the loads being carried largely on the backs of sheep.

Almora is the second largest entrepôt of the Indo-Tibetan trade, the largest being Kalimpong. The latter is the capital of a tract in the eastern Himalaya, which was annexed from Bhutan in 1865 and now forms part of the Darjeeling district. Half the entire trade between Tibet and India passes through this thriving town. To many it is known as the centre of that inspired organization, the St. Andrew's Colonial Homes, which rescues and trains children of European and mixed parentage. Founded and fostered by the love and genius of Dr. Graham, these homes have carried his name throughout India and Scotland.

The route from Kalimpong to Lhasa passes through south-eastern Sikkim and crosses the frontier into Tibet via the Dze-lep La. Four miles to the north-west of this pass is the Na-tu La on the road to Gangtok, the capital of Sikkim. During recent years this village on the mountain side, one of the world's smallest capitals, has acquired a share in the Tibetan trade. When I was in Sikkim, we arranged camping-grounds with fuel, fodder, and water at convenient stages along the mountain tracks, a site for warehouses in the vicinity of Gangtok, while the administration of the State was regularized more or less on British lines. So the Tibetan traders, who value just laws and a stable administration, even though of foreign make, have begun gradually to use Gangtok as a trading centre.

But to return to the Kalimpong route. Descending the Dze-lep La into the Chumbi Valley, the home of the prosperous Tro-mo-was, it is soon joined by the road from Gangtok and ascends the valley to its source. Thence it crosses a plain to Pa-ri, a thriving village, albeit dirty beyond belief. The houses, built of sods, have their floors two or three steps below the level of the ground outside, a device which keeps out the devastating wind and gives much-needed warmth, for the village is fourteen thousand three hundred feet above the level of the sea. Being just on the Indian side of the Himalayan divide, the wind is touched with dampness, so that you feel the cold here more keenly than at somewhat higher elevations in the dry interior of Tibet.

At Pa-ri an important trade-route diverges into Bhutan, whose frontier, at the Tre-mo La, is only a couple of miles or so away. Here one may see the Bhutanese bringing their wares on their backs, especially rice for the few in Tibet who can afford it, and paper for printing the sacred books. Sturdy folk are these Bhutanese, many of them armed with two swords and a dagger, which they are not slow to use. Hot-tempered and physically powerful, they are disliked and feared by the peace-loving traders of Tro-mo. Tibetans also bear arms when their consignment of goods is large or especially valuable. Formerly Tibetan matchlocks were carried, but nowadays modern rifles are coming into use more and more.

The route to Lhasa crosses the main axis of the Himalaya by the Tang La, 'The Clear Pass', nine miles beyond Pa-ri. Thence the main stream of the traffic passes along the eastern shore of the 'Otter Lake'.[1] It avoids Gyangtse, taking a route to Lhasa, which is more direct and provided with better pasture.

Between Kalimpong and Pa-ri mules carry most of the stuff. From Pa-ri to Lhasa yaks and donkeys are the chief beasts of burden. The yak, though his long, shaggy hair exaggerates his massive proportions, is yet much larger than the little Tibetan donkey. But each of them, and the mule also, carries the same load, about a hundred and seventy pounds. The mule will take its burden twenty to twenty-five miles a day, the donkey ten to fifteen, the yak a similar distance or rather less.

[1] Hram Tso in Tibetan; the Bam Tso of the maps.

A most sensible animal is the donkey. If too heavy a load be laid on its back, it will sit down quietly until the load is lightened. The mule travels about three miles an hour, the donkey two, the yak one and a half. The last-mentioned marches, as a rule, for only six or eight hours. He needs a longer time at the grazing than the others, for, unlike them, he receives no daily ration of grain.

The muleteer's whip has a thick, but somewhat short, handle of cane and a long thong. A leather band goes round the wrist to prevent the whip from falling. The traders and the gentry often use riding-whips with shorter stocks and thongs than do the mule drivers.

From Gyangtse to Pa-ri, a distance of a hundred and two miles, the laden mules used to take four days; the donkeys seven in winter and ten in summer. They travelled faster in winter because they carried their grass fodder with them then, none being available on the road. During summer they grazed and so were slower. The yaks took nine or ten days to cover the distance. The hire of a mule from Gyangtse to Pa-ri was eleven rupees, two annas; of a donkey two rupees to three rupees, six annas, the rate being higher in winter. Yaks were not much used over this stretch of country, for they depend on grazing, and the grazing was poor.

An early start is the rule, often before five in the morning, though most of the trade passes through during the winter months and some of the trading-places are at altitudes little lower than the summit of Mont Blanc. At five o'clock the thermometer may well register fifty degrees of frost on the Fahrenheit scale. But the Tibetan driver knows nothing of thermometers, and does not fear the cold. What he does know is that by midday the wind will be blowing fiercely, and he seeks therefore to complete as much of his day's march as possible during the hours of morning calm.

By far the largest export from Tibet is wool. More than three-fourths of the animals are laden with this alone. And very useful it is when the muleteers halt for the after-

noon and night on the windy plain, perhaps between
midday and two o'clock. The drums of wool are built into
a wall, along three sides of a square, to keep the wind out.
At one of the corners the watch-dogs are tethered. When
approaching an encampment the dog will dart out from
within. So you must allow for the length of the chain;
otherwise you will find his teeth in your throat.

The drivers stay contentedly inside the square under
the open sky. They sit and talk and cook their food; at
least some of it, for they eat a good deal of their meat raw.
When darkness falls, they snuggle under their blankets.
The starry heavens are above them, the temperature is
twenty degrees below zero, but they sleep well, and are
up at four or five o'clock next morning. On their way
back from India with miscellaneous goods the drivers
must manage as best they can. Perhaps some of the sacks,
at any rate, can be piled into a low wall, against the wind,
so that the men can lie down under its lee.

On arrival the yaks and donkeys are usually turned out
to graze and summoned in before starting with calls of
Sho, sho, sho, sho (Come! come! come! come!) in the
peculiar Tibetan intonation, which carries far across valley
and plain.

In western Tibet sheep and goats are used for transport
purposes. Twenty to twenty-five pounds is the load of each,
probably wool, salt, or borax, and with this they make
long marches across the mountains towards India. Often
they do not return to their own country, being killed and
eaten when they have completed their toilsome journey.

A European merchant at Kalimpong used to inform me
that the Tibetans resorted to various devices to increase
the weight of the wool. A great deal of rope was used,
nominally to prevent theft by the muleteers *en route*, but
really, as he averred, to increase the weight. Consequently he had an agreement with them by which every
so-called maund [1] of wool should contain forty-one seers,

---

[1] An Indian weight, between eighty-two and eighty-three lb. avoirdupois.
It is divided into forty seers, each seer thus weighing a little over two pounds.

Muleteers encamped for the night on the 'Three Brother Plains',
fifteen thousand feet above sea-level

Yaks carrying wool

of which not more than three should be rope. For any weight of rope beyond this nothing was paid. Even then the remaining thirty-eight seers were not all wool. Bits of stone and skin would be found inside. Sand also, a quantity of dust, and occasionally an old boot. Mrs. Graham among her manifold activities found time to supervise a factory for making Tibetan floor-rugs. These are made of Tibetan wool. She found that from each maund purchased not more than sixty-five pounds of cleaned wool emerged, and sometimes only sixty.

The trade is worked on a system of advances. European and Indian buyers advance loans to the larger Tibetan merchants, though not to the small traders who bring down only two or three hundred maunds. For these advances they charged 1 per cent. monthly. During spring and summer the Tibetan merchants give advances to the owners of the sheep in Tibet, and arrange to take delivery from the following October. By giving these loans six months or more before taking delivery they are able to buy the wool at a rate per maund three or four rupees lower than would otherwise have been possible.

The Tibetan merchants prefer a steady price for their wool to one that fluctuates greatly, even though higher. In the former case they can settle their rates with those who own the sheep on a firmer basis, and know better how they stand.

But even so the Tibetan merchant does not gain complete stability. For he buys the wool from the sheep-owners in Tibetan money and sells it in Indian rupees. During the last five years the Tibetan *trang-ka* has risen as high as three and a third and fallen as low as seven per rupee. It varies from year to year, from month to month. If there is a large wool crop and the price is good, more rupees come to Tibet and the value of the rupee falls. Conversely, if the crop is poor, the value rises. And so also with other exports, but, these being on a far smaller scale, their influence is correspondingly less.

Another factor, which works steadily to reduce the

value of the *trang-ka*, is to be found in the large number of copper coins that have been minted during the last seven or eight years. This tendency has been further strengthened by the recent counterfeiting in India of such coins, which are smuggled across the Tibetan frontier.

The Indian merchants at Kalimpong, who control the Indo-Tibetan trade there, are nearly all Marwaris, members of a race whose home is in Rajputana and the southern Punjab. Banker, moneylender, and cloth merchant combined, the Marwari of Kalimpong is an exceptionally shrewd man of business. Their fellow Indians will laughingly maintain that a young Marwari is already making calculations and gaining a profit when only a few years old.

The main import from India to Tibet consists of cotton goods. Other articles of import are woollen goods, hardware, corals, precious stones, tobacco, dried fruits, sugar, molasses, and miscellaneous domestic utilities such as matches, needles, and soap. The total import, both in volume and in value, falls considerably short of the export. The balance is made up by Indian rupees which, during recent years, have poured into the country. This coin is readily taken up on account of its stability, and all the more because Tibetan coins are not accepted in India, and are therefore of no use in commercial dealings with that country. In the trade between Tibet and China the balance is against Tibet, which has therefore to remit coin or bullion to cover the difference.

The commodities going up, cotton goods and the like, have greater value, load for load, than the raw wool coming down. So many animals go up empty, and the transport rates are consequently lower.

From Nepal and from Bhutan a fair amount of rice is imported. Salt is exported to Nepal, but not much else, so the balance has to be remitted in specie. But with Bhutan, whose people are closely akin to her own, Tibet both imports and exports on a considerable scale.

There is a large colony of Nepalese in Lhasa and there

are smaller colonies in Tse-tang, Shigatse, Gyangtse, Lha-tse and at places in the province of Kong-po. By a treaty made between Tibet and Nepal in 1856 these enjoy the right of extra-territoriality. Another provision of this treaty grants the extraordinary privilege that, 'Henceforth Tibet shall not levy taxes on trade or taxes on roads or taxes of any other kind on the merchants or other subjects of the Gurkha Government'.[1]

The population of Nepal is made up of many tribes, among which the tribe of Gorkha—by Europeans styled Gurkha—is dominant since A.D. 1769. Before that time the ruling tribe was that of the Newars, and it is the people of this tribe who go to live in Tibet. They work in metals, and make some of the images in the temples, especially those in Sikkim. They are bankers and keen in various departments of trade. Many of them are Buddhists and may be seen any day worshipping at the shrines in the great temple at Lhasa. Indeed, one met them everywhere in the Holy City.

They go not only to Nepal but to India also on commercial business. I remember meeting one of them during one of my frequent rides with Ku-sho Pa-lhe-se outside the city. This Nepalese merchant was riding on his way to Calcutta, and was accompanied by seven or eight donkeys in the charge of two Tibetans. The donkeys were all carrying rupees, with which he would buy his wares in Calcutta. I asked Pa-lhe-se whether he was not liable to be robbed *en route*.

'There is not much danger,' replied Pa-lhe-se. 'Three men are enough to guard the cash, for they will travel only during daylight. At night-time they will always stay in a good house and bar the door of their room. But, of course, he is not free from anxiety till he gets the money down safely. There are not many among the merchants in Lhasa who have banking facilities in Calcutta.'

The Newars seemed mostly to carry skins, musk, and

[1] For the full details of this treaty see my *Tibet Past and Present*, Appendix IV (Oxford University Press).

money. One party which we met on our way to Lhasa was going first to Shigatse with tea for sale, and probably on to India afterwards.

The Nepalese in Lhasa were not, as a rule, on good terms with the Tibetans. Feelings of dislike and jealousy came into play.[1] Towards myself and my party they were guarded and suspicious, especially at first. Having been for many years the intermediaries between British and Tibetans, it was natural that they should view with dis-approval the coming of the white foreigner, who was received into a close and friendly relationship by the Dalai Lama and his subjects. Their position of advantage was lost. However, as time went on, they thawed.

But there were, of course, a number who were amicable throughout. When riding with Ne-tö Dzong-pön one day, we met a smiling Nepalese, who gave us a friendly greeting. Ne-tö told me that he was called 'Inserted Light' (Ö-juk-juk), adding,

'He brushes the dust off his clothes, and oils his hair freely.'

'Does the nickname annoy him?'

'Not at all,' he replied. 'Everybody calls him that; he has lost his own name.'

During the period that I spent on the north-eastern frontier of India, namely, from 1900 to 1921, with a few intervals, the Indo-Tibetan trade was quietly but steadily increasing. Between Sikkim and India the growth was rapid, the trade having increased from ten lakhs[2] to sixty lakhs of rupees during the same period. The trade between China and Tibet, on the contrary, declined greatly during the latter years of my residence on account of the hostilities between the two countries and the consequent blocking of trade-routes.

The main road to China goes from Lhasa to Tachienlu via Gyam-da, the capital of Kong-po, and then on through Cham-do. From the latter village there are two routes to

---

[1] See my *Tibet Past and Present*, chapter xxv.
[2] A lakh is one hundred thousand rupees.

Tachienlu, one going to the east through Kan-ze, the other south-east through Ba-tang and Li-tang. Tachienlu is on the border between Tibet and China. The political frontier lies, indeed, a long way to the west of it, but the population to the west is purely Tibetan; to the east it is Chinese.

By these routes the tea which is the chief import from China pours into Tibet. It is pressed into the shape of bricks for convenience of carriage. These are packed securely in coverings of yak-hide and conveyed on the backs of yaks or other cattle, ponies, mules, and donkeys throughout the length and breadth of Tibet, maybe for a journey of three thousand miles across the snowy passes and deep ravines of this difficult country. As the yak, which is one of the chief beasts of burden, travels only ten to twelve miles in an average day's march, the journey takes a long time, and the tea must of necessity be well packed.

Five kinds of Chinese tea are drunk in Tibet. In the Chumbi Valley, whose people have become prosperous through trade, the second best found most favour, the fourth kind was drunk only by the poorest classes, the last kind not at all. Bhutan, however, lived on the two lowest kinds.

The farmers and shepherds of central Tibet drink the third variety mainly; the gentry and merchants the second, mixing a little of the first quality with it. The difference in price of the various kinds is not so great as it seems, for, when inferior, you must use more tea. In Lhasa the second quality costs the equivalent of two shillings per lb., the third one shilling and sixpence. Considering the large quantities consumed, the Tibetan expenditure on tea is enormous.

When tea is bought in large quantities, e.g. five hundred pounds' worth at a time, credit of four or five months may be given. Lhasan firms buy large quantities from eastern Tibetans and retail them in western Tibet.

Until the British Expedition to Lhasa in 1904 the im-

port of Indian tea into Tibet was prohibited by the
Chinese. From 1904 it was allowed, but the Tibetans did
not and do not like it. They find the Chinese tea more
nutritious, more wholesome, and more pleasant to the
taste. Consequently, they rated the Indian varieties only
slightly above the lowest grade of Tibetan tea. There is
unlikely to be any real market for Indian tea in Tibet, until
it is made like Chinese tea in appearance and flavour. The
yearly import from China is estimated at a weight of fourteen or fifteen million pounds.

Tachienlu is, as stated, on the Sino-Tibetan border. Of
the trade centres inside eastern Tibet the most important
is Jye-kun-do, pronounced Kye-gu-do by the people of
central Tibet. Though but a village, routes lead from it
to central Tibet, Mongolia, Kansu, and Szechwan.

After tea the chief imports from China are silks, satins,
brocades, cotton goods, and a few miscellaneous articles
such as matches, buttons, &c. Ponies come too, the best
being those from the region of Sining in Kansu. The
chief exports are musk, gold-dust, wool, sheep-skins, furs,
medicinal herbs, and deer horns. The last named are
taken in the velvet and are highly prized in China as
medicine. It is believed that they strengthen the body and
prolong life. But the chief exports are musk and gold-dust.

Between Lhasa and Mongolia two caravans go and
return each year, one in the summer, the other in the
winter. The members of the caravan, merchants and pilgrims, unite near the Koko Nor on the north-eastern
border of Tibet, and travel together—for mutual protection against the brigands that infest these wilds—as far
as Nag-chu-ka, some ten days' journey north of Lhasa.
From Nag-chu-ka to Lhasa the caravan dissolves into
small parties; this part of the country holds more inhabitants and is outside the ordinary attentions of the robber
bands.

From Mongolia comes Chinese silver, especially in the
shape of horses' hoofs, some gold, too, in the same shape
but much smaller. Silk also comes in plenty, and a

A joke's mixed reception

Indian official seated. Behind him two Indian men and one Tibetan. Four Tibetan women

moderate number of ponies. Sining sends ponies and hides. Am-do, the holy land of Tsong-ka-pa, sends pilgrims, but not much of worldly goods. To Sining go in return woollen cloth and otter skins; to Mongolia woollen cloth, sticks of incense, and copies of the Tibetan scriptures.

The summer caravan arrives in the Holy City during August–September; the other during January–February. Traders come in one or other of these two caravans. For riding and pack animals across the lofty, desolate Chang Tang camels are used, and yaks in summer. Traders in the summer caravan are sometimes detained for a time by the larger rivers between Nag-chu-ka and Lhasa. When in flood from one of summer's heavy rainfalls, they swirl down rapidly between their broadened banks. But they fall as quickly as they rise.

From Am-do to Lhasa pilgrims and others sometimes come in small parties. But not from Mongolia, for the distance is very great, deserts have to be crossed, and there is preponderating fear of brigands. In the Chang Tang a wild yak (*drong*) will sometimes hold up a party of travellers, when the valley is narrow. They then go up the hill-side and kill it from above. So the Dalai Lama told me. And he knows the Chang Tang, having crossed it twice.

During August 1921 Colonel Kennedy and I left Lhasa on a visit to the north. We could not go more than seventy miles, as, being on a diplomatic mission in Lhasa, I could not afford to be indefinitely removed from the nearest telegraph office, from which Lhasa itself was then one hundred and forty-five miles distant. I timed the visit so that we might find members of the summer caravan on their way from Nag-chu-ka to Lhasa. We accordingly met men and women from the distant province of Gya-rong in the extreme east of Tibet under Chinese rule. Parties of Mongols also came along, but most of all, people from the Koko Nor and from the province of Am-do in the northeast. Very religious are the Am-do-was (inhabitants of

Am-do). They come down from Nag-chu-ka, as a rule, before the Mongols, perform their religious duties and their few commercial transactions in Lhasa, and return quickly.

But none may leave Nag-chu-ka for Lhasa until the date fixed by the Dalai Lama for their departure. For Nag-chu-ka is one of the main gateways to Lhasa. It is therefore necessary to prevent any unauthorized foreigners or other suspicious persons, among whom the Chinese are now included, from pushing their way into the heart of Tibet.

XI
A MERCANTILE NATION

THE preceding chapter has dealt with the mercantile community, and especially that portion of it which is engaged in foreign trade. But it must here be observed that, though there is a regular mercantile class, still almost all the people from time to time engage in commerce. For the Tibetan is a born trader.

During autumn and the early days of winter, after the crops have been reaped, the herdsmen journey away from their upland pastures and descend to the villages, bringing salt and soda, the latter for tea, with them. A little wool, too, they bring; this is for the most part sold separately to the regular merchants.

They barter their salt and soda for the peasants' grain, buying qualities that are inferior and mixed in some degree with dust, the empty ears of the *yok-po* weed and so forth. They pour this into the yak-hair bags which brought the salt and soda and ram it down with their hands and heavy rods, for they must carry a year's supply with them.

The nobility have their commercial agents, who go to Peking, Mongolia, and other distant lands, buying rare and valuable articles for their employers. In the Pa-lha household, and no doubt in others also, records of the more valuable purchases are kept in the family archives. When I was in Lhasa, one of the Tibetan ministers had an agent in Mongolia. Having succeeded in eluding the attentions of a Mongolian priest, who had taken to brigandage, he arrived in due course at Lhasa.

The large monasteries trade widely, and are able to do so because each has its administrative department, known as the *Lab-rang*,[1] which has charge of the monastic properties. As an example of these miscellaneous activities

[1] བླ་བྲང་ lit. 'Lama's residence'.

I may quote the case of Re-ting, sixty-three miles north of Lhasa, a large and important monastery which in a past century exercised for a time a sovereignty of its own.

Colonel Kennedy and I visited Re-ting, on the Dalai Lama's invitation, in August 1921. While there, I had several walks and talks with the chief executive officer of the monastery, who held the significant title of 'The Holder of the Keys' (*Di-chang-nga*). Re-ting is connected with the Shi-de Monastery in Lhasa, which the Chinese burnt and looted, while they were fighting with the Tibetans in 1911 and 1912.

So the Key Holder was sent to Sining, in Kansu, to gain profits by trade, in order to help in repairing the ravages. He borrowed money from the Dalai Lama and went to Sining, but as the trade there was unsatisfactory, he journeyed on to Urga, the capital of Mongolia. This town he found very hot during its brief summer and extremely cold in winter, but the commercial prospect was more promising. Accordingly, he spent over two years there, and was absent for five years altogether on this trading venture. He bought incense sticks, drugs, and woollen cloth from his fellow Tibetans, silks and other articles from Chinese, and, selling what he bought, made some profit on the sale. From these profits fresh images were fashioned for Shi-de and funds were provided for a part of the cost of restoration.

The Maharaja of Bhutan, both before and after he assumed the secular headship of his country, always had his agent in Lhasa, employed mainly for trade and known as Lo-chak-pa, 'He who Stays through the Years'. Under him are his servants or trade assistants, known as his 'Trade Children',[1] at several places including Pa-ri, where the trade between Bhutan and Tibet is large. The Pa-ro Pen-lop, the leading subordinate chief, had his own agent there for a similar purpose.

The Tibetan Government have many such agents throughout Tibet and beyond its borders in China, Mon-

[1] *Tsong-truk.*

golia, and India, making necessary purchases for the Government. On the Tachienlu route the private traders used necessarily to pay customs duties to the Chinese authorities, but the Tibetan Government's commercial agent was exempted from these. He was a *tse-trung*, i.e. an ecclesiastical official. He had several agents under him and sometimes farmed out the advantages which his position as the Government trader gave him. To the Tibetan mind there is nothing incongruous in a governmental agent selling his official privileges in this way. He has had to pay the high officers of government for his appointment, and this is how he recoups himself—and is expected to recoup himself—and make such profit as is reasonably possible. The relations, in fact, between such officials and the Government are largely on a contractual basis.

Even the robber tribes issue from their haunts and go to other districts to trade. Perhaps the most prominent among these are the Go-lok-pas, i.e. the people of the Go-lok territory. Though they habitually rob traders and travellers that pass through their part of the country, yet they go themselves as peaceful traders across their eastern border into China, as well as westwards through Tibet. We met some in Lhasa and could not fail to notice their prosperity. The backs of their womenfolk were plentifully adorned with huge silver plaques. No doubt they find the combined occupation profitable, trading in other districts and robbing in their own.

It is noteworthy that when the Dalai Lama travelled through their country he was not molested. On the contrary, they flocked to him for his blessing. Brigands, indeed, they are, but brigands after a method that is governed by the needs of this world and the next.

Women may often manage the shops and the retail trade generally. Especially is this the case in Lhasa. Men take charge of the commercial dealings which necessitate journeys. And in any case in which the trade transaction is a large one the decision as a rule rests with the man.

I have shown above [1] how in the payment of rent money is but little used, the greater part being settled by grain payments and by services rendered. In trade transactions also the use of money is in a measure restricted. Buying and selling is often effected by direct barter. Or, instead of money, other commodities may be substituted, these varying in different districts. Rockhill notes the use of boots as a medium of exchange in the Tsai-dam area of south Mongolia and in the Koko Nor region. And in many parts of Tibet tea is used in the same way, the vendor perhaps quoting the price in money, and the purchaser offering so many tea bricks in settlement of the demand.

I paid many visits to the market at Gyangtse, which is held every morning. One such visit, in August 1915, in the company of my wife and the British Trade Agent, may be briefly noted. We found bricks of tea from China, soda for flavouring the tea, and Tibetan salt. The soda, like the salt, comes from the plains of northern Tibet. Dyes of various kinds from Tibet, Bhutan, and Sikkim were in evidence, especially the madder, which grows profusely in the last two countries. Glue for the rough Tibetan paper was made up into small engraved slabs known as 'mouth-glue', because it is put into the mouth and then rubbed on. It was noticeable that three-fourths of the matches came from Japan, the remainder mostly from Sweden. The cups, used for food as well as for drink, were fashioned in the main from the wood of the silver birch brought from Bhutan. In Sikkim maple is commonly used. We were interested to see salted fish from the Yam-dro Tso, three days' journey away. It can be kept for nine or ten months in good condition, for such is the climate of Tibet.

Books of an ordinary kind are sold in the markets, but the more valuable ones can hardly be obtained except through the high lamas or through laymen of the upper classes.

Gyangtse has its own market-place. The goods are laid

[1] See p. 83.

' One of the wealthiest merchants in Gyangtse, a woman
who owned valuable landed property '

Stalls in Gyangtse market

'They gossip over the events of the day.' Floor rugs for sale

out on the ground, or on planks and boxes, or on banks of
stone and earth. Often a large umbrella or a tent-like
awning is erected to keep off the sun and glare. The vendor, usually a woman, sits on the bank with the things for
sale grouped round her. Sometimes a wall of sun-dried
brick runs along the back, affording welcome support
when trade is slack. Those who dispose of the picturesque
little Tibetan floor-rugs, again chiefly women, have a
corner to themselves, where they gossip over the events of
the day until a purchaser strolls up.

It is not only the poor who sit and chaffer in the petty
sales of the market-place. One of the wealthiest merchants in Gyangtse, a woman who owned valuable
landed property, took her seat with the others for a time
each day.

Ponies, mules, and donkeys stand here and there,
ready to take the unsold surplus away. Dogs wander in
and out, looking for whatever they may pick up. It is a
leisurely, peaceful scene. No Englishwoman peering into
the shop windows in Oxford Street gains greater pleasure
than these purchasers and sightseers who saunter along
from stall to stall.

In Lhasa the goods are exposed on stands, or laid out on
the ground in front of the shops. Let us take one typical
of many. In the centre are cartridges. On the near side
of them are bridles and stirrups. Beyond and to the right
is the stall-keeper's food, a teapot, a cup, and a basket
containing barley-flour. On the extreme right is a large
wooden chest for storing the more valuable articles. In
front to the right are sacks which serve for carrying away
the unsold surplus after the day's business is ended. The
keeper of the stall sits on a rug of white felt behind his
cartridges.

Going one day down the streets of the Holy City on
my way to the Temple, to hear—though not to understand—the disputations of the doctors learned in the law,
I passed a Chinese barber. A secretary of the Dalai Lama
was with me, and I learned from him that such barbers

charged ordinary folk a sum equivalent to one penny.
The gentry paid eightpence.

During my time in Tibet the chief Tibetan merchant
was a man named Pom-da-tsang. I met him in Lhasa.
He had branches in Calcutta, Shanghai, and Peking, and
formerly had maintained a branch in Japan also. His business with India was chiefly in wool, but he exported also
yak-tails and other commodities. To Peking he sent woollen cloth, as well as the skins of fox, stone marten, lynx,
marmot, &c.

He imported great quantities of Chinese silk. During
the last twelve years he had obtained this via Calcutta,
instead of, as formerly, along the overland routes through
China and eastern Tibet. As the years go forward, more
and more grows the tendency for the Sino-Tibetan commerce to pass oversea, forsaking the tracks overland across
the mountain ridges and deep ravines of the border country.
The long, lingering hostilities between these two peoples
have strengthened this tendency, but they have done no
more than this. Were there profound peace on the Tibetan
marches, even then the sea route would continue to grow
in favour.

Pom-da-tsang emphasized the necessity of knowing the
different patterns on the silk, for some districts in Tibet
favour one pattern, others another. The silk which came
from Russia, he asserted, was of good quality only; there
was nothing second-rate. It was more costly than the most
expensive Chinese silk.

I have described the ordinary day, as it may be spent by
the herdsman, by the peasant, and by the official of the
upper class. Regarding the typical day of the merchant
or trader not much need be said. It will be somewhat after
the fashion of the official, but on more modest lines.

Let us take the case of a Tro-mo-wa merchant, keen and
fairly prosperous, not a half-timer, but one who lives for
commerce alone. He spends a good deal of his day going
round and settling business matters with other merchants.
He must see that his muleteers are looking after his mules

Grounds of the Serpent Temple
Regarded by the Chinese as one of the five beauties of Lhasa

Stall in Lhasa market with cartridges, &c., as described in the text

A street in Lhasa. Shops in foreground, *chö-ten* in middle distance

and other animals that carry the merchandise from Pa-ri to Kalimpong and back again.

Our merchant friend, like the gentry, is very probably fond of gambling, having his parties for this purpose in the evening. The man who wins the round puts a *tang-ka* (about fourpence) or, if the stakes are high, three or four *tang-kas* into the pool. At the end of the evening the pool is given to the host in return for the supper which he gives to the party. Different members of the gambling set act as host in turn, now one, now another, but not all. Those only are chosen who provide good gambling apparatus and good fare.

XII

BEGGARS

THE professional beggar is a familiar spectacle in the East. In Tibet he is professional and hereditary through generation and generation. No doubt some of the workers, through loss of a leg or the like, being unable to earn their daily food, may take to begging. But these are a small minority.

While beggars are ubiquitous throughout Tibet, they are mostly to be seen in the towns, and especially in Lhasa. Cynics, indeed, aver that the Holy City is tenanted by women, beggars, and dogs.

When you come to stay in Lhasa, you cannot disregard the beggars. Though they swarm, you must give to all—once. Having done so, you are free of them for a season. If they are still importunate, a reminder will move them away, for they, too, recognize the rules of the game. But once you *must* give. If you attempt to evade your obligation, you will be cursed, and every one fears the curse of a beggar.

The monks, who go a-begging, are, of course, on a different footing. Their lives are devoted to religion, not only for their own spiritual advancement, but also for the benefit of all humanity and the whole animal creation, birds, beasts, and fishes, for all are 'mind-possessors' (*sem-chen*), and can therefore in time attain to the status of the Buddha. Working thus as they do in the service of all, it is recognized that the labourer is worthy of his hire. With staff and begging bowl the monk—or nun—passes from village to village, from door to door, especially during autumn, the favourite season for mendicant monks and nuns.

The monk is not always begging for himself. A lama has several disciples, and these may beg for him. In a Tibetan history [1] we read of a priest named Jeng, who lived

[1] Tep-ter Ngön-po, vol. iii, folio 35.

in the eleventh and twelfth centuries of the Christian era,
being born about the time of the Norman conquest of
England:

'Finding that Ba-gom (his spiritual Guide) was a worthy
Teacher, Jeng, instead of returning home, went towards Sang-ri
collecting alms. He bought a sack, and filling this with the barley
which he had obtained on this begging round, went to his Teacher
and offered it to him.

'But the latter said, 'You have served me; I do not want this.
Use it while engaged in your devotions. I have a rare text, called
Dor-je Sam-pa, by means of which you can master the truth of the
"Transient", and obtain Buddhahood in a single lifetime. There
has been an unbroken line of saints, who left no particle of their
physical bodies behind. This testament I have not hitherto im-
parted to anybody. Now I will give it to you." '

Jeng continued to press his Teacher to accept his offering, saying that, as it had been mentally dedicated to him
(the Teacher), he must be kind enough to accept it. As
for food while engaged in his devotions, he would be sure
to receive it somehow. His Teacher then laid his left
hand on Jeng's head, and with his right hand patted Jeng's
shoulder, and said, 'You are full of faith; I am greatly
pleased. The text is sure to prove of great use to you.'

The history goes on to record that by teaching, by
astrological divination, and by performing rituals for
guarding against evils, Jeng obtained enough to last him
through his devotional period.

Three miles above Gangtok, the capital of Sikkim, on
the road to Tibet, I used to pass a bamboo pole with a
cross-bar. It was in a place whence several high peaks
were visible. At one time it held cloths of various
colours. These were offerings to the spirit of a high
mountain peak, the practice being to put them up in
places whence many mountains could be seen. Mendicant
priests, when they passed, would remove these fragments
of cloth for patching their own garments. To this no
objection was taken; it did not destroy the value of the
offering.

In Tibet such are always printed with prayers, and then no one meddles with them. Indeed, it would be a sin to use these holy pieces for patching clothes, and a very heinous crime to apply them to patching or lining boots. It is forbidden to throw writing, even unwanted letters, on the ground; they should be burnt in the fire. For letters and writing, it is held, owe their origin to the Buddhas of the past. As for the books, they have been written by revered priests and contain the teachings of Gotama, the present Buddha.

But to return to the lay beggars. Though there are many in Tibet nowadays, the popular report maintains that it was not so at the first. Among the common sights of Tibet are the *men-dongs*, low buildings like thickened walls. They are erected in the names of deceased persons by their heirs and successors, or by others for their own spiritual advancement. In them are placed the offerings decreed by the lama, e.g. images modelled in clay, sacred books, and other religious objects.

But there are other buildings, somewhat similar in appearance, which are not *men-dongs*. In olden times cakes of barley-flour, &c., used to be placed on these that the birds might eat of them. In former days, tradition says, Tibet was so prosperous that there were no beggars and nobody would accept alms. Accordingly, as an outlet for their charity, the people used to feed the birds.

A beggar's form of address is peculiar. No doubt a wide diversity marks the forms of salutation current in different countries of the world, but few can be more out of the ordinary than that used by the humbler classes in Tibet towards their social superiors. Peasant, shepherd, or labourer will put out his tongue when addressing—or addressed by—one of the gentry. A beggar adds the further compliment of putting up his two thumbs, thus signifying that the person addressed is of the first quality, and may be expected to give a present in accordance with his quality.

The beggars in Lhasa often sue in the following terms,

Beggar man, woman, and child

Tongue and thumbs. The beggar's salute

'Great mercy, Learned Sir! A little present, please, for me.' Those in the Chumbi Valley will sometimes say, 'Officer, Buddha, please give me a present.' But I was never addressed in such terms in Lhasa.

Places of pilgrimage are much frequented by beggars. Round many of the sacred edifices in Tibet run sacred roads or paths. At Lhasa, as befits the Holy City, there are no less than three sacred ways. The 'Inside Circle' (*nang-kor* [1]) runs round a cloister inside the Temple. The 'Intermediate Circle' (*par-kor* [2]) is the road which encloses the Temple buildings. The 'Park Circle' (*ling-kor* [3]) is about four miles in length, as it takes in not only Lhasa City but two low hills nearly a mile away. These are surmounted, the one by the Dalai Lama's palace, known as the Potala, the other by the Temple of Medicine.

The largest circle would naturally have been named the 'Outside Circle' (*chi-kor*) in contradistinction to the Inside and the Intermediate. But the word 'outside' is ill-omened. It is applied to the 'outside man', i.e. the non-Buddhist (*chi-pa*), and to the unbeliever from abroad (*chi-ling*), a term that carries with it almost the meaning of 'foreign devil'. It could not, therefore, be applied to the Sacred Way-round the Holy City. So it is called the Park Circle. It passes by several of the parks or groves (*ling-ka*) that fringe the town. These add greatly to the amenities of town life, especially during summer when the trees, willow and poplar, are in leaf, the air is warm, the wind is moderate, and the dust storms do not come in the overwhelming fury of winter. Then the call of the out-of-doors receives a ready response from the town dwellers of a people accustomed to life under the open sky.

These Sacred Ways are happy hunting-grounds for the beggars. The stranger from another district, intent on treading the religious round, can hardly forbear the small act of charity that they demand. And of course they throng the frequented roads into the city. I never failed to find some seated by the bridge, known as 'Turquoise

[1] ནང་འཁོར་   [2] བར་འཁོར་   [3] གླིང་འཁོར་

Roof Bridge', which spans a small arm of 'Middle River' (Kyi Chu [1]) between Lhasa and the Potala. It is on the main road between the two. Often there were three beggars in this coveted position. A woman sat in the middle telling her beads. A man sat on each side, one partially seeing and turning a prayer wheel, the other stone blind, telling his beads. As you passed on your pony, tongues were extended, thumbs were raised. Their large black dog sat in front, quietly scanning the passers-by; their staves lay around them, for all were old.

One meets beggar fiddlers all over the countryside. The fiddle (*tse-tse*) has usually four strings, and the fiddler is often accompanied by a small boy; sometimes by two or three, boys and girls. The young assistants join in the dance, and solicit and collect the alms to the accompaniment of a plaintive whine that is universal and never varies. One such party that I met in the 'Valley of Taste' (*Nyang* [2]) consisted of the fiddler with two small boys and one small girl. These three danced; the man played his fiddle behind them, lifting his foot only to kick any of his small dependents who showed a slackening in effort. The dance was that known as the Dance of the White Devils.

A beggar frequently goes farther than this and actually assumes the part of a White Devil (*dre-kar*). He puts on a mask, such as the actors wear, and goes alone or with one child to a festival, a market-place, or other frequented spot. He makes the people laugh by his absurdities. Though poorly housed and poorly clad, a White Devil's role is to describe himself as rich and powerful. 'I have arrived', he will say, 'from a far-distant country, where I visited one of the mansions of the Lord Buddha, and come now to bring blessings to you all.' The audience laugh and give him presents, some a little flour, some coins

[1] European writers have translated Kyi Chu as 'River of Happiness', evidently on the understanding that Kyi is spelt སྐྱིད་ a word meaning happiness. But I am assured by well-informed Tibetans of Lhasa that both in books and in letters the spelling is དཀྱིལ་ which means 'middle'.

[2] ཉང་ Nyang Chö-jung, folio 3.

'The walls of their huts are built with horns'

worth a penny or two. Any one who refuses fears the beggar's curse, and that would bring ill fortune.

There lived in bygone times a Bhutanese priest, known sometimes as 'The All Good Bhutanese' (*Druk-pa Kün-le*) from the good that he achieved, and sometimes as 'The Mad Bhutanese' (*Druk-ngön*) from the unconventional methods by which he achieved it. This priest taught many religious refrains to the beggar fiddlers. His idea was that religious words being sung, others would hear, and the religion would be benefited.

Sometimes we shall see a beggar seated on the ground revolving a small pole with pieces of cloth attached to it. On the cloth prayers are written. To turn these round and round, the way of the sun, is tantamount to offering the prayers. So spiritual benefit accrues.

On the outskirts of Lhasa there are shelters for beggars. A usual type is a circular stone wall, three to four feet high, surmounted by an old awning of yak-hair, stretched upwards to a peak or ridge. Those in more prosperous circumstances may possess a yak-hair tent of their own in a moderate state of preservation.

There is a community of beggars in Lhasa, known as *Ra-gyap-pa*. The walls of their huts are built with the horns of animals, yaks, other cattle, and sheep. They are the scavengers of the city. It is their duty to carry the corpses of poor people to the appointed places where the corpses are broken up and given to the vultures. They must also take outside and cast on the surrounding plain the carcases of animals that die in Lhasa. Another duty, which the Government entrust to them, is to search for Lhasa thieves who flee into the country. They used also to be placed in charge of convicts, but this practice has been discontinued. During the Dalai Lama's stay in India from 1910 to 1912 it was noted how prisoners are set to work in the Indian jails. Accordingly, since his return to Tibet, such convicts are usually employed in the Government workshops.

The Ra-gyap-pas are insistent people. Where others

beg, they demand forcibly. The countryman feels that he
has no option but to give. Should he hesitate, he may be
told that he will not live to reach his home, and his corpse
will be dishonoured.

To the gentry they go on festivals and holy days, and to
officials at the times of promotion, but often keep off
ordinary beggars from importuning their hosts at the
same time. Gentry from Shigatse and elsewhere give to
them once on arrival in Lhasa, and once on departure.

The Ra-gyap-pas wear the hat of respectability, called
bok-do,[1] but ordinary beggars do not wear this. In fact,
a Ra-gyap-pa amasses a fair competence by following his
varied occupations.

A poor person, who claims to have been the subject of
a miracle, may use this as a means for soliciting alms.
Now and then in Tibet is to be found a man or woman
who claims to have risen from the dead. Such a one is
known as *De-lok*, 'Passed away and returned'. I met a
de-lok one day on the Lhasa *ling-kor* behind the Potala.
She was an old woman from eastern Tibet, and she
claimed to have come back to life five or six days after
she had died. So she sat by the Sacred Way reading
prayers, and pious pilgrims gave her alms. Tibetans
always respect a miracle, though they are not unduly
surprised by it.

Ne-tö Dzong-pön and Ku-sho Pa-lhe-se were with me
at the time. The former remarked, '*De-lok* are usually
imbecile. They make absurd statements and seem wrong
in their heads. There was one in the Töm-pa family (one
of the noble families of Lhasa) some time ago.'

The *de-lok* must not be confused with another type of
apparent return to life, the 'Standing Corpse' (*ro-lang*).
Tibetans hold these in great dread. Tsa-rong Shap-pe
told me in 1915 that there had been a case recently, when
he was away at the Re-ting Monastery with the Dalai
Lama. There were six monks attending a funeral service.
Just as the corpse, in accordance with Tibetan custom,

[1] See p. 20.

was to be broken up, it stood upright. The monks fell
down from the shock. The corpse also, after standing up
for an instant, fell down.

'Such cases', said Tsa-rong, 'occur chiefly when a person dies during a thunderstorm. There are no thunderstorms during winter, and the corpses of those who die
in winter never show signs of coming back to life again.

'The Tibetan belief is that the *ro-lang* can walk straight
ahead only. It cannot turn to the right or left. A stone
thrown at it will not hurt it; the only way to kill it is
by throwing a boot at it. Anybody who is touched by the
ro-lang dies.'

XIII

ROBBERS

It is natural that there should be brigands in Tibet. It is a wild country with vast empty spaces, rendered still more wild and difficult by high mountain ranges and deep ravines. By tradition and instinct the people are nomadic, and the means of subsistence among all nomadic peoples are precarious. Disease among the flocks and herds, a drought that kills the scanty pasture, drive the herdsmen to repair these ravages at the expense of others. The strength and endurance bred of their healthy life combine to empower them, and so we find that brigandage is innate in all nomadic communities.

The political and social order of Tibet is several hundred years behind that which now holds in England; it corresponds to a period when highway robbery was rife in this country. The ordinary folk of Tibet are hardy, living the simple life in clear, cold air, courageous, mobile, and fond of adventure. It is not a matter for wonder that there should be brigands, but rather that they should not. be more numerous than they are.

The robber tribes are said to be able to bend down sideways and fire under their ponies while the latter are galloping. Firing from under their ponies' necks is but a small matter to them. These feats are shared by some of the herdsmen.

Side by side with their characteristics recorded above, the Tibetans have the instinct for orderliness. It lies deep down in their nature, and is one of the qualities which has helped them to establish their hierarchy on a firm basis. And the hierarchy, thus established, repays its debt by aiding in the maintenance of order. One sees this respect for rule and custom on all sides.

In England it would not be possible to determine when winter will begin and when it will end. Our Cabinet

Ministers, officials, and clergy would resent being compelled to wear an overcoat on a warm day, or forbidden its use when an icy north wind was blowing. But Tibet, in this as in so many other matters, does things differently. On the anniversary of the death of Tsong-ka-pa, who in the fourteenth century reformed the Tibetan Church and inaugurated the sect of the Yellow Hats, winter commences. On the eighth day of the third Tibetan month it ends. This places winter between a date in the first half of December and another in the last half of April. Between these two dates, all officials, lay and ecclesiastical, must wear fur hats and cloaks after prescribed patterns. Outside these dates, however cold the day may be, they are debarred from doing so.

So strong within certain limits is the instinct for orderliness, that even the brigands are governed largely by rule. Many of them are robbers on the highways and byways of their own districts for a part of each year, but peaceable traders when they visit Lhasa and other centres of commerce. Nobody attempts to interfere with them on these trading expeditions, provided that they conduct themselves honestly then. The people of Go-lok in the east of Tibet are notorious robbers, and those of Nya-rong scarcely less notorious. Yet you will find the men and women of both districts in Lhasa and elsewhere. Occasionally the predatory instinct is too strong, driving one to snatch something off a stall in the market. But this does not happen very often. Pliny noted that the Arabs were equally addicted to theft and trade. And so it is, and from time immemorial has been, with the robber tribes of Tibet.

As one travels in Tibet, one's Tibetan companions point out places on the road where robbers from time to time descend on unarmed travellers. More likely than not it is a valley which has narrowed into a rocky ravine. Such a one is the gorge in the Nyang Valley above Sau-gang, and the ravine leading up to the Cha La on the road going north from Lhasa to Ta-lung.

In 1914 robberies were prevalent in Gya-de, a province one hundred and fifty to two hundred miles north-east of Lhasa. Till 1912 this province was under Chinese administration, but in the latter year the Tibetans drove the Chinese out of central Tibet, and ended such privileges as the Chinese possessed there. Accordingly the Tibetan Government sent a priest from the Se-ra Monastery, one of the three great monasteries near Lhasa, as its delegate to inquire into the brigandage in Gya-de. On arrival the priest demanded ten of the ringleaders, but the robbers came and told him that they would kill him. 'That', he said, 'will not make this affair smaller; it will make it larger.' However, they killed him.

The Ka-lön Lama—as the ecclesiastical member of the Supreme Council is called—was in command of that part of the country. He advised the Tibetan Government to dispatch a military expedition against the brigands. This was done, and the troops ravaged the country. They killed all whom they captured among those who fought against them, and destroyed their property. Those who surrendered, promised obedience to the Tibetan Government, and gave up all arms and ammunition, were spared, as is the custom in such cases.

Among the crowds which flocked to Lhasa for the New Year ceremonies I noticed a party from Am-do, a province on the north-eastern border of Tibet. They were carrying long iron spears, which they find useful when crossing the Northern Plains, for this ice-bound desert is infested with brigands.

There have been instances of monasteries taking to robbery. The important monastery of Cha-treng, known to the Chinese as Siangcheng, and situated in south-eastern Tibet under Chinese rule, used frequently to dispatch marauding expeditions. But it was actuated largely by the desire to rise against the hated Chinese. When I was in Lhasa, the Cha-treng force had grown to large proportions, of whom only two hundred or so were monks. The balance was made up of deserters from the

Go-lok man and his wife in Lhasa

Chinese troops, and of men from eastern Tibet and from Gya-rong, a large province containing eighteen Tibetan tribes on the Sino-Tibetan border and governed by the Chinese. These men from Kam and Gya-rong were scally-wags, destitute and desperate. An expedition so composed took to loot and pillage as a matter of course.

Indeed, during the British military expedition to Lhasa in 1904, the troops from Kam, who had been summoned to assist in repelling the British, habitually looted the Tibetan villages through which they passed. Such troops often fought bravely in their cause, but seemed to regard themselves as entitled to plunder those whose hearths and homes they had been called to defend. As for the expedition from Cha-treng, during my time in Lhasa, the Dalai Lama appealed to it to return to the monastery. And it obeyed the call of the Head of the Faith, though flushed with victory over the Chinese foe and well placed for plunder.[1]

Cha-treng, Am-do, Gya-rong, and a large part of eastern Tibet were all under Chinese rule. There was much more brigandage and unrest in the parts of Tibet under Chinese control than in those under the Tibetan Government. This was noticed by several travellers, including Mr. Teichman,[2] of the British Consular Service in China, who travelled up and down through eastern Tibet in 1918.

From about 1912 to 1915 there was a large increase in thefts throughout Tibet, because the crops had been poor for several years in succession. People in want of food became desperate. Hermitages and nunneries, being de-fenceless, were often despoiled by robbers.

'Thieves do not scruple to rob even saintly lamas, if alone,' I was told. 'They have no religion, but seek only their own needs. They will, however, hesitate to rob any-body, even a woman, belonging to a family that exercises power, such as that of an official or wealthy landlord, for fear lest they should be caught later on and punished.'

[1] See *Tibet Past and Present*, p. 251.
[2] *Travels in Eastern Tibet*, by Eric Teichman, p. 193 (Cambridge University Press).

A partial failure of crops for two or three years is met in some measure by the numerous granaries owned by peasants as well as by landlords. If there should be a heavy failure for three or four years in succession severe famine results. Then those who are starving, in the power of their great number, seize the food of their wealthier neighbours with such completeness that the latter are likely to starve first. And so the popular saying runs:

> Though they're the country's ornaments, the rich
> Die first by hunger's knife when famine comes.[1]

Of course, thefts are sometimes due in part to personal reasons. During my stay in Lhasa the Commander-in-Chief had many enemies, especially among the monks. There was deep enmity between the priesthood and the new army, which curtailed the priestly power and prestige. So, during the Tson-chö festival which took place early in April, when the city was overrun by monks, the latter broke the windows in the Commander-in-Chief's house. He was one of the few who had imported the foreign luxury of glass windows, for most fill their window-frames with white cloth, sufficiently thin to let a modicum of light through. A little later on his wife's jewellery was stolen to the value of about three thousand pounds.

The Tibetan histories say that in olden days robbers were sometimes held in check by magical means. We read in the Blue Record of an Indian Buddhist, who had been a Hindu king in southern India, was converted to Buddhism, and relinquished his royal state in order to don the robes of the mendicant monk. While returning to India through Nepal, a favourite resort of Tibetan students, he and his party encountered a band of robbers. His disciples were anxious, for they carried some gold with them. However, the royal monk, we are told, 'cast a charm on the robbers, who fell to dancing, and the party escaped while the robbers were yet under the spell'.[2]

---

[1]   Chuk-po chem-po yül-kyi gyen-cha yin;
            Mu-ge chung-na, tok-ri ngen-la chi.
[2] Tep-ter Ngön-po, vol. vii, folio 19.

The Bhutanese have long been feared by the Tibetans for robbery and other violent crimes. With them, therefore, outbreaks of brigandage needed sterner measures. Writing of the times of the first Dharma Raja,[1] who ruled Bhutan between two and three hundred years ago, the leading Bhutanese history [2] informs us:

'About this time the borders towards Ta-ka-na were infested by robbers and thieves, who plundered the neighbouring settlers and wayfarers. The Dharma Raja sent armed men to roam over the mountains and forests, rocks and caves, to hunt these pests and to suppress them. Most of the robbers were killed and thus peace and security were established.'

Of this Dharma Raja we are told:

'He introduced law into lawless Bhutan. His chief cause for self-satisfaction was in the knowledge that he had not wasted any time. He was wont to say, "I could not relinquish the glory of being called the Bhutanese, but I have never wasted any time in selfish idleness." '

Of his Deputy, to whom in his old age he entrusted the secular government of Bhutan, we read:

'His guiding principle was, "Actions, if unadulterated by self-interest, bear good fruit in the future, though they may at the time appear to be harsh or even sinful." Thus, acting upon that simple and straightforward principle, he made Bhutan a land of security, so that even an old woman might carry a load of gold in safety.'

Possibly the zeal of the historian led him to rate the improvement too highly. Or perhaps the standard has declined since the first Dharma Raja passed away. At any rate, Bhutan's neighbours would not put it so high nowadays, for the Tibetan saying still runs:

No handles to their pots,
No law in their land.

But the late ruler of Bhutan, Sir U-gyen Wang-chuk, an administrator wise and tolerant but firm, did much towards bringing his vigorous, if turbulent, subjects into line with modern standards of law and order.

[1] Dharma Raja is an Indian term, though generally used by Europeans. Bhutanese. and Tibetans style him *Shap-trung Rim-po-che*.
[2] Lho-hi Chö-jung.

From time to time I used to accept the invitation of the priests in the Ka-gyü Monastery, the chief monastery in the Chumbi Valley, to visit them. During a visit of this kind in 1917 an old monk came out of his religious retreat (*tsam*) to have a talk with me. In accordance with the Lhasa Convention of 1904 the valley had been taken under British administration until 1908. It was my duty to administer it for the first fourteen months of this period, and the old man remembered me from those days. In 1916, when in retreat, his cell had been invaded by Bhutanese brigands. His property was looted, and he himself was beaten. 'It was not so, when the great Sahibs governed the valley,' said the old monk, 'but under our own Government these things happen.' The British rule lasted for three years only, during which some two hundred Indian soldiers were stationed there. The turbulent elements were probably afraid to kill or steal under conditions which they had never known before. They preferred to wait till affairs resumed their normal aspect.

Some of the robber tribes in Tibet have religious feelings, which restrict robberies in some degree. Should they raid cattle or other animals, which are afterwards found to belong to a monastery, they return these. The Dalai Lama's friendly reception by the Go-lok brigands has already been recorded.

The punishments in Tibet for brigandage and other crimes of violence are severe. Both Chinese and Tibetan magistrates used sometimes to order that the hand of one found guilty of habitual theft should be severed at the wrist. Robbers and other convicts are to be found wandering about the market-places with heavy irons on their legs begging for their food. Yet even in such an uncomfortable predicament you may find them incurably cheerful.

'You may find them incurably cheerful.' Convicts and beggars

XIV

THE WOMEN

WHEN a traveller enters Tibet from the neighbouring nations in China or India, few things impress him more vigorously or more deeply than the position of the Tibetan women. They are not kept in seclusion as are Indian women. Accustomed to mix with the other sex throughout their lives, they are at ease with men, and can hold their own as well as any women in the world. But I will come back to this subject. Let us first see what they look like.

As to standards of beauty, who shall decide? Many English people deny beauty to the generality of Tibetan women; the almond eyes, flat noses, and high cheek-bones are causes of offence. But to many Tibetans it appears that some of the European features are abnormal and ugly. A Tibetan lady in a recent book [1] has written:

'The average European is not good-looking according to our ideas. We consider your noses too big, often they stick out like kettle-spouts; your ears too large, like pigs' ears; your eyes blue like children's marbles; your eye-sockets too deep and eye-brows too prominent, too simian.'

The great majority of men and women have the almond eyes, flattened noses, and prominent cheek-bones common to the Chinese and other nations of eastern Asia. As recorded above, a Sikkimese saying regards a long head as a hall-mark of aristocratic birth.

In many parts of the country the hair is worn in a number of little plaits which descend from the crown of the head to the waist. In other parts, e.g. in Ba-tang and Tachienlu, one large plait hangs down the back. Married and unmarried women living in the same district dress their hair in the same way, but those who are married wear more ornaments. The women of central Tibet wear their

---

[1] *We Tibetans*, by Rin-chen Lha-mo (Seeley Service), p. 131.

hair divided right and left, fluffed out on each side, and increased artificially to make a good show.

It may at any rate be said of most Tibetan women that they are of strong physique, and that their cheerful faces break readily into smiles, radiating health and intelligence, and showing to advantage their strong white teeth. The ladies have fair complexions, and of their complexions they take great care. In the lower elevations, those below an altitude of eleven thousand feet, the young girls' faces are as fair as those of northern France. But almost all have dark eyes, and dark, straight hair; curly hair is regarded with disfavour. Some of the people are disfigured by goitre, but, except in parts of eastern Tibet and along some of the valleys in Bhutan, this is not common. Of Bhutan, one may say that it always strikes one as a man's country. The men are endowed with great physical strength and determined wills, though too prone to sudden outbursts of anger, when swords are freely drawn. But their womenfolk are plain according to our ordinary standards, and all the more so from their habit of wearing their hair close-cropped.

As we have seen above, many of the ladies stay in their houses as far as possible during winter for the sake of their complexions. Throughout Tibet it is a general custom for women to smear caoutchouc on their faces. Some writers have explained that this custom was ordained by the Tibetan Government in former days to prevent the women from being unduly attractive, as their too easy morals had led many men astray. I did not find acceptance of this explanation in Tibet. As one of my Tibetan friends remarked:

'I never heard that. It is the duty of women in all countries, whether Britain, China, Tibet or other, to be as good-looking as possible.

'Some women put caoutchouc on their faces to ward off toothache, neuralgia, &c., caused by the cold winds. Many also apply it because they believe that, when they wash it off, it makes their skin whiter. So they put it on

when at home by themselves, and wash it off when they
go out among friends and when they attend festivals.'

Rockhill notes [1] that rouge pads of felt, which have
been soaked in a red colouring matter, are used by both
Mongol and Tibetan women. A portion of this is transferred to the cheek by moistening the pad slightly. Such
pads are prepared in China. The Mongol women use these
pads much more than their Tibetan cousins, whose mountain air is more generous to them in the gift of rosy cheeks.

When we were in Lhasa together, Colonel Kennedy,
being a doctor, used constantly to visit the Lhasan households to render necessary medical assistance. During such
a visit to one of the leading families, an elderly lady, the
head of the house, pointed to a mole on her cheek. She
asked whether there was any way by which she might be
rid of it, for people told her that it was an insidious thing
which might kill her one day unless she could contrive its
removal. He gave her some lunar caustic and told her
to use it sparingly as it would blacken the skin.

A few days later, when he called again to vaccinate
some members of her household, she arrived with her face
muffled up. It soon became apparent that she had two
large smudges where the lunar caustic had been applied
with far too free a hand. The picture was completed when
another member of the household arrived with her nose
blackened, almost completely blackened, by her endeavours to remove a mole from it. At this spectacle
Kennedy could not refrain from laughter, in which the
ladies joined him with great heartiness. It may be that
the removal of blemishes rather than the fear of disease
had increased their efforts. And Tibetans of both sexes
can usually join in a laugh against themselves.

The dress worn by Tibetans, both the lower and the
upper classes, men as well as women, has found mention
above.[2] I will, therefore, limit myself here to a brief
description of the main ornaments worn, and chiefly those
worn by the women.

[1] Rockhill, *Ethnology of Tibet*, p. 722.   [2] See pp. 20, 21, 67–69.

The woman's chief ornament is her head-dress. The shape of this varies in different parts of the country. In central Tibet it consists of a wooden framework, ornamented with corals, turquoise, and seed-pearls. Even a woman of the labouring classes has a few corals and turquoises in this important adjunct to her attire.

The head-dress of the Tsang province, that in which Shigatse and Gyangtse lie, differs markedly from that worn in the province of U, the centre of Tibet, itself centring in Lhasa. In the former one wooden branch rises as a semicircle above the head, another branches out behind. But Lhasa favours a pattern which clings much closer to the hair.

When travelling on horseback, ladies screen their *patruk*, as this head-dress is named, to keep it free from dust. The Tibetan air is almost always dusty, as it must be in a land where the air is so dry and the wind is ever scouring the ground.

Numerous other ornaments are worn. Rings of gold, silver, or shell in the hair. Earrings of gold or silver, or of seed-pearls threaded on a wire loop, with a few corals or turquoises in addition. Necklaces of coral and turquoise with seed-pearls, interspersed with gold or silver pendants delicately chased. Other necklaces of light green jade and corals with strings of glass beads. The strings of beads are hooked to the left shoulder and hang vertically. A few of the Tibetan ladies of high family own necklaces of jade having the appearance of emerald or approximating thereto. A Lhasan lady of my acquaintance owns one such, which is the envy of all who see it. Chatelaines of gold or silver are suspended from the breast and end in a toothpick, an earspoon, and tweezers. Needle-cases of silver, brass, iron, or red leather are also fastened to waist-belts. The best iron cases come from Der-ge in eastern Tibet; it is in Der-ge that Tibetan metal-work finds its highest expression.

Neck-clasps of gold, buttons of gold and coral, bracelets of silver minutely carved, or of shell, girdles round

Wife of Lhasa official in gala attire

The head-dress is mainly of pearls with a few large corals; the earrings of turquoises. The charm-box on the chest is of gold, set with diamonds, rubies,
sapphires, and turquoises

'That of a lady of Kong-po shows wide variations
from the costumes worn around Lhasa'

Working-class girls wearing Tsang head-dress

the waist with clasps of silver and gold, finger-rings of gold or silver set with turquoises and corals, all figure in the toilet of Tibetan ladies.

A pair of silver or gold chains may be worn hanging from the hips, one at each side. Such a chain with three arms, set with turquoises in the centre, is used for tying up a woman's shawl or cloak. It hangs in front and is known as 'The Scorpion' [1] because the hooks at the end are reminiscent of scorpion's claws.

The dresses of the women vary in different provinces and districts. For instance, that of a lady of Kong-po shows wide variations from the costumes worn around Lhasa, though the two provinces are close to each other.

Charm-boxes (ka-u) are worn almost universally by the women. They are laid on the chest, immediately below the throat. The charm-box is studded with turquoises and other precious stones. These, if of good quality, are by some people believed to strengthen the bones, so that in the event of a fall, from one's horse or otherwise, injury is averted.

Into the ka-u is put as a talisman [2] a small image of a deity, perhaps of Chen-re-si, Lord of Mercy, or of Je-tsün Dröl-ma, the Lady Deliverer. Very often, indeed, of Je-tsün Dröl-ma, for, says my informant, 'She works quickly. So, too, when ill, we pray much to her, for there is need of quickness then.'

For the talisman the wearer goes to a lama, who writes one out for her. It will, as a rule, be for protection against illness, for long life, or for wealth, or indeed for all these blessings. The talisman is a writing and picture combined, and it varies according to the work demanded of it.

A common one is that known as Gong-dü's [3] charm. Gong-dü is the name of a god who cleanses from evil and gives you the good things of life. Ta-shi-ding in southern Sikkim is believed to be the Palace of Gong-dü, according to Gong-dü's book, a work of thirteen volumes composed

[1] Dik-ra.

[2] Sung-wa (སྲུང་བ), meaning literally 'Guardian'. [3] དགོངས་འདུས

under the direction of Padma Sambhava at Sam-ye Shem-po, a cave near Sam-ye.

When the book was finished Padma Sambhava asked who would preach it. A girl, living near, came and threw all her ornaments at the saint's feet and said that she would do so. This girl, who was subsequently killed jumping down a mountain side, is held to be the guardian of the book.

The Buddhist religion was then flourishing in Tibet. So the book was hidden in a mine with the idea that, being discovered when the religion was waning in power, fresh life, fresh power would result. The mine was at a place called Puk-ri Puk-mo-che, a large rock in the province of Kong-po or Po.

It was subsequently discovered by a miner, named Sang-gye Ling-pa, to whom its resting-place was revealed in a vision. With the book were some grains of mustard seed in a horn, placed there by Padma Sambhava to keep demons from the book, for the seeds were invested with the power of killing any being in whose direction they were thrown. The miner gave the seeds to a lama of the Kar-ma-pa sect.[1] He tested them by throwing a few towards a vulture flying overhead. The vulture fell down dead. Then the people of the district put the seeds back into the place whence they had been taken, fearing that they would cause many deaths, and so render many people guilty of the heinous sin of taking life. Later on, others endeavoured to recover the seeds, but failed. For the stakes, used for digging them out, all snapped off. And thus it came to be understood that Padma Sambhava would not give the seeds a second time.

Sometimes a charm-box contains a small disk of earth. The Tashi Lama may consecrate some earth by uttering incantations over it. The earth is then divided into disks and stamped. Such is known as *sa-nga*, 'incantation earth'. One in my possession has the imprint of the thunderbolt (*dor-je*) of the God of Rain on one side, and of a devil-dagger (*pur-pa*) piercing a serpent spirit (*lu*) on the

[1] One of the earliest reformed sects in Tibetan Buddhism.

other. The thunderbolt affords protection against epileptic fits; the dagger and serpent denote power over this class of serpent, and thereby protection from skin diseases, a malignity which lies within the latter's province.

Consecrated earth of this kind has other uses. For instance, a small fragment may be taken internally to cure a cold or a cough, or applied externally to remove a sore or a swelling. So a charm-box of this kind is not for ornament alone.

The ivory ring that encircles the thumb of the left hand is worn by men, but not women, of the poorer classes. It is a protection against witches (*sön-dre-ma*). A witch appears at night in dark, deserted spots. Probably in the distance it takes the form of a beautiful young girl. But as it draws near it changes into an old hag of terrifying aspect with long hanging breasts and two long tusks. You must then touch her head with your ivory thumb-ring. And you must do this without fear in your heart, saying to yourself that she can do you no harm. For none, who is afraid, can succeed in touching a witch. But having so touched her, she cannot injure you.

The richer classes do not wear these ivory rings, for they do not go out so much into deserted places at night. And when they do go, they have servants with them, and witches do not appear in such circumstances. Instead of ivory rings they often wear rings of jade, which serve the double purpose of ornament and of toughening the bones, just as they are toughened by the precious stones in the charm-box.

Many indeed are the ornaments with which Tibetan women bedeck themselves. Even the men wear a not inconsiderable number. They too, especially the shepherds and herdsmen, let their gaiety speak in their hair, to which rings of ivory, silver, &c., may be attached. They sew on a narrow band large turquoises and small charm-boxes, fastening the band on that portion of the queue which would normally hang from the shoulder to the waist or lower. However, the queue is usually disposed round the head, and thus the decorations are effectively displayed.

It is only in a few districts that men adorn themselves with necklaces. Charm-boxes and finger-rings are common, earrings are very common, and among the official classes universal. The official earring is of a standard pattern. It hangs from a gold ring attached to the left ear; it is long and narrow, with a pearl in the middle. For the rest it is a string of turquoises, except that an inflexible rule requires the elongated lower end to be not a true turquoise but an imitation. In the right ear a rough turquoise is worn, and this by all classes, official and unofficial, rich and poor.

Purses of leather covered in red silk with a blue border, Chinese spectacle-cases of blue silk with red cloth inside, hang from the dress of a man and set it off. A knife is carried for cutting meat and other purposes, and often a sword also. The scabbards of the knives as well as of the swords may be highly ornamented. A Bhutanese often carries two swords, one across the small of the back, as well as a dagger in his waistband. The best Bhutanese swords are unsurpassed in Tibet. Their sheaths are worthy of them, of polished silver, gilt here and there, a red cloth belt with clasp and pouch and blue and red tassels. The handles and iron sheaths of the daggers are deeply and delicately carved.

Rosaries are carried by both men and women. Though used for devotional purposes, they are also ornamental. Usually they are wound two or three times round the wrist; sometimes they are worn round the neck also. The number of beads is one hundred and eight. This is a sacred number. The Kan-gyur, the Tibetan scriptures, are often bound in one hundred and eight volumes. And happy is the family that can claim an ancestor or ancestress, who, having died when one hundred and eight years old, has thereby set the seal on a virtuous life.

Rosaries may be made of wood, of seeds, of bone, of glass, or of crystal. They may be made of coral, turquoise,

Lhasa nobleman and wife with servants

He and the men servants wear the official earring

or ivory. One in my possession is of white stone beads, believed by Tibetans to be pieces of ice fossilized. They should be worn in warm weather, when they will always be cool to the touch, cooler than glass beads. This rosary, which came from the house of one of the old nobility in Lhasa, should be worn wound three or four times round the wrist.

XV

THE POSITION OF WOMEN

THOSE who have studied domestic life in Tibet can hardly fail to agree that the position of women in Tibetan society is remarkably good. Such is the verdict recorded in the books of the late Mr. Rockhill, an American, and of Shramana Ekai Kawaguchi, a Japanese, both of them among the leading foreign authorities on Tibet. It is no less the verdict of Mrs. Louis King, a Tibetan lady. Rockhill, a scholarly and careful observer, says that the 'pre-eminent' position of women in Tibetan society has been from of old one of the peculiarities of this race.[1] Kawaguchi considers that, 'The condition of Tibetan women with regard to men, especially in the provinces, may be considered as surpassing the ideal of Western women, so far as the theory of equality of rights between the sexes is concerned '.[2] Mrs. King writes that, 'Men and women treat each other as equals'.[3] Chinese writers, too, have noted the high status accorded to Tibetan women.

But one reservation must be made. A girl does not, as a rule, choose her own husband. The choice rests with her parents, subject to certain limitations which will be explained later.

The Tibetan woman is brought up with boys and men. She is physically strong; she is undeniably intelligent. When still a girl, she may hold charge of part of the household. Later on, a grown woman, she will probably have a great influence with her husband. And if her husband be absent or dead, she may manage the estate till her son grows to manhood. If there be a daughter in a home, but

[1] W. W. Rockhill, *The Land of the Lamas*, p. 213 (Longmans, Green).
[2] Ekai Kawaguchi, *Three Years in Tibet*, p. 475 (Theosophical Publishing Society, Benares and London).
[3] Rin-chen Lha-mo (Mrs. Louis King), *We Tibetans*, p. 125 (Seeley Service).

no son, this daughter's husband marries into her family, adopts the family name, and takes a position subordinate to his wife in the management of the family estate.

In an ordinary household the husband appoints the menservants, the wife appoints the maids and has the chief power indoors. The ordinary domestic work is done by the mistress, her daughters, and the maidservants. The relationship between mistress and maid, master and man, is generally good; the servants in an old family are proud of the connexion and regard themselves as sharers in the glory of the house. The mistresses know their maid-servants well and work with them; feudalism is tempered with a strong democratic instinct. In addition to the ordinary work of cooking, sweeping, &c., women spin the yarn and weave the cloth. When cooking of a higher order is needed, as at the New Year feasting, it is usually done by men, while the women may prepare the soup and the tea. Men take the larger share in sewing, much of it being in garments of leather and stiff cloth.

Wives, sisters, and daughters plait the hair of their menfolk, and help them to wash it. A gentleman may wash his hair once every month or six weeks. His women-folk plait his queue for him every three weeks or so. The ladies help their husbands to dress in the mornings, and tidy their husbands' hair at that time.

There is a curious custom in Tibet according to which ladies of good position, known as *gyen-sang-ma* (literally, 'She with good ornaments'), serve the wine to the guests of high rank at dinner parties. When Colonel Kennedy and I dined with the Commander-in-Chief in Lhasa, two young ladies, belonging to families of the upper middle class, came round the table from time to time pressing us to drink wine. They stayed outside the room during most of the time, entering at intervals for this purpose. They were dressed in very expensive clothes; they were further beautified with turquoises, corals, and pearls in a generous profusion.

I asked a young friend of mine, a member of the Sha-

tra family, about this matter. 'They are employed', he
said, 'on account of both their rank and their sex. They
can press the guests to drink, when servants could not
presume to do so, and being of the feminine sex, can
crack jokes with the guests, and press them more insis-
tently than any man can do. It is the object of every host
and hostess to make their guests drink as much as possible,
and, best of all, to see them in a state of complete intoxica-
tion. This is the highest compliment, for it shows that
the wine was so good that they could not abstain. It is
an auspicious event; the party is then held to have been
a complete success.

'If a guest', he continued, 'is so drunk that he cannot
rise from his seat, a ceremonial scarf (*ka-ta*) is occasionally
put round his neck as a compliment.

'In return for their services these ladies receive a present. This sometimes takes the form of money, but more
often is an article of dress, e.g. a shirt or an apron.'

The guests, especially the higher ones, give money
presents not only to the lady waitresses, but also to the
ordinary serving-men and maids, and even to the cook
and his assistants. The heavy drinkers are apt to pour
out their money freely. Such presents are given on the
conclusion of the entertainment, which may last for three
days or even more. The guests come at about ten in the
forenoon. They have a light meal at midday, a heavy one
at four or five in the afternoon, and usually disperse to
their homes between seven and nine o'clock in the
evening.

Women milk the cows and make the butter. Ploughing
is man's work; other agricultural operations, as mentioned
above,[1] are shared between them. Both men and women
carry water, employing for this purpose a short, wooden
barrel with a hole in the board that covers the top.

Some writers have asserted that Tibetan garments are
not washed. But numerous small gatherings of women
may be seen washing clothes. Those of Lhasa do their

[1] See p. 42.

'A short, wooden barrel with a hole in the board that
covers the top'

work on the edge of the river, and in the various ponds scattered here and there.

Women whom one meets on the road are treated much the same as men of similar position. Riding with a Tibetan official, he calls out to a woman, who is measuring her length along Lhasa's Sacred Way, 'Woman! Arise!' (*Mo! Long-shik!*) A man of the same low social position would be addressed in corresponding terms. When riding with another Tibetan friend, he calls to an elderly peasant woman to move to the side, and in doing so addresses her as 'Mother' (*A-ma*). This is suitable for women of the lower middle class and upwards. Those between about thirty and fifty years of age we may accost as 'Elder Sister' (*A-chi*); the younger ones as 'Daughter' (*Pu-mo*).

The Tibetan custom of polyandry, by which, when a woman marries a man, she takes as joint husbands some or all of his brothers, is followed in many families. In such cases the wife is the centre of the family, whose interests pivot round her. It follows naturally that her influence is thereby augmented.

Probably Buddhism also has had a share in elevating the women's position to some extent. The Buddha, though at first unwilling, admitted women into the religious order. During the early days of Buddhism women were influential; in Tibet, as we shall see presently, some held high religious positions. In Burma and Siam, Buddhist countries, the standing of women is high; during the period when Buddhism was powerful in Japan (A.D. 800–1100) a number of female writers came to the fore.

As mentioned in a previous chapter, the Tibetan women are active and shrewd in commercial matters. Most of the shops are kept by them. They do not work in gold, silver, and other metals. But they help the butchers to kill the animals, as I have seen a few miles outside Lhasa.

They work as porters, carrying heavy loads for long distances. They turn out and take their share of the *ula*, the forced labour due to the Government and to the landlord. The men and women receive equal treatment. The weight of the load does not depend on sex, but on the chance of the garter. These garters, which are tied round the high Tibetan boots below the knee, are of multifarious colours and designs. So, before starting the morning's march, each porter puts a garter into the general heap. The distributor of the loads picks them up and throws a garter haphazard on every load. Each porter resumes his —or her—garter and takes the load with it. As to the relative strength of the sexes, who shall say? The story, recounted for so many years at Darjeeling, of the Tibetan who carried a piano up the mountain side, is usually told of a woman.

During my long service in Tibet and the borderland, my head groom was a Gurkha. Like most Gurkhas, he was a hard worker and knew what hard work meant. Being of the Tamang tribe, he was a Buddhist; and, having been much in Tibet, he spoke Tibetan and understood the people. As a patriotic son of Nepal, between whom and Tibet there is constant rivalry, he was not predisposed to praise the Tibetans. But he freely admitted the industry of their women. Said he, 'These Tibetan women work hard. Their menfolk are constantly away at Lhasa, Shigatse, and other places engaged in trade, while they, the women, carry on the labours of the farm in addition to their varied household duties. They work very hard, do the women of this country.'

Such was the verdict of 'Third Son Tamang'. He was fourteen years in my service, but neither I, nor his fellow-servants, knew him by any other name. Tamang was the name of his tribe. Gurkhas usually take these name-substitutes, for they consider it unlucky to call a person by his or her real name.

In the government of different portions of their country the Tibetan women have here and there occupied commanding positions. As you ride through Tibet you frequently notice ruined forts, a memory of the old days when the country was split up into a number of petty principalities, each ruled by its own chief. Some are pointed out to you as having been formerly under the rule of women. There is one of the latter variety a few miles from Lhasa down the valley of 'Middle River' (Kyi Chu).

Sometimes, when a chief died young, and his widow had the necessary vigour and intelligence, she seized the power and wielded it herself. Sometimes, also, the daughter of a chieftain, being employed by her father to aid him in his administration, took an ever-increasing share, and finally took over the reins of government altogether.

One of these chieftainesses lived at Lho-mo, four or five miles north of Lhasa. She introduced the Ra-mo-che Prayer Festival, an important event which precedes the 'Great Prayer' of Lhasa by a few days.

One who dwelt near Lhasa, farther down the valley, lived in the time of the great reformer, Tsong-ka-pa, in the fourteenth century of our era. Both Nan-kar-tse Dzong and Pe-de Dzong, its neighbour, knew women rulers. And no doubt there were many others. In the sphere of government, as in other spheres, Tibetan womanhood was to the fore, though the times were hard, and they had constantly to deal with wars and uprisings.

A Chinese history of eastern Tibet in former times, entitled *Nü Kuo* (Tang Shu, Bk. 122), tells of a Tibetan queen who ruled a large territory. She kept several hundred women near her person, while men tilled the soil and provided the soldiery.[1]

Even in modern days many chiefs, ministers, and officials in all grades consult their wives in their official work. It not infrequently happens that the wife is the real ruler. The rulers of Sikkim are of Tibetan birth, taking their wives almost invariably from Tibet. During my first few years in Sikkim the queen—from the Lhe-ding family of Lhasa—was a woman of exceptional intelligence and charm. She had withal a strong will, while the king was easy-going. The latter was not disposed to bother about the administration, especially as, in accordance with the

[1] Rockhill, *Land of the Lamas*, p. 340.

policy of the British-Indian Government of that period, but little was left to him. What share was left, the queen in large part administered. She even kept the State Seal. From time to time the king asserted himself and took matters into his own hands, but in the daily round of affairs it was the queen that governed.

We have discussed the position of women in the home, in industry, and in the government of their country. It remains only to consider how they fare in that which to the Tibetans is the most important of all, the religious life.

Here the signs of an inferior status are not wanting. A priest in close attendance on the Dalai Lama explained to me the varying grades of blessing which His Holiness accorded to different suppliants. He places both hands on the heads of those of the highest rank, both lay and ecclesiastical. These are but few. Similarly with one hand he blesses each ecclesiastical and civil official; and thus, too, he blesses every monk, even the lowest.

The heads of all others the Dalai Lama touches with a tassel, held in his hand. This is the last and commonest form of blessing. The right to the two-handed blessing is granted to very few; the one-handed to somewhat less than two hundred laymen, though to several thousand monks; for the remainder, the tassel. And in this last class are included all women, except only one, Dor-je Pa-mo, 'The Thunderbolt Sow', of Sam-ding Monastery on the great Yam-dro lake, between Lhasa and Gyangtse. She, the only female Incarnation in Tibet, is one of the highest of all Incarnations. She is reputed to have the power of transforming herself into a sow. And to her the Dalai Lama gives the blessing with one hand on her head.

'For all other women,' said my priestly informant, 'it is just the tassel. Even the Prime Minister's wife and the wives of the highest nobility receive no more. Laymen generally are considered common and unclean (*kyü-ma tang tsok-pa*),[1] and so are all women, even nuns.

---

[1] དཀྱུས་མ་དང་བཙོག་པ་

'Women are lower than men. The very word "kye-men",[1] i.e. "the lower birth", shows that we Tibetans think so.'

The monastery of Ta-lung, 'The Tiger's Prophecy', fifty miles north of Lhasa, is one which has wielded a very high position and power in centuries now past. Of this monastery in its spacious days a leading Tibetan history, written during the fifteenth century,[2] says:

'Although many years have elapsed since the monastery was first founded, yet even till now the strict priestly rules are so well observed that no female is allowed to enter the monastic premises, nor indeed does any female even dare to look towards the monastery. This is attributable to the Hierarchs, who were all of saintly charac-ter and pre-eminent learning. Two hundred and ninety-seven years have elapsed since the founding of the Ta-lung Monastery to the present Fire-Monkey year.'

Perhaps stringent rules in this respect were necessary, for in another place we read [3] that a young woman rushed naked into the presence of a novice in a monastery. In this case, however, good befell. The young man became a fully fledged monk, vowed to a celibate life, and rose to the headship of the great monastery of Dri-kung,[4] revered both for his learning and his piety.

Writing of Burma, another Buddhist country, in *The Soul of a People*, Fielding Hall records that it is to some extent believed there 'that a woman must be born again as a man before she can enter on the way that leads to heaven'.[5]

In some measure Buddhism may have helped the Tibetan women, strong, intelligent, capable, to maintain their position; but it does not give them such power in religious affairs as it does to the men. And perhaps they do not want it. They are religious up to a point, more so than the men. But it is a part only of their daily life, along

[1] སྐྱེས་དམན་ the ordinary Tibetan word for 'woman'.
[2] Tep-ter Ngön-po, vol. viii, folio 109.   [3] Ibid., folio 85.   [4] འབྲི་ཁུང་
[5] Fielding Hall, *The Soul of a People*, p. 231 (Richard Bentley & Son).

with the home, the family, the friends. They are not willing, to the extent that the men are willing, to renounce all in the quest of the great deliverance. For every nun there are thirty or forty monks.

Still, when I went from chapel to chapel in the great Temple in Lhasa, and came to the shrine of the Goddess Dröl-ma, the Deliverer, I used to see a crowd of women there, especially on the evening of the full moon, singing praises and prayers. They asked for preservation from illness, and besought other blessings also.

Religious services are held in Tibet, especially on the eighth, fifteenth, and last day of each month; that is to say, at the first quarter, the full moon, and the new moon. These are attended largely by women, and especially by the elderly women. Such services are of two kinds, one termed *nyam-ne*,[1] in which the woman takes only one meal in the day; the other, *nyung-ne*,[2] in which she fasts completely, taking neither food nor even water throughout the day. If a man or woman—for both may vow themselves to it—should break the vow of *nyung-ne*, it must be made good the next day by numerous bodily prostrations in the religious style.

Sometimes, indeed, women have ventured all in their zeal for religion. In the same 'Blue Record' quoted above it is recorded [3] that when Atisha—the great Indian teacher, who came to Tibet during the eleventh century of the Christian era—was nearing Lhasa, a girl gave him as an offering the ornaments from her head, thus giving probably most of her worldly wealth. 'Her parents took her to task, and she committed suicide by leaping into the river.' Atisha performed her funeral ceremonies, and announced that she had taken rebirth in one of the Heavens.

One of the first heads of the Ka-gyü sect of Buddhism was a saint named Mar-pa, a name held in great reverence

---

[1] བསྙམ་གནས་   [2] སྨྱུང་གནས་

[3] Tep-ter Ngön-po, vol. v, folio 8.

in Tibet, especially by those who belong to this branch
of the Tibetan Church. Of one of Mar-pa's chief disciples, named Ngok, it is thus recorded.[1]

'Once, while holding a conference of several celebrated Lamas,
a grand-daughter of the Lord Mar-pa came by chance. Begging the
permission of all the great Lamas there, Ngok put this lady in the
highest seat for a day, and allowed her to preside at the rites.'

Her relationship to the saint gained for her this honour.
But occasionally women, who rose to the highest positions,
did so apparently by their own exertions. A woman held
the headship of the Pa-druk Monastery.[2] In Bhutan also,
after the death of the high priest of a monastery his sister
occupied his seat during her lifetime.

The Bhutanese history [3] then tells of the wife of a high
lama. She was regarded as an Incarnation of Dor-je
Pa-mo, 'The Thunderbolt Sow', and received initiation
from leading two lamas. We read that 'She passed several
years in meditation in the solitudes of Jong-ka, and was made
perfect in the Faith. After this she visited the chief holy
places in Bhutan. In them she left miraculous impressions
of her hands and imprints of her feet, produced fountains
and wells and worked other miracles. . . . She conferred
initiation and instruction on Lha-cham Kün-le and nomin-
ated this lady as her successor in Tam-go'.

Another of her disciples was a priest who 'was the best
painter in the whole of Bhutan. It was he who worked
the great silken picture of Chen-re-si, entitled "See and be
saved" (*Tong-dröl-ma*)'.

It is evident from the above instances that even in
religious careers the Tibetan women have come to the
front from time to time. The standing modern example
of this is to be found in the monastery on the peaceful hill
overlooking the 'Lake of the Upland Pastures' (*Yam-dro
Tso*) and facing the eternal snows of the Himalaya. Not
inaptly is this monastery called 'The Soaring Meditation'
(*Sam-ding*). Both the situation and the character of its

[1] Ibid., vol. viii, folio 4.
[2] Ibid., folio 125.   [3] Lho-hi Chö-jung, folio 57.

occupant justify the name. For here resides the holiest woman in Tibet, the Incarnation of the goddess Dor-je Pa-mo. The present is the eleventh Incarnation. When one dies, or 'retires to the heavenly fields', her spirit passes into a baby girl, and thus the succession goes on. The ninth Incarnation was the most famous of the line.

It was my privilege to visit her on my way to Lhasa, accompanied by Mr. Dyer, our doctor from Sikkim. We were the first white men to be received by her, indeed the first she had seen. We had halted at Nan-kar-tse, and Sam-ding was some seven miles away. During the last three miles before we reached the monastery, the well-trained monks sounded in our honour the monastic trumpets, ten feet long, which gave out a deep full note that calls appealingly in this mountain land.

Outside the door of her private apartment the goddess received me. She endeavoured to put the white silk scarf of ceremony round my neck—the prescribed greeting for Tibetan ministers—but it fell on the top of my head. This, with their unfailing courtesy, my Tibetan friends informed me, was an auspicious sign betokening a long life, continuing even when the hair on my head should be as white as the scarf.

Her robe was after the pattern of the priests', maroon coloured with red edging at the top, showing an under-robe of yellow silk. The boots were of white leather with silk tops.

Her seat was a long and broad one, used also as her bed, raised but little from the ground, and surrounded with lacquered woodwork. Next to this, towards the centre of the room, which is somewhat small, but not unduly so, was her throne, four feet in height. It, too, was enclosed in lacquered woodwork, and was overspread with a woollen cloth of maroon colour. Dor-je Pa-mo spends the greater part of each day and sleeps the night also in this one room.

Twenty-four years of age, a pleasing face, bright,

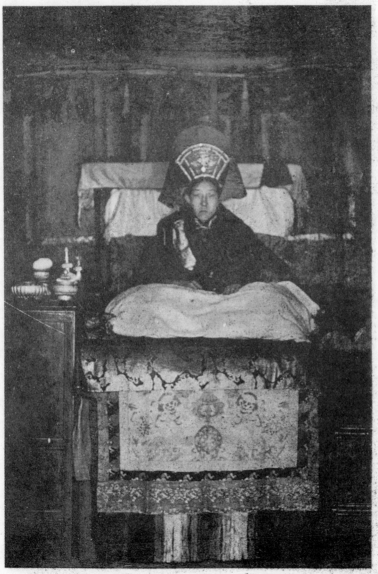

The holiest woman in Tibet, Dor-je Pa-mo

rounded eyes, a low, broad forehead, high cheek-bones, and a rather heavy mouth with small, regular teeth. Such was Dor-je Pa-mo, who, though of humble parentage, ranks above all the women, and nearly all the men, in Tibet. Her hair, parted in the middle, was passed above her ears and tied in a knot behind. She was slightly pock-marked from the dreaded disease that attacks so many in Tibet, high and low. I know not whether a jury of my countrymen—or countrywomen—would find her fair of face. Perhaps not; but her sweet, though pensive, smile, her youth, her quiet dignity, invested the young abbess with a charm that was all her own.

Our clerks, our servants, and Ku-sho Pa-lhe-se himself, though of noble birth, all bowed low before her and presented their offerings, while she blessed them, one by one, touching each on the head with her hand.

After the polite inquiries that etiquette demands, she asked me how long I intended to remain in Lhasa. A natural question to ask a white man going to her Holy of Holies, but difficult to answer. For I was being sent on a diplomatic mission, and could not say what turn the mission might take. She herself had been only once to Lhasa, and never to Ta-shi Lhün-po, but hoped to visit Lhasa again within the next two or three years.

It was interesting to learn that there are no nuns in the monastery, except herself. All are monks. There are fifty-nine of them. Another point worthy of note was that in this number are several different sects, including the old, unreformed (*Nying-ma*), the semi-reformed (*Ka-gyü*) sect, and the fully reformed (*Ge-luk*). Yet all were living and working in harmony together, and this is often so in Tibetan monasteries, for whatever else is found or is lacking, tolerance is there beyond a doubt.

As we talked Mr. Dyer was called away to attend on her mother. He found her suffering from indigestion and chronic bronchitis.

Dor-je Pa-mo occasionally visits monasteries in western Tibet. In the summer she moves here and there, but not during the arctic cold of the Tibetan winters. The climate of western Tibet, high and exposed, is especially severe.

The leading priests showed me all over the monastery, which possesses a fair assortment of books in addition to the Tibetan Canon (*Kan-gyur*) and the Commentaries (*Ten-gyur*).

We then returned to our hostess, who hospitably regaled us with a Tibetan lunch. When we left, she accompanied me to the door of her room, and gave me a second scarf in token of farewell. She presented me also with a piece of cloisonné. I sent her a watch as a return present, for she told me that she could not tell the time except at sunrise and sunset.

One of my orderlies, Rab-den Lepcha, had already to some extent learnt from me how to use my cameras, and was taking my photographic work more and more into his own hands. After I left he stayed behind under the aegis of Pa-lhe-se, and the goddess very willingly allowed him to take a photograph of her. One of the Dalai Lama's men had photographed her some time previously, but without success. To Pa-lhe-se she expressed surprise as well as pleasure that I was able to converse with her in Tibetan, 'for', said she, 'to talk to one who cannot understand and reply easily is like one simpleton babbling to another.'

Though there are vastly more monks than nuns in Tibet, yet the number of nunneries is not inconsiderable. They are smaller than the large monasteries, and are often situated in secluded valleys where, alas! they are sometimes despoiled by hungry brigands. You will often see the nuns travelling between their religious and worldly homes, carrying their luggage on their backs and halting here and there during the nights. Those who belong to the reformed sect (*Ge-luk*) shave their heads; but the members of the old, unreformed (*Nying-ma*) wear their hair long, though not as long as those classes of priests who are immured in their cells for the period that covers three years, three months, and three days. Few nuns are good

'Nunneries are often situated in secluded valleys'

'Clear, Pure Spring' nunnery

looking; the shorn heads of many, and the dull, severe garb of all, emphasize still further the contempt for worldly attractions.

There is in Tibet a class of deity known as Chö-kyong, i.e. 'Protector of the Religion'. A Chö-kyong from time to time enters the body of a medium, known as Chö-je. Thus inspired, the Chö-je makes the oracular pronouncements of the god, giving prophecies and advice. Such may be of general application to a district, or of special application to one who has consulted the god on his own account. I hope to deal with this subject more fully in a subsequent volume on religion, and have mentioned it here merely to say that women also take part in this work. A woman Chö-je is possessed by one of the goddesses or by one of the Serpent Spirits (*lu*). Goddesses and Serpent Spirits but seldom enter male Chö-jes, nor do gods often enter female Chö-jes, though both events occur occasionally in the Tsang province.

There is one such woman Chö-je, for instance, in a small house, like a hermitage, in the vicinity of Lhasa, between the Oracle Temple of Ne-chung and the Drepung Monastery. Such women are not nuns. They marry husbands, and a daughter becomes Chö-je when the mother dies. The succession thus goes through the daughters. Female Chö-jes do not usually shave their heads.

XVI

WOMEN'S WORK AND RECREATIONS

WE have seen something of the manner in which Tibetan shepherds, peasants, merchants, and nobles pass their time. So a few words as to how a Tibetan lady spends an average day will not be amiss. We will assume that she is the wife of an official, for most men in the upper classes enter the service of their Government.

If she has been brought up in the country, that is to say on the family estate, she will be an early riser, as work begins early on the land. But if town bred, whether in Lhasa, Shigatse, or elsewhere, she will keep later hours. In any case, after she has dressed and performed her religious exercises, she must see to the servants' work. Between eight and nine o'clock breakfast comes.

Breakfast finished, or even during its continuance, visitors may come to see her husband and herself. A merchant perhaps comes to borrow or repay money used in some trading transaction, in which the official—whom we will take to be the governor of a district (*dzong-pön*)—and the merchant are partners. For Tibetan officials are allowed to engage in trade. Or perhaps a dealer in turquoises or other goods calls to show some of his recent purchases. In this case keen bargaining ensues before the governor or his wife will buy anything from him.

At midday she goes, not infrequently, to visit relations and friends. The talk perhaps turns on some fascinating piece of jewellery, which, being for sale, one of them wishes to buy; about the beauty or otherwise of their lady friends, which of these go about with their male acquaintances more than is seemly, and so forth.

During the afternoon, if there be archery, of which Tibetans are very fond, she may be present at it, but only if held near the house. If Chinese dominoes, known as *ba*, is played, she may very likely join in the game, or assist one of the guests in playing. *Ba* is a favourite pastime. It continues sometimes throughout the afternoon and even through most of the night.

In the evening there may be singing and dancing. If the husband or wife can sing or dance, he or she or both will join in freely with such of the servants as can. This is not considered in any way derogatory to the master or mistress, and it helps to pass the time after supper for an hour or two. Then, in the absence of special attractions, to bed at nine or ten o'clock.

Women of all ranks are fond of entertainments, religious and secular. They delight in theatricals, they delight in picnics. All these entertainments take place in the open air. The Tibetans are by nature an out-of-doors people. During the summer they often spend the whole day in picnics and other outdoor entertainments; sometimes under awnings, sometimes under the open sky. The time is spent in feasting, singing, dancing and gambling, in good fellowship and jollity. Towards the end of summer theatrical entertainments take place. The Dalai Lama starts the ball rolling in the Jewel Park with a series of plays that continue for a week. During my year in Lhasa I followed this with an entertainment to my Tibetan friends that lasted for three days, a separate play being performed daily. The performances took place in a park near Lhasa. The plays were not short; each began during the forenoon at about ten o'clock, and ended with the daylight nine hours later. Even then they had to be curtailed; if rendered in full, each would have required several days for its performance.

The Tibetans, men and women, take naturally to singing. Walking or riding, working or resting, they pour out deep-throated song. 'Tibetan women', said Ku-sho She-sur, 'usually sing when they work. They work better when they sing.' The song often makes sport of some person or class. No people in the world are more devout in their religion than the Tibetans, and none are more ready to deride laxity in the priesthood.

The various branches of the Mint are placed here and there in the neighbourhood of Lhasa. During a visit to the Gold Mint I found the furnaces for melting the metal being kept in life by bellows worked by women. As they worked they sang:

> Cut my child's hair, East Bhutanese!
> All Good One, hear my prayer!
> A child who as a servant works
> Can work without his hair.[1]

Some monks, in spite of their shorn heads, the badge of priesthood, go into service or trade and so make money whereas they ought to devote themselves entirely to the religious life. The verse is a skit on these.

The songs are often of topical import. This bald rendering reproduces the Tibetan metre of one as well as the meaning:

> In the Lhasa market
> Shü-tsi boots I purchased; .
> While the right danced well, the
> Left foot raised a dust storm.[2]

Here the reference is to the friction between the priesthood and the army, while I was in Lhasa, culminating in an outbreak at the great Dre-pung Monastery.

'Verses of this kind', says Ku-sho She-sur, 'are sung by men and women as they pass along the roads. The women drawing water at the wells, especially during the festival of the Great Prayer, love singing them. Large numbers of monks and lay people are then assembled, so that much water has to be drawn. It is believed that Pal-den Lha-mo, the tutelary goddess of the Tibetan Government, incar-

---

[1] Shar-chok Druk-pa Kün-le,
A-lö trä-lo chötang;
A-lo mi-yok gyuk-ken,
Tra-lo gö-pa min-duk.

[2] Lha-sa trom-ne nyö-pe
Lham-ko Shü-tsi ko-po;
Shap-ro ye-ne gyap-pe,
Tel-tsup yö-ne gyap-chung.

nates herself at this time as one of these women, and passes on the topical songs to them.'

In one form of entertainment the men of the party align themselves along one side of a room or open space, and the women range themselves along the opposite side. The men sing a verse; the women counter it in their reply.

For instance, 'I will leave you, unless you treat me better'.

Men. The yaks graze on the meadow-land,
 The grass is their delight;
For them the grass grows; should it fail
 They'll seek a better site.

Women. The hinds graze at the valley head,
 There is but scanty grass;
Water on this side there is none,
 And so they cross the pass.

Again, 'Love pretended but not sincere.'

Men. The pony courses o'er the plain;
 But though it's fair above,
There's bog below. He slips and falls.
 So is it with thy love.

Women. I drink the stream so clear, but mud
 Comes oozing up above.
I cannot clear the poison out;
 So is it with thy love.

The Lhasa women of the lower classes, especially those who belong to the trading community, drink a good deal of barley-beer. The wives of the gentry drink but little, nor do their husbands as a rule drink much.

A Tibetan nobleman expressed himself to me thus as to the duties of Tibetan ladies:

'She will love and obey her husband. She will show kindness to her relatives.

'She will not be harsh to her servants, will explain their faults to them, not punishing hastily. She must avoid making favourites among them. She will not trouble her husband with the faults or disputes of the servants, but will settle these herself. She must be an adept in all household management.

'She must avoid making favourites among her children. Tibetans do not rank a son as higher than a daughter, but both as equal. The crime of female infanticide, though found in some countries, has never found a home in Tibet.

'She ought to go to plays and spectacles, be sociable and not keep to herself. She ought to visit her friends frequently and give them presents and entertainments, thus showing a friendly and affectionate disposition. They will of course give presents and entertainments in return.'

The above opinion would probably be general among the men of the upper classes. And it may be safely said that on the whole the Tibetan lady fills the part well.

Some of the characteristics of Tibetan womanhood have been portrayed above. For the rest, we cannot forget her cheery disposition, easily moved to laughter, her kindly heart. And she has an undeniable capacity for friendship.

Two Mongol merchants in Lhasa

XVII
MARRIAGE

ALTHOUGH the Tibetan woman enjoys so great a measure of independence, yet in the choice of her husband, the most important event of her life, she is apt to have little, if any, share. A son is consulted by his father as to the bride proposed for him. But the parents consult a daughter hardly at all.

'The daughters always say', a Tibetan nobleman informed me, 'that they wish to stay at home and not to marry. For this reason there is no help for it but to keep them in the dark, if possible, as to their marriage until a day or two before the wedding takes place. Not but what they suspect something when they see their steward going frequently to a house to which he used not to go before.'

It is the same in Bhutan. The History of Bhutan, when setting out the laws that hold in that country, is emphatic that ,'Marriages must not be contracted in defiance of the wishes of the parents'.[1]

Little by little, however, this strict rule is slackening in modern times. The practice of young men choosing their own brides is growing; it is commoner among the peasants and the traders than among the landed gentry.

In some parts of the country, if the young people cannot get their way they may elope. Two Sherpanis—women of a Tibetan tribe who live within the north-eastern frontier of Nepal—whom I met in Sikkim, were returning from the pursuit of the daughter of one of them. She had eloped with a Nepalese, one of the Thami caste. After a lot of search they had run the pair to earth, and had left the daughter with the Thami. If the latter came to ask forgiveness, they would pardon him; if not, they would institute a complaint, and have him fined. These peasant

[1] Lho-hi Chö-jung, folio 112.

women did not take the matter too seriously, though determined that the parents' position should not be disregarded.

In Tibet itself, however, Western influence being almost negligible, elopements are rare. If a boy has set his heart on a girl other than the one chosen for him, his parents may be brought to agree and to accept his choice, provided that she has good qualities of mind and body,— e.g. not markedly deficient in education or personal charms—and is not of unduly low position. Should the girl be beyond the pale in these respects his parents will give him a share of the property and send him out of the family to join his bride.

So, too, with the girl. If it should occasionally happen that she is firmly set on an undesirable young man her parents may perforce make the best of it, give her a share of the family's goods, and let her go.

When the young woman is an only child she is on a stronger footing. For her husband will join her family, live on its property, and take its name. She herself is, as the Tibetans say, the 'root' of the family, and has the chief power in the management of its affairs when her parents die. But she, too, usually follows her parents' wishes in the choice of a consort.

The Tibetan fondness for singing extends to love songs also. These often have alternate verses for the girl and the man, as in the singing parties described in the last chapter.

Here is part of one which I received from the King of Sikkim's talented uncle, the late Lha-se Ku-sho, a lover of music and painting:

Girl. Be thou the tree, my best beloved,
　　　　Firm rooted 'neath the mould;
　　　　Then I'm the leaf that shelters you
　　　　From heat and biting cold.

Man. On drifts the cloud, nor fleetest horse
　　　　Can e'er that cloud outrace;
　　　　No parents, if our hearts be one,
　　　　Can sunder our embrace.

Girl.   In this white cup a pure heart's milk
      I pour; 'tis ours to drink.
      But do not from above let fall
      Polluting drops of ink.

Man.   To my roof overhanging there
      Let thine be joined, my love;
      Then, like a cock with comb erect,
      I'll step in from above.

Girl.   For you I'll dare the narrow path
      That overhangs th' abyss;
      For you I'll cross the river's flood,
      I'll scale the precipice.

Man.   Though poor your dress, with jewels none,
      Yet grant we never part;
      For like a peach tree by my house
      You stand, and steal my heart.

Girl.   The people gossip. And 'tis true
      A dog did bark close by.
      I cannot thread those narrow lanes,
      However hard I try.

Man.   We must have incense for the peak,
      And for the river too;
      And just a quiet, little track
      For me, my love, and you.

Girl.   The people talk; on me they cast the blame.
      They tell me I must give you up. Ah! No.
      For when the hunting dog has caught the stag,
      Her teeth grip fast, nor ever let him go.

The Lhasan nobility from time to time give their daughters in marriage to the princes who govern states in Tibet and on the Tibetan border. In the south-east of Tibet is the rugged country of Po, merging into the Himalaya. Its people are partly Himalayan, partly of the Tibetan uplands. They are a sturdy, lawless folk, almost independent of the Lhasan Government, but greatly under the influence of the Holy City.

During May 1921, when I was in Lhasa, an Envoy

from the Chief of Po was lodged in the city. He had come
to seek, as wife for his Chief, the sister of a man newly
ennobled. For, as Pa-lhe-se told me, 'These rulers of Po [1]
often take a Lhasan lady to wife, but are unable to win a
bride from the highest families, partly because their country
is a long way off, but still more because it is rough and
ignorant of law. Sikkim, on the contrary, though distant,
is quiet and law-abiding. And so it comes that the rulers
of Sikkim are able to marry into the noblest families in
the land'.

The preliminaries to a wedding and the wedding ceremony itself necessarily vary to some extent in the different
provinces and districts of Tibet. But the basis and the
general observances hold constant throughout the country. Let me describe briefly what happens in an upper-
class family of central Tibet, seeking a bride for their son.
I quote from a Tibetan squire whose estate is near
Gyangtse. Being an official he has often lived in Lhasa
and is well acquainted with Lhasan customs.

'First of all, inquiries are made among girls who are
eligible for marriage and who belong to a good family and
social position. The parents then ascertain which girl is
desired by their son. Now they ask the parents of the girl
who is named, let us say, Lha-chik Kün-sang, to give her in
marriage to their son, named, perhaps, Rin-chen Chö-pel,
provided that the horoscopes are in agreement, and that
the advice of the lamas and the gods is favourable.

'After ascertaining the date of the girl's birth, the relatives of the bridegroom will consult either His Holiness
the Dalai Lama or His Holiness the Ta-shi Lama or some
other high lamas, in addition to their own deities, as to
whether the girl is suitable for the boy to marry or not. The
revelations made by these, if favourable, will be shown to
the parents of the bride to prove that everything is well.'

It seems necessary to interpolate here a few words about
the horoscopes. Time in Tibet is reckoned by cycles of
sixty years. There are five elements, viz. earth, iron,

[1] Called *Po Ka-nam De-pa* in Tibetan.

water, wood, and fire, arranged in the above order. These are combined with twelve animals in the following order: dog, pig, mouse, ox, tiger, hare, dragon, serpent, horse, sheep, monkey, and bird. Each element comes twice, first as male, then as female. Thus we have

Male Earth Dog
Female Earth Pig
Male Iron Mouse
Female Iron Ox
Male Water Tiger

and so on.

Now, if the boy was born in one of the water years and the girl in one of the fire years, it will not do for them to marry, for water and fire cannot go together. Earth and wood are friendly; and so, among the animals, are horse and sheep.

My friend continues:

'If the horoscopes agree, the boy's parents visit those of the girl and offer them a ceremonial scarf (*ka-ta*) and presents. When the latter have given their consent to the proposal, both sides will join in fixing an auspicious day for the bridegroom's party to go to the bride's house. When they do go, they are entertained lavishly for a whole day.

'This visit is named "the begging beer" (*long-chang*), i.e. the beer given when asking for the daughter in marriage. On that day the parents of the bridegroom offer five hundred to two thousand *ngü-sang* (fifty to two hundred pounds) as "the price of the breast" (*nu-ring*) to the bride's mother, and an apron is also given to her. Thus it is recognized that she has nourished and brought up their son's wife. After the conclusion of this ceremony the two fathers and the two mothers, with their relatives and witnesses and the bridegroom, draw up an agreement concerning the future conduct of the bridegroom and bride, and put their seals to it.

'The bridegroom's party then give a suit of clothes and other presents, accompanied in each case by the scarf of ceremony, to each member of the bride's family, father, mother, brother, sisters, &c. They give also a scarf and some money to each of the senior servants in the family, the steward, the butler, the bailiff, and others, varying perhaps from one to ten pounds in each case, according to their means and the rank of the servant. The ceremony of the "begging beer" is thus concluded.

'The next step is to fix a date of good omen on which the bride will leave her home to go to the bridegroom's house. When this day arrives, the bridegroom's party array themselves in fine attire and with some ten attendants betake themselves to the bride's house. Here they are entertained sumptuously, tea and beer and rich food being set before them.

'When the bride is ready to leave the house, one of the senior servants of the bridegroom's party puts a turquoise in the top of her head-dress (*pa-truk*), and plants an "arrow-flag" (*da-tar* [1])—that is to say, an arrow adorned with silk streamers of five colours, red, yellow, white, blue, and green—on her back near the neck. This elderly retainer then describes the good qualities of the turquoise and the *da-tar* in suitable terms. Before and after this ceremony there is dancing, and the singing of songs, historical and other, without intermission.'

Here I should make clear that at this stage her parents give the dowry, which is mainly in ornaments and to a lesser extent in clothes and money. A well-to-do family may give to an out-going daughter a set of ornaments on the following scale, namely: a gold charm-box, a pair of gold earrings, a head-dress of coral and turquoise for daily use, another set in pearls for use on occasions of high festival or ceremony, a necklace of jade, coral and pearls, and other varied adornments. They may add a pony for riding, and ten to twenty *do-tse* (£40 to £80) in money. A mule is not given as a present on such occasion, for a mule has no offspring. It would be, therefore, a bad omen for their daughter. Indeed, useful though the mule

[1] མདའ་དར་

is, one should be careful in using them. When a Tibetan official has received a step of promotion in official rank, and as a consequence proceeds on the appointed day to offer a scarf of ceremony to the Dalai Lama and the Ministers, he must not ride a mule, but a pony. For a mule is of lower rank than a pony, and it would be unfitting for him on this day to disregard the call of rank by riding the lowlier animal.

'The time has now come', continues my friend, 'for the bride to leave. A party comes from the bridegroom's house to fetch her. She rides away on a mare with a foal, for this is a lucky sign. Her saddle-cloth must be an especially good one. As she leaves the cry is raised, "Be not lost luck!" (*yang ma shor*), or words to that effect.

'On the way she is twice offered beer from a small pot. She does not drink, but flicks a little out with the thumb and finger of the left hand as an offering to the gods. And she takes with her a Wheel of Life. This is a picture scroll that portrays, as on a wheel, the six worlds, the twelve signs of existence, and, on the hub of the wheel, a cock, a pig, and a snake, typifying lust, greed, and anger.[1] For these are the three primal causes which chain all beings to the relentless round of miserable existence with sin and sorrow and death repeated again and again.

'Arriving at the bridegroom's house, the bride dismounts upon a stack of twenty or thirty loads of wheat and rice and other presents. The servants are in attendance but the bridegroom's parents do not come out. They, with the bridegroom and other members of the family, sit in order of seniority on their cushions in a large sitting-room. The bride, entering with her retinue, sits down by the bridegroom, but neither he, nor his family, rise at her entrance. Tea and beer, barley-meal, rice, &c., are served. The good qualities of the *da-tar* are described again, and songs are sung. On this day the bride wears choice and costly garments.

'The parents now give presents and ceremonial scarves

1 See p. 300.

to the bride and bridegroom, and add their blessings. After that, all the relatives and friends give them presents and scarves, and wish them prosperity and every joy. The guests then leave. Those friends who are unable to be present at this time may come later on and give their presents to the bridegroom and the bride.

'In the evening a good room is selected for the bride and bedding is provided for her. To it she retires when permitted. After a short time the bridegroom is permitted to join her. The servants give him some beer and sing three songs. Then they close the door and retire.

'The members of the family gather in the central hall with the bride and bridegroom three times a day, a ceremony which is continued for about seven days. They invite all their relatives and friends, including the parents of the bride, and entertain them sumptuously for a period, which, as a rule, is not less than ten nor more than thirty days.

'The bride, having left her family, has lost the protection of her household gods. She must accordingly be brought under the protection of her husband's deities. Husband and wife therefore pay a visit to his Oracle together, and make offerings in the chapel of his Guardian Deity (*Gön-kang*).

'After the bride has been married some six months or so, her husband and she pay a visit for a few days to the bride's parents, for the latter are naturally anxious about their daughter's welfare.'

In the Tibetan history known as 'The Blue Record' we read [1] of a Tibetan lad:

'He was handsome, endowed with a sweet voice and very fond of singing. He had listened also to discourses from various learned instructors in religion.

'It happened once that at a wedding feast a party of four singers sang a new song, the chorus of which ran as follows:

> With Chö-je Gya-re of Ra-lung is found
> All good, all bliss for this life and the next:
> Let us, a band of friends, to him depart,
> Search out our hearts and live the Sacred Text.

[1] Tep-ter Ngön-po, vol. viii, folio 122.

A wedding group

Left to right, seated, bridegroom's assistant, bridegroom, bride, bride's assistant

The last is a servant who attends the bride after marriage

'On this bare hearing of Gya-re's name, he was moved to the highest pitch of faith. Taking his father's permission, which was readily granted, he went to Ra-lung with but a small offering, and arrived there while Gya-re was preaching a religious discourse before the assembly of monks. He was subsequently ordained a priest under his own name, Gön-po Dor-je.'

And so the wedding feast turned Gön-po Dor-je to religion, and he became in time one of the pillars of the Tibetan Church.

Officials are forbidden to take fees in respect of marriages. Says the Bhutanese history,[1] when discussing the rights and duties vested in the deputies of the district governors,

'A deputy is not entitled to any presents or fees from parties contracting a marriage, or from married couples who are wedding or separating of their own free will.'

The wedding preliminaries and the actual wedding ceremony, as practised in Sikkim by the Sikkimese branch of the Tibetan race, are in the main on the above lines. The go-between, the 'begging beer', the horoscopes, and the auspicious days fixed by the astrologer, the prayers, blessings, ceremonial scarves, presents, and feasts, the da-tar, the bridal journey, &c., all find their place. But Sikkim has its own specialities.

Let us take the case of an upper-class family in Sikkim. My authority is the unpublished History of Sikkim compiled in part by the late King Tu-top Nam-gyal, but mainly by his talented queen. The History bears the king's seal. The English translation from which I quote was made under their Highnesses' instructions.

If the astrologers find the horoscopes of bride and bridegroom to agree, the first present given by the bridegroom's parents goes to the maternal uncle of the bride. For the Sikkimese proverb runs:

The maternal uncle is half the person;
The sleeves are half the cloak.

[1] Lho-hi Chö-jung, folio 112.

So a present of a few rupees, a bamboo jug full of Sikkimese beer and a presentation scarf (*ka-ta*) are sent to him
through the go-between. 'The latter must be a man of
substance [I quote from the History] endowed with
wealth and children, as he has to play an important part
throughout the whole business until it is brought to a
successful issue.'

After the begging beer has been accepted by the bride's
parents, 'then the intended bridegroom', says the History,
'is received into the house of the bride and is expected to
work as a member of the house for three years, in accordance with another proverb,

'A son-in-law, though not of the slave class, is still of the class
who must be made to work for three years.'

'When this period of probation is finished, and the consent for the final marriage ceremony is given, the maternal
uncle comes in for another treat, a good dinner. After this
is over, the bridegroom's parents, as well as those of the
bride, make vast preparations for a grand feast, and provide large stores of rice, beer, a live bull, &c. These
being ready, an auspicious day is fixed by the astrologer.
On this day all the relatives and connexions of both
parties assemble at a spot mid-way between the houses of
the two parties, selecting a site where a stream or spring
issues from a rock, with a view of rendering the lives of the
bridegroom and bride as stiff as the rock, and their progeny as long and continuous as the course of the stream.
The marriage feast is given in such a place as described
above.

'At this ceremony either the headman of the village, or
the Bijua (a wizard with power of prophecy), or a priest of
the Pön religion, rises up and offers oblations of beer to
the Three Chief Rare Ones, to the local deities, and to their
own usual tutelary gods, invoking blessings of long life,
progeny, riches, health, &c., on the couple.
'The price of the bride is also paid that day. This is
generally a milch cow with a calf, the value of which is put

down at fifteen rupees,[1] (though it may be far more valuable), and other presents in cash and kind, whose value may total from about one hundred and twenty to two hundred and forty rupees. Even bronze and copper vessels are accepted as value. It may also be in the shape of more valuable ornaments, as well as ponies or cattle.'

A year or so after that event the ceremony of conducting the bride to the bridegroom's house takes place. The astrologer not only fixes the day and hour for this, but 'he also names the years in which the bridesmaids must have been born, the colour of the bride's cushion and pony, what food she will have to take first in her new home, as well as the birth-year of the person who serves her with the first article of food. And if a suitable person of the age, so divined, be not forthcoming, he also prescribes the necessary steps to be taken to counteract the evil that might arise from such discrepancies.'

The bride's progress to the bridegroom's house is peculiar.

'The female members of the bride's party, intending to make the occasion as auspicious as possible, go about it in a strange way. Wishing that the bride should have many sons, who will all be bold and heroic and as quarrelsome as possible, they bar up the path of the bridegroom with a fence of thorns, and treat the comers to a fine beating with thorns. The severity of this ceremony may be modified by the bridegroom, if he offers a present of five rupees as a fee for withholding the force, while on the other hand the bride's parents give one rupee to the "effacer of the thorn-wounds". The leader of the bridegroom's party is also treated to a good dinner and made much of privately.'

A grand feast follows and presents are given by the parents and friends of both bride and bridegroom. 'Then the parents of the bride, according to their means, give a dowry to their daughter in the shape of ponies or cattle, ornaments, raiment, and vessels of copper, brass, or bronze.'

[1] A rupee may be taken as worth about one shilling and sixpence.

'When the bride is on the point of setting out, the parents put a scarf on her with their blessings and instructions, beside invoking blessings from the gods, &c. After she has left, they keep a priest of the Pön or of the Buddhist religion to perform the *Yang-kuk* ceremony, so that their luck may not depart with their daughter during these three days of her absence. At the same time the bridegroom's parents have to keep a lama, called Ta-shi Lama, meaning "The Lama of the Auspicious Event",[1] who performs a great ceremony of worship in the house.

'The party that escorts the bride is received and entertained in a separate lodging. The doors are ornamented with flowers. Vessels filled with water are ranged along the road, as well as loads of fuel in the most tasteful and auspicious manner. A deputation bearing beer and other food is sent out before the bridal party arrives at the house. The leader of the bridal party receives the beer, offers oblations to local deities and other gods, and invokes blessings. To the head of the food-bringing deputation he gives a ceremonial scarf, and addresses him in a mock-imperious manner. He says that he must furnish the means of making merry for eighteen days, during which time all lodging, bedding, food, drink, seating according to rank, plates and cups and dining-stools must be served to each and all according to his position without any blunder or confusion.

'When the bride approaches the house, she is given a cup filled with flour and butter and an arrow adorned with silken streamers before she crosses the threshold. The Ta-shi Lama performs the exorcism, and hits her on the head with a volume of the sacred book, in retaliation for which the leader of the bridal party gives a tap to the lama with a stick, which of course furnishes the matter for a laugh.'

The reason for the exorcism is that the bride, when she

[1] Not to be confused with the Grand Lama of Ta-shi Lhün-po, who is styled Ta-shi Lama in western countries. The latter is not so known to Tibetans. To them he is 'The Precious Great Pandit' (*Pan-chen Rim-po-che*), 'The Precious Sovereign', and so forth.

left her home, lost, as we have seen above, the protection
of the gods of her home and district. Thus, unprotected
on her way to the bridegroom's house, evil spirits may
have entered into her. These must be expelled before she
enters her new home, and, in so doing, comes under the
protection of the bridegroom's guardian deities.

'When the bride is seated, she is addressed thus, "Oh
mother! welcome and blessings!" A bowl filled with
flour, surmounted by a slab of butter, boiled sweet yams,
rice, beer, oil, and curds are arranged in front of her.
These items should be either five or seven in number.
Then the leader of the bridal party rises, and, taking the
slab of butter, offers it to the ancestral gods, the maternal
gods, and the five kinds of household gods. Having done
this, he hands them to the bride, who takes a little of each
daintily, and puts them down.

'Although the usual brag is that the wedding feast
should extend over eighteen days, yet practically it lasts
only three days. The day on which the bride arrives
is called "Face beer",[1] i. e. "the beer on seeing the face".
The second day is "Beer drinking and play".[2] The third
day is called the "Accompaniment to beer".[3]

. . . .

'On the day of the big *chang-tung*, the real festive day,
the Ta-shi Lama puts the rice cake of the ceremony on
the heads of the couple and confers his blessings on
them, wishing them long life, prosperity, health, wealth,
and progeny.'

And so the feasting and merriment go on. On the third
day the cooks, wine servers, and other servants 'turn up
and challenge the guests and the bridal party to a lively
banter and a warfare of witticisms. The elders may air
their laid-up store of maxims and proverbs, quoting
freely from "The Precious Rosary of Wise Sayings".[4] At
night they bring out all the old songs they can think
of, e.g. "Sikkim, the Golden and Happy".[5] On such

[1] *Dong-chang.*   [2] *Chang-tung Tse-mo.*   [3] *Chang-se.*
[4] *Tam-gyu Rin-chen Treng-wa.*   [5] *Den-jong Ser-len Yang-cha.*

festive occasions old songs are held to be the most appropriate.'

On the third day the bride has to give various presents, including the head of the slaughtered bull or pig to the elder women. These in their turn entertain the leader of the bridal party, who gives them small presents. The bridegroom's family gives something to the stewards, cooks, servants, and helpers, including of course the singers, who receive a present from the Ta-shi Lama also.

'Having finished this feasting and drinking, it is customary to allow the bride to go back once to her parents' house.'

I have dealt at such length with the marriage customs of the central Tibetans and of their Sikkimese cousins that I forbear to extend the survey into the domain of the Lepchas, whose wedding preparations and rituals partly agree with and partly differ from those of the Sikkimese.

XVIII
MARRIAGE (*continued*)

WEDDING celebrations are the occasion of much feasting and jollity, and these appeal to the laughter-loving people of Tibet. But the spiritual side of the Tibetan character is touched by the spectacle of those who deny themselves the pleasures of married life at the dictates of their religious law. In the histories we read of many such. And the Lho-hi Chö-jung tells of one—Tung Tam-cho by name—who 'observed the rules of priestly celibacy very strictly. As a proof of this, a sweet scent used to pervade the air wherever he went, and his body cast no shadow.'[1]

Many priests, however, marry, including those of the Ka-gyü sect which prevails in Bhutan. Of Mar-pa, who was the highly revered leader of this sect soon after its earliest beginnings, it is recorded that he was heavily married. He was returning to Tibet from India, where his spiritual guide had passed away. Says the Blue Record,[2]

'He was then forty-two years old. On his arrival in Tibet, he took Dak-me-ma to wife. He is said to have had eight other female disciples who were also his spiritual consorts. And these nine were believed to have been the manifestations of the nine female deities of the Kye Dor-je Mandala.

On my way from Ta-lung Monastery to that of Re-ting, I saw, high up on the mountain side above, a dwelling with the familiar red band which indicates a house of religion. It was built into the face of a precipice. An inquiry elicited that it was the abode of a priest from Ri-wo-che, north-west of Cham-do, in eastern Tibet. He had taken up his abode there at the request of Ta-lung Monastery, to whom the house belonged. Ta-lung is of the Ka-gyü sect, but is nowadays turning more and more

[1] Folio 58. [2] Tep-ter Ngön-po, vol. viii, folio 2.

to the reformed sect known as the Yellow Hats, that to which the Dalai and Ta-shi Lamas belong. This priest, however, belonged to neither, but to the old, unreformed sect, known as the Red Hats; an interesting fact, for it shows how the different sects can combine and work together.

Being of the Red Hats he was married and had children, for the rules of the sect permit this. But he had a wide reputation for learning and sanctity. So parties of young monks, ten to twenty at a time, came to stay with him, sometimes for a few months, and sometimes for a year or so. And, having done this, they carried the fruits of their instruction to their homes throughout Tibet.

And the nature of his instruction to these young men? Well, he told them the good and the bad in humanity; what is virtuous, what sinful. He would read the sacred books to them and explain the meanings. Sometimes he would merely read without explaining. For, as he had attained a great height in religion, by his mere reading he gave them the blessing, known as *lung*,[1] which they could not gain by reading themselves.

Though married, he was a Living Buddha (*Trü-ku*). At the time, when we passed by, he was leading a life of stern asceticism, for he had remained seated, Buddha-wise, continuously for the preceding twelve months, with the result that he was unable to stand upright.

'A lama's wife', Pa-lhe-se tells me, 'is known, not by the same designation as the wife of a layman—*cham*, *kye-men*, &c.—but as proprietress (*dak-mo*).[2] The lama and his belongings are in her charge, so that he is free to devote himself to religion.' Thus marriage is, as it were, excused.

In the Blue Record is narrated [3] the story of a young man, named Dröl-gom, who was married when fifteen years of age. This denotes an actual age of thirteen or fourteen, for Tibetans, in reckoning age, count both the first and the last years. Thus a baby born in, say, October,

---

[1] ལུང་   [2] བདག་མོ   [3] Tep-ter Ngön-po, vol. viii, folio 29.

'It was built into the face of a precipice'

becomes two years old with the New Year in the following February.

Losing his wife during the first year after marriage, the lad was so overpowered by the blow, that he took to the religious life, choosing as his spiritual guide a priest, named Gam-po-pa, who had been one of the leading disciples of the famous poet-saint, 'Cotton-clad Mi-la' (Mi-la Re-pa). His marriage, according to the history, did not prevent him from attaining to miraculous powers in his religious career. For we read that he attained the power of soul-transference (*drong-juk*).[1]

'One Pal-chen Ga-lo', says the history, 'exhibited the power of balancing his entire body on one of his big toes. Dröl-gom, seeing that Pal-chen wanted to overawe him, determined to show his own power. He transferred his consciousness to the body of a dead goose. The goose flew round the place thrice, and then, coming in front of Ga-lo, uttered many cries. After this Dröl-gom left the body of the goose, re-entered his own and held long converse with Ga-lo. He called Ga-lo's exhibition the medium power of suppleness according to Gam-po-pa's standard.'

In Tibet, as elsewhere, the course of love too often does not run smoothly. A girl with two lovers—or a man with whom two girls are in love—wishes to meet the best beloved, but the other intervenes. So she (or he) sings:

> I threw a stone on yonder hill,
>   The owl on this side stirred;
> Ne'er had I thought that fear would fall
>   On that ill-omened bird.

A young man of lower birth who pines to marry a girl in a higher family or one whose father holds a high official position, expresses his woes with a sad and helpless simplicity.

> The choicest blossoms all are found
>   Placed high upon the tree;
> I could not reach to pluck them, but
>   To leave was misery.

[1] འགྲོང་འཇུག་

Monogamy, polygamy, and polyandry are all found in Tibet. Polygamy is for wealthy men, who can afford two, and occasionally even three, wives. In the course of conversation a Tibetan gentleman expressed surprise that our King-Emperor was allowed only one wife, and seemed to think that it was somewhat useless to be a king if one was limited so narrowly.

The second wife is sometimes a sister of the first one. At the marriage with the first wife incense is burnt. And, as we have seen above, those friends and relations who come and offer the ceremonial scarves must be feasted.

'A member of one of the highest families, such as the Do-ring family', a Tibetan gentleman informs me, 'will have to feast some two or three hundred; a landlord (*gerpa*) of comparatively low social position must entertain thirty or forty. Families who have heavy obligations in this respect will divide these wedding guests into parties of twenty to thirty at a time. Each party is entertained for a whole day, three meals being given.

'If the husband marries a second wife, the feasting will be on a smaller scale. Should there be even a third marriage, the feasting will be smaller still.'

Where polyandry holds, the husbands are brothers. Having married one of the brothers in a family, the wife marries also the other brothers who are younger, but not any that are older than him. As to the classes that practise polyandry, there is considerable divergence of opinion. Rockhill, writing of eastern Tibet, states that polyandry prevails largely among the peasantry, but not among the nomads. He writes:

'The tillable lands are of small extent and are all under cultivation, so it is extremely difficult for any one to add to his fields, which as a general rule produce only enough to support one small family. If at the death of the head of the family the property was divided among the sons, there would not be enough to supply the wants of all of them if each had a wife and family. The secular experience of the whole human race showing that several families cannot live in peace and concord under the same roof, the only solution of the problem in this case was for the sons of a family to

POLYANDRY   193

take one wife among them, by which means their ancestral estate
remained undivided, and they also saved considerable money.

'Among the nomads, where existence is not dependent on the
produce of the soil, where herds of yak and flocks of sheep and goats
are ever increasing and supply all their owners' wants, this necessity
of preserving the family property undivided can never have
existed.' [1]

It is of course easier to increase flocks and herds than
to augment the outturn of the crops. But, so far as my
experience went, the grazing-grounds are carefully divided
off and regulated. The grass is poor; each flock requires
much land for its grazing. Any family, therefore, that
largely increases its flocks and herds is regarded with dis-
approval by the co-sharers in that grazing-ground. And
in central Tibet at any rate the population has been decreasing for the last hundred years. There is consequently a large area of land which has fallen into disuse
and is available for those who wish to extend their holdings. So much is this the case that a special Agricultural
Department has been formed in order to dispose of these
vacant lands.

Mr. Combe, quoting, I think, Paul She-rap of Tachienlu, gives the same opinion as Rockhill. But he adds a foot-
note by the Reverend J. Huston Edgar, who spent over
twenty years in the regions west of Tachienlu, which
affirms that 'the nomads around Li-tang seem peculiarly
given to polyandry'.[2] And Mr. She-rap himself says that
of the sharing brothers one will perhaps join the nomads.

Such inquiries as I made on the subject lead me to
believe that polyandry is frequently practised by both
farmers and herdsmen. Ku-sho Tsen-drön, the 'Peak
Secretary', that is to say, one of the Secretaries of the
Dalai Lama, was attached by His Holiness to my mission
in Lhasa. A man of exceptional intelligence, he had
travelled a good deal in Tibet, and had found polyandry
to be common among the communities of herdsmen in the

[1] Rockhill, The Land of the Lamas, pp. 211, 212 (Longmans, Green).
[2] G. A. Combe, A Tibetan on Tibet, p. 73 (Fisher Unwin).

Northern Plains, as well as in western Tibet, where the bulk of the people are herdsmen. A landed proprietor in the Tsang province, where polyandry is on all hands admitted to be exceptionally prevalent, was of opinion that it was common among both the peasantry and the graziers.

One reason assigned by the Peak Secretary for the prevalence of polyandry among the herdsmen was that among them men were needed to go to the lower countries to buy grain, as well as to go to the higher lands to procure salt for consumption and sale. The herdsmen do not eat much grain, but some they must have. And no doubt in the nomad's wandering life women and children are somewhat at a disadvantage.

Often, too, one heard the explanation, given by Ku-sho Pa-lhe-se as applicable rather to the farmers than to the graziers. He said 'Polyandry is due to the fear of the family splitting up and of the family property being divided. This would impoverish the people. Polyandry is more prevalent in Tsang, where the soil is poorer, than in the U province. Estates and holdings in Tsang are larger and therefore require more persons to look after them. Polyandry is thus particularly suitable for the Tsang province'.

All were agreed that, taking Tibet as a whole, monogamy was more prevalent than either polyandry or polygamy. The Peak Secretary estimated that in the province of U out of every twenty households one might say that fifteen would be monogamous, three polyandrous, and two polygamous. In the Northern Plains he estimated the proportions at ten polyandrous, seven monogamous, and three polygamous.

Speaking of divorce, the History of Sikkim, already quoted, defines the custom among Sikkim-Tibetans as follows:

'Should the matrimonial connection have to be severed, then before either the villagers' law court, or the landlords' court, or even before a higher court, the party who applies

The Peak Secretary in his ecclesiastical robes with two attendants

for separation has to pay a penalty of eighteen golden *shos*, if male; and twelve, if female. Each *sho* is reckoned at five rupees and is paid in rupees. In addition to this it is necessary to pay the actual expenses in cash and in kind incurred during the marriage as price of the bride, &c. Payment need not be made for the beer, rice, and other food consumed during the feasts.'

Adultery is regarded less seriously in Tibet than in Europe. The laws of the Dharma Raja, recorded in the History of Bhutan, do, however, prescribe that a man who commits adultery with 'a woman having a recognized husband' [1] must pay compensation. [2]

---

[1] *Dak-po-chen kyi tsung-ma.*   [2] Lho-hi Chö-jung, folio 103.

XIX

THE CHILDREN

THE Tibetan children are jolly little people, merry, and mischievous. And as they grow a little older, the mirth and the mischief remain. I well remember the four Tibetan boys of the upper middle class whom their Government sent to England in 1914 for a few years' education. They were from twelve to fifteen years of age. My wife and I were able to see something of them as they passed through Gangtok, my head-quarters, and we could not fail to recognize their similarity in many respects to British schoolboys. Their open-hearted natures, their love of a joke, and their robustious health seemed to fit them well for the battle of life. And when they were in England, though they worked perhaps harder than the average English boy, yet they possessed also in some degree the latter's healthy instinct against overtaxing the young brain.

It is a general Tibetan belief that it is bad for people to sleep in the daytime, for it is thought that doing so, especially during summer, induces fever. When the Ta-shi Lama visited India, he suffered from the journey in the mountain train down the Himalaya. The British doctor in attendance wished him to have a little restful sleep, but this his own people vigorously opposed. And so, too, with the Tibetan mother. The sleep that is her due after her baby is born is apt to be curtailed or denied on account of this same belief. Even an invalid is not allowed to sleep except at night. Should he do so, the relative who looks after him sprinkles water over his face.

Mothers often suckle their young until they are two or three years old. Large families are the exception in Tibet, not the rule as among the Gurkhas in the neighbouring country of Nepal. If the mother dies, a relative or maid-servant acts as foster-mother, and only in default of these is cow's milk used. Apart from this milk they receive scraps of their parents' food.

The death-rate among young children is heavy. Venereal disease is prevalent and is regarded but lightly. This no doubt is in a large measure responsible for the smallness of the families. And the little children themselves are sometimes put to hardships, which are destructive even to those born of Tibetan parents. A Tibetan officer of high family left Ya-tung for Lhasa with his wife and family. Their baby, two and a half months old, was carried in a box, covered with a waterproof sheet to keep out the rain. This covering allowed but scanty ventilation. A maid was in attendance on it, but it became ill the next day at Pa-ri, and died on the following day at Tu-na. Let it not be thought that Tibetan parents are wanting in affection towards their children. They are not, but the people generally are inured to hardships, and babies are sometimes tried too high.

In eastern Tibet a child's name is not chosen for it by its parents, but by a lama who is a Living Buddha (*trü-ku*), or other priest of high reputation; and sometimes by an Oracle. But a pet nickname often takes the place of the real name. In central Tibet, however, the parents always name the child. In a few cases a lama gives a name some years later, and, if so, this takes the place of that given by the parents.

Two names are given, of which the first is frequently the day of the week on which the child was born. For instance, a boy born on a Monday may be called *Da-wa Tse-ring*, i.e. 'Moon Long-Life'. Or, where the day of the week is not used, *Ta-shi Tön-trup*, i.e. 'Prosperity Purpose-accomplished'. Girls also have two names, of which often only one is a woman's name, the other being applicable to men as well as to women, e.g. 'Lotus', or 'Prosperity'. 'Goddess Long-Life' would be an appropriate full name. Very many are named after Dröl-ma, the 'Deliverer', the most popular of all the goddesses. The second name is in no sense a surname. The nearest approach to such is to be found in the name of the family or house, e.g. Do-ring or Yu-to.

Another ceremony is known as the 'Life Power' (tse-wang). In some parts of the country it is performed on the third day after birth, but is often postponed. Like many other customs, it varies in different districts of Tibet. The object of the tse-wang is to promote long life. It is done not only to children, but to people of all ages, especially when sickness supervenes. The lama's servant makes up life-giving pills and brews life-giving beer. The lama himself offers prayers, which may take a week or even longer. After this a service is held in which sometimes an image of Tse-pa-me, the god of 'Measureless Life', is placed on the head of the suppliant. The service lasts for an hour or more according to the number of suppliants. This ceremony may be performed several times during a person's life.

When a lad enters the priesthood, the hair on his head is shaved, except one lock in the middle. A lama cuts off this lock at the time when he gives the boy his priest-name. The ceremony is known as 'The Giving of the Hair as a Firstfruit Offering'. The new name is known as 'the golden name', the term 'golden' being habitually applied to the priesthood.

It is believed that a young child can recollect its previous life. But as it learns to walk and talk, the power weakens and finally disappears. Many stories are told in the histories and other Tibetan books of small boys, little more than babies, who display this knowledge. A boy, only seven months old, is taken into a temple where there is an image of a Black Hat lama of the Kar-ma-pa sect. 'The child burst out laughing. On being asked the reason, he pointed to his own heart, thus indicating that he was a rebirth of the lama.'[1] This power is believed to be possessed in the highest degree by Incarnations (Trü-ku), i.e. those who by the sanctity of their lives have attained the right to Nirvana, but consent to be reborn into the

[1] Tep-ter Ngön-po, vol. viii, folio 49.

world to aid all animate creation on the upward path. Many Tibetans credit these with powers of recollection until they are seven years old. Such a one identifies some of his possessions in his previous existence, this being one of the tests by which he is known to be the desired Incarnation.

If a boy is to be a priest, he is educated in a monastery. The Tibetan histories are full of boys who insist on a religious career. Of one boy, a magician's son, striving for Buddhahood, the Blue Record says,

'Being too poor to pay for a higher education, his mother urged him to abandon his study, but he, though only a child, replied, "All truly great men have borne hardships and difficulties." Thus he entreated his mother not to stand in the way of his attainment of Buddhahood.

'So saying, he set forth, and, putting himself under many Lamas of note, gained knowledge of the philosophy of the Middle Path and of the Peace-making Doctrine.' [1]

The first of the Dalai Lamas was, according to his biography, moved in a similar fashion.

'Although a mere boy, he considered that if one follows religion in the way that a layman does, it is like sitting in a house that is on fire. But if one follows the religion as it is lived by the holy priesthood, it is like dwelling in a cool house. The Buddhas of the Three Times (Past, Present, and Future) followed and will follow the religion of the holy priesthood.

'His mother said to him, "Generally that is so. But how can you be a priest? All that we have is half a woollen blanket; we have nothing else. Your father has passed away, your brothers and sisters are young. It is better to wait for some time.' [2]

But the young boy would not wait. He persuaded his mother, became a priest, and rose to be the first of the 'Inmost Protectors' who still control the destinies of Tibet.

Many miraculous accounts are given. One child has visions and is surrounded by supernatural beings.[3] A baby performs miracles when only seven months old.[4]

[1] Ibid., folio 7.
[2] Biography of Gen-dün Trup-pa, folio 8.
[3] Tep-ter Ngön-po, vol. v, folio 27.   [4] Ibid., vol. viii, folio 49.

Another receives profound teaching on religious subjects from his fourth year.[1] This—taking into account the Tibetan method of reckoning—would probably be his third year of actual age, and a similar deduction should be made in the ages now to be recorded. Another boy can read and write when five years old, and so on. It is no matter for wonder that, when a child of this kind is called to the bedside of his dying mother, she should thus address him, 'My venerable one! Regard me with gracious compassion.'[2] A boy, aged eleven, reaches that stage of religious meditation by which he is able to recognize the illusory nature of all phenomena.[3] One, aged twelve, receives an inward revelation by which he also perceives the illusion and impermanence of all things. But this light is dimmed after receiving initiation from some powerful magicians of the Black Hat sect.[4] Another child composes poetry and hymns when thirteen years old.[5] Of another the Blue Record says,

'Being entered as a novice and given some religious instruction at the early age of five by the Lama, he was restless and playful. The Lama reprimanded him, saying, "Child, do you hold me in contempt, or my religion?"

' "Why do you ask that?" replied the boy.

' "Because you are playing all the time I am teaching you."

' "But is there any harm in moving my hands and feet, when I listen with my heart?"

'On being told that it would be difficult for him to listen if he played, he at once repeated everything that the Lama had taught him during the preceding three days.'[6]

Intellectual and devotional exercises are combined. Of one young priest we read,

'He learnt the five divisions of the Maitreya's doctrines and the seven divisions of metaphysics. Having mastered every branch of scriptural lore, and having become known as a pre-eminently learned scholar and devotee, he next passed five months alone in a dark cell.'[7]

---

[1] Tep-ter Ngön-po, vol. viii, folio 46.   [2] Ibid., folio 50.
[3] Ibid., folio 27.   [4] Ibid., vol. v, folio 24.   [5] Ibid., vol. viii, folio 88.
[6] Ibid., folio 10.   [7] Ibid., vol. iii, folio 45.

Instances like the above might be multiplied indefinitely from the Tibetan histories. These are written, of course, for believers, for whose benefit are thus portrayed the lives of the great saints and teachers in their Church. An overwhelming proportion of Tibetans have an unquestioning faith in the Tibetan form of Buddhism. Mystery they welcome, miracles they easily believe. Many are nomads, following their yaks and sheep across the mountains and arid plains. So they have the genius for religion that is born of the desert.

But in actual practice many of the young monks abandon the religious career when they grow older. They find that they do not want to be priests.

Secular education is meagre, but is not entirely lacking. In the towns such as Lhasa, Shigatse, and Gyangtse there are schools with whole-time teachers. But in other places, and sometimes in these towns also, the teacher is a man with other work of his own, and can attend to teaching only for part of each day. During his absences the head boy in the school takes his place.

The parents, too, have their duties. As the couplet says:

> To eat, to sit, to walk in seemly style;
> These three a child is by his parents taught.

In an earlier chapter [1] I have outlined the education which a nobleman gives to his children through his own private tutor, and along with his own children to those of his servants and neighbouring peasantry. Let me now say a little about the boy who, though of lower social position, yet achieves some measure of education. Very few are the girls who share his privileges.

By the age of eight or nine many Tibetan children have learnt to say long prayers and praises, e.g. to the goddess Dröl-ma, 'The Deliverer'. Also another prayer called 'Clearing of Obstructions from the Path',[2] by which is meant the removal of misfortunes, bodily, mental, and

---

[1] See p. 104.   [2] *Par-che Lam-sel.*

spiritual, that would otherwise happen. At the age of six a boy is often able to repeat prayers for half an hour without stopping. But he will understand nothing, or almost nothing, of what they mean.

When six or seven years old a boy may go to a teacher and stay till he is fourteen or fifteen. The teacher takes in this way a few boys who do domestic work of various kinds in return for the teaching. There may be girls also; these can serve tea and do other jobs to pay for their tuition. If the teacher lives a long way off, the boys board in his house: girls do not generally board with him, unless he is related to them.

The teacher is usually, as mentioned above, a man who has business of his own outside his teaching; a trader perhaps, or a peasant educated above the average. In addition to the domestic services of his students, he receives useful presents, e.g. tea or cloth from their parents from time to time, and especially when the period of tuition comes to an end. But no fixed fees are paid to him.

Later on, the parents may possibly arrange to send the boy to a larger school with a whole-time teacher at Lhasa, Shigatse, Gyangtse, or other large centre. This is feasible only if they can arrange for their boy to stay with a relative or friend.

A young friend of mine, who was at a large school in Lhasa, spent most of his time there in reading and writing, and a little in arithmetic. The Tsa-rong Shap-pe's wife was at this school at the same time. Three or four girls attended it.

Even those in Lhasa were not all fortunate enough to command the services of a whole-time teacher. One young man described to me his education in Lhasa for three years, from the age of eight to that of eleven. He was during this time at a school—if it can be so called— kept by a subordinate clerk in the office of the Supreme Council.[1] There were about forty boys in the school.

Before going to his work in the Council office each

---

[1] *Ka-sha.*

morning the clerk gave the boys so many lines to write in Tibetan from copy-books. These consisted chiefly of letters of the Tibetan alphabet, written at first in large letters, succeeded by others becoming gradually smaller and smaller. On returning from the office in the evening the clerk made a somewhat hurried scrutiny to ascertain whether the boys had written the required number of lines, and for every line short gave the offender a flick on the cheek with a springy piece of bamboo.

A little reading was also done, all the boys reading aloud together. The time allotted to this exercise was short, the noise of the voices was great, and there was only one master. These causes combined to render the instruction almost useless.

'It was writing', said my informant, 'on which the greatest stress was laid. In fact, during those three years at school I learnt practically nothing except how to write the Tibetan alphabet. Tibetans attach the highest importance to a neat handwriting.

'The number of boys at this school was much less than usual owing to the fighting with China, which took many parents away from Lhasa. But even when there were far more boys, there was still only one master, and he spent only a short time each morning and evening at the work. What I learnt, I learnt chiefly from my own parents.

'These Tibetan copy-books are bound in cloth and have to be kept very carefully until they literally fall to pieces. The boys write on wooden slates and make their own pens from bamboos, cutting the points finer and finer as the letters become smaller and smaller.'

I was often reminded of the high value set on a good handwriting, which must be both neat and of an undeviating regularity. As many hours are spent on this as by an English public schoolboy on Latin or mathematics. When the Ta-shi Lama gave me a coloured photograph of himself, I had considerable difficulty in persuading him to put his name to it, as he considered his penmanship to be inferior.

Learning by rote is also greatly practised. Tibetans are able to memorize prodigiously. Monks in monasteries commit to memory every year hundreds of pages from the sacred books. Nomads from the grazing-lands of the far north recite the epic of Ke-sar throughout many days in succession without once repeating themselves. Writing may be difficult, but memory seldom fails.

As for arithmetic, it is evident that the Tibetans as a race are weak in even its simplest forms. The beads on the rosaries are often used in addition and subtraction. This weakness may no doubt be due to absence of effective instruction, but one seemed to notice the same trait among the other hill races, Gurkhas and Lepchas, in the eastern Himalaya. Among all three races those who were otherwise well educated could not calculate the details of even petty contracts for building, road-making, and the like. Consequently, they often made losses on such undertakings.

But for drawing and painting, for designing and engraving on metal or wood, many Tibetans appear to have a natural instinct, which can be guided to a high standard under capable tuition. They have also considerable aptitude as doctors. We sent two Sikkim-Tibetan lads to Kalimpong and Patna for an elementary medical course, such as their scanty education permitted. On completing this, one was posted to Gyangtse and the other to the Chumbi Valley. Being the only Tibetans who had received a training in Western medicine, they rendered valuable service in those districts. A few Lepchas, similarly trained, volunteered to a man for service in the World War, when very many of other races were holding back. They were sent to Mesopotamia, and proved their worth in those torrid plains as in their own cool mountain land.

Reading, too, must be difficult when all the other boys in the little room read aloud at the same time. On my way to Lhasa I halted for two nights at Nan-kar-tse. A small school adjoined the enclosure of our staging bungalow.

A small school in Lhasa

Boy showing writing to teacher. The backward boys write on broad, wooden slates ;
the more advanced on narrow strips of paper

Each morning, before sunrise, commenced the sing-song, which showed that a reading lesson was in progress. It was winter, with a temperature of forty to fifty degrees of frost, and the room was entirely unwarmed.

There were no regular schools in the Chumbi Valley. Village schools are sometimes maintained, as we have seen, by private landlords. But the land in this area was owned by the State. Where the State is the landlord, it does not maintain any school; the parents have to find private tutors for their boys. The only schools in central Tibet kept up by the Government are two in Lhasa, namely, the 'Peak School' (*Tse-Lap-tra*) for teaching boys and youths who intend to become ecclesiastical officials, and the Finance Office (*Tsi-kang*) for those who intend to become lay officials.

Beating is frequently used as an aid to instruction. Tibetan villagers living in the north of Sikkim used to tell the missionary lady working among them that it was useless to try to teach them without beating them.

As mentioned in an earlier chapter, students in the Finance Office at Lhasa are taught accounts and general correspondence. The latter subject includes the writing of letters and other correspondence in the prescribed styles. For each class or occupation a separate form of address is deemed suitable, and this too must be varied for different occasions. For each of the highest lamas, e.g. the Dalai Lama, the Ta-shi Lama, those of Sa-kya and Cham-do, as well as for Dor-je Pa-mo, a special form of address is appointed. Lengthy and high-flown compliments are poured out in each case.

The chief authority on the correct styles of epistolary correspondence is a book styled *Yik-kur Nam-sha*, i.e. 'The Arrangement of Correspondence'. It contains a selection of letters written by an ancestor of the Sha-tra family who was Regent of Tibet eighty years ago. The letters are regarded as models of correspondence. In the introduction to this work it is stated:

'One's moral merits of this and of future existences are in-

creased by the use of suitable complimentary expressions towards
great and holy persons.

. . . .

'Prayers made with fervent love, respect and faith, expressed in
writing, remove the defilement which is inherent in speech. Moreover, sages have freely stated that one may attain to Omniscience by
such means.

'When the person addressed is highly exalted and awe-inspiring,
you should not venture on such words as "to your honourable hand"
or "to your honourable person". Expressions such as "to your
honourable lotus feet" or "to the honourable lotus foot-stool" are
applicable.

'We, the commoners, when addressing the class worthy of honour
and praise, or those by nature holy and pure, as well as rich with
profound wisdom, scholarship, and talents, or who are noble by
lineage . . . to whom we cannot ordinarily offer our salutations
personally, should use complimentary expressions such as "To the
feet of", "To the presence of".

'To the humble also polite words and pleasing expressions should
be used. In addressing the three classes, high, intermediate, and
low, complimentary expressions as befitting their respective positions, conformable to time and circumstance, ought to be employed.

'The Supreme Ruler of China being a great Emperor will be
addressed with the highest formality. Profound veneration will be
shown to the Dalai Lama, the All-seeing, Powerful King. . . .
Compliment the learned or the wise with the word "Ocean", such
as "Thou Ocean of Learning". . . .

'That which fulfils one's desires should be respectfully compared
to the Wish-fulfilling Gem (*Yi-shin Nor-pu*) or to the Wish-fulfilling Tree (*Pak-sam Kyi Shing*). One who is of high birth or who
holds an exalted office address as "Chief of men". Compare the
illustrious and the intelligent with the sun, the steady with the
earth, the unchangeable with gold, the sincere and candid with milk,
and the magnanimous with the sky. Address the beloved one as
"Flower Anthers of the Mind", and one who is beautiful as the
"Moon" or the "Lotus".' [1]

During one of my numerous conversations with the Dalai
Lama, the talk turned to this school in the Finance Office.
'I have insisted,' said His Holiness, 'that those who enter

[1] See Sarat Chandra Das's edition of the *Yik-kur Nam-sha*, printed at the
Bengal Secretariat Press, Calcutta.

our Government service must have better literary qualifications; the standard in this respect was formerly too low. Examinations are held twice yearly; one in summer and one in winter. Those who do well are rewarded.'

It is inevitable that Western education should in time permeate Tibet. But it may be hoped that it will come gradually, not in an overwhelming flood. A beginning has been made. The training of two Sikkim-Tibetans as doctors has been recorded above. About the same time the Dalai Lama sent four Tibetan boys to England to gain such education as was possible in a limited period, and these on their return did such work as their training allowed.

The little State of Sikkim has been longer in touch with the outer world. In 1916 I talked with the head of the Yangtang family—landed proprietor, magistrate, and member of the Sikkim Council—and asked him his opinion as to what subjects the sons of the Sikkimese aristocracy should learn when at school.

'English, Hindi, and Tibetan,' he replied, 'especially English. They should learn both to read and to write these languages. They should commence learning English when quite young; the younger they begin, the better it is for learning foreign languages.

'Hindi is also necessary now that the great majority of our peasantry are Nepalese. It is better to learn Hindi than Nepalese, for it enables one to speak to Indians and to read their petitions, and most Nepalese are coming to understand it also.

'Our boys should learn sufficient arithmetic to enable them to understand the estate accounts. They should learn a little geography and history, for these subjects broaden the mind. And they should be taught games, as well as jumping and other athletic exercises, for these benefit the body.'

Tibetans believe, too, in home training and believe in heredity. For, as their proverb tells them,

If the father's qualities do not come to the son,
How does the hare get his split lip?

XX

CHILDREN AND OTHERS

IT has seemed best to deal at some length with the education of the young, for it would otherwise be impossible to understand the Tibetans and their outlook on life. Scanty, indeed, their training is from the European standpoint, and scanty must necessarily be their knowledge of the world outside their borders.

Apart from those who go to India to trade, visiting the large centres of commerce, especially Calcutta, the chief interest of Tibetans in India is fixed on those places that are hallowed by their associations with the life of the Buddha. Bodh Gaya in southern Bihar they know, for thousands have been there, to see the place where the founder of their Faith became the Buddha, 'The Enlightened One'. Sarnath near Benares they know, for there the Buddha preached his first sermon. But the whereabouts of many of the places mentioned in their sacred books are unknown to them. Such information as they have they gain from the Tibetan beggars who roam through northern India during the cool season. These beggars are of course uneducated. Accordingly, much incorrect information is given, and Tibetans are misled.

The Tibetan book on geography, a modern work, known as 'The Mirror that shows the Extent of the World' (*Dzam-ling Gye-she Me-long*), has been mentioned in an earlier chapter.[1] It makes a brief reference to most of the countries of Europe, of which continent it remarks that the manufactures are numerous and váried. It adds, 'The people are white in colour. They are wise and are unequalled in religious and temporal work. The religion is the religion of Christ'.[2]

'North-east of "Kamshatha" . . . after crossing the

[1] See p. 8.
[2] Dzam-ling Gye-she Me-long, folio 119.

ocean for a distance of tens of thousands of fathoms one arrives in America.' [1]

'In the southern ocean there is Mahasagera Island, inhabited by Indians and owned by Holland. And there are numerous islands rich in jewels.' [2]

'There is Africa, belonging to the Feringhi (i.e. Europeans), and there are many islands in the ocean belonging to the English.' [3]

'In the western ocean of Africa there is an island where the crops grow without being sown. There is another island, where there is no water. Here the people and animals drink the dew which falls on the trees.' [4]

A little history too is put forward, but it tends to be fabulous or twisted. Archimedes of Syracuse and his burning glass do not escape attention.

'Near Italy there is Sicily Island, which belongs to Italy. The people are very intelligent and are clever in the making of goods. It is said that no other kingdom ever conquered it, because the king had made a glass, and the light of the sun coming from the glass burnt tens of thousands of ships.' [5]

Of Napoleon we read, 'About twenty years ago there was a commander called Nepoliya. He conquered most of Europe, but was caught by the Russian king, Alexander, and was imprisoned'.[6]

There are several historical works in Tibetan. But they deal almost entirely with religious happenings, which to the Tibetan mind are the only things of real importance. Of war or administration we find but a few lines here and there; of racial, industrial, economic movements there is hardly any mention. On the other hand, schools of religious thought, names of saints and scholars, what they did and said and thought and dreamt and the visions they saw, these are recorded in detail. And with it all a strong tendency to the miraculous.

---

1 Ibid., folio 92.   2 Ibid., folio 96.
3 Ibid., folio 97.   4 Ibid., folio 101.
5 Ibid., folio 127.   6 Ibid., folio 128.

Allied to these histories are the books known as *nam-tars*, or at least the historical section of them. A *nam-tar* of this kind is a biography, or semi-biography, of some great personage. The same tendency to miracle and marvel is found in it also. Such books are widely read, and are popular subjects of conversation.

The dramas and some of the religious ceremonies show the doings of the early kings, those who lived between the seventh and the ninth centuries A.D. These, too, are naturally tinged with poetry and legend. In the war-like achievements of these early kings Tibetans take a great and legitimate pride, for in those days the Tibetans were mighty in battle and achieved wide conquests. But even of those stirring times the spread of the Buddhist religion in Tibet is what interests them most, for to the Tibetans religion comes first of all.

One afternoon I entered the great Temple in Lhasa for a short visit. The day was the fifteenth of the Tibetan month, the day of the full moon, and therefore holy. The courts and chapels of the Temple were thronged with worshippers. In addition to these crowds the main court was occupied by three hundred monks from Gyü, the strictest of all the Lhasan monasteries. There was to be an eclipse of the moon that night, a bad omen, and the service was designed to counteract its evil effect.

On the way home the Dalai Lama's Secretary said, 'The popular belief among Tibetans is that eclipses of the sun and moon are caused by the planet Dra-chen, which moves through the sky and sometimes crosses the path of the sun or moon, covering them wholly or partially from sight, and thus causing total or partial eclipses. Our astrologers can foretell the dates of these eclipses.' In this matter, as in others, Tibetan astrologers appear to follow those of China and India.

Though their form of education permits them but little knowledge of outside events, there are Tibetans here and there who have a wide acquaintance with the literature of their own country. In Lhasa the man with the widest knowledge of all was perhaps he who was known as the Tsen-shap, the chief librarian to the Dalai Lama. He was reputed to be acquainted with all the histories, both secular (gyal-rap) and ecclesiastical (chö-jung), in addition to the religious and philosophical works. He was in charge of the Dalai Lama's large library, and constantly attended His Holiness, to whom he must read and explain passages when called upon to do so. He was in attendance for that purpose, so the Dalai Lama's Chief Secretary told me, for several hours every day. Few, if any, Tibetans can have a wider knowledge of Tibetan literature than he has.

Some continue their studies long after they are grown to manhood. To attain the prized position of a Ge-she, a priest must toil at his books for about twenty years, and even then success is not easy.

The children learn many wise sayings and proverbs when they are young. These serve them in later life. Books of maxims are general favourites among adults, and a proverb is often more potent than an argument.

Before I served in Tibet I made a land settlement of the Kalimpong district. The inhabitants are Gurkhas, Lepchas, and Tibetans; the land belongs to the Government. Fields were measured and classified, rents fixed, disputes settled, vested rights inquired into; in fine, all the arrangements, which are usual in Indian land settlements, were made with a view to promoting agricultural peace and prosperity.

Among other arrangements I reserved land, both woods and grass lands, in each village. These were to be kept as village common lands. They served for grazing the plough cattle, and for increasing the villagers' store of fodder and fuel. The Government gave these lands, but to round them off it was sometimes necessary to take back, as the law allowed, a small piece from one or other of the villagers. These nearly always consented. But one Gurkha, from whom I wished, in the public interest, to take a fragment of rough, uncultivated land, was obdurate. Arguments he controverted; appeals he ignored.

So I made use of a proverb, quoting a line of one well known among the Gurkhas. I said, 'There is no medicine for death.' The village headman and other villagers standing round at once took up the other line, 'There is no answer to an order.' The field was yielded without further demur, for a proverb is not the argument of man but the wisdom of high Heaven.

Here are three characteristic Tibetan proverbs taken at random.

'A little knowledge'

Those with a little learning are proud;
The truly wise are humble.
The brooks are noisy,
But the ocean is quiet.

'Gossip'

Gossip is the scum of water;
Action is the drop of gold.

'Leave well alone'

If your mind is free from care, stand surety for a loan!
If your body is free from pain, stamp on a dog's tail!

We have followed the young people through their educational stages far along the road of manhood. It is time now to return to them as children. And here it must be made plain that, except those destined for the priesthood, most of them, especially the girls, grow up without receiving any outside teaching in monastery or school. What they learn, they learn at home from their parents and others. Meanwhile, they are set to work at an early age. Quite small children, girls as well as boys, will look after sheep and goats and cattle. They go out also to gather for fuel the dung of yaks and other cattle, throwing it into the baskets on their backs. If the district lies at a sufficiently low altitude, say below eleven thousand feet, for firewood to be available, this must be collected. The girls, besides taking part in the above work, help in the house, and, while but small children themselves, look after those that are still younger.

At an early age both boys and girls take their share in drawing water from the well. Morning and evening a daily routine, but a pleasant one. For there is news to be had of other households, high and low; and conversation is pleasant, interspersed with snatches of song.

It was early on a January morning, when Colonel Kennedy, the Peak Secretary, Ku-sho Pa-lhe-se, and I rode out from Lhasa to visit the district across the river, where Tse-chok-ling, the smallest of the four privileged *Ling* monasteries, sheds its kindly influence. Near the tall obelisk below the Potala is a well from which, the ice having been broken, several are drawing water. A small boy, some seven years of age, passes us, carrying his wooden bucket of water to his home. As he steps along, he sings heartily, 'There is only one thing to say; there is only one thing to say'.[1] We turn off to the right, and the childish treble, piping always, 'There is only one thing to say', dies away in the distance. A line perhaps out of a popular Lhasa song, the only line which his youthful mind can retain.

In addition to the ordinary occupations of Tibetan childhood there is one to which I have seen no reference made in books on Tibet, that of the Dance Boys (*gar-truk*) of Lhasa.

Colonel Kennedy and I were fortunate in being the first white men to witness the Dalai Lama's great yearly Reception, known as 'The King's New Year', held in the Potala on the second day of each Tibetan year. This Reception is accompanied by various ceremonies and spectacles, which follow each other in their prescribed order. Among them is a dance performed in front of His Holiness by thirteen boys, each carrying an axe. They are said to represent the sons and daughters of gods who appeared to King Song-tsen Gam-po. But deification is not uncommon in Tibet, and so perhaps the scene really

[1] *Lab-gyu chik-le min-du.*

symbolizes warfare or victory in the old days of those fighting kings.

These lads are recruited, willing or unwilling. Likely boys seen in the streets of Lhasa are seized from time to time and taken before the Dalai Lama, who picks out some of them. These become dance boys, whether their parents desire this or not. Some fathers, however, manage to get their children off by saying that they are making monks of them, for it would not be right to forbid a spiritual career. In addition to the actual performers a reserve is maintained in order to take the place of those who are ill, and to work as messengers. All serve for about three years, after which those who show aptitude become musicians, performing in the religious dances.

The Tibetan children, merry and mischievous as they are, do not lack amusement. Not for them are the complicated and costly games evolved in Europe and America. They make their own.

During summer we shall see the boys wrestling, throwing stones as far as they can, and pitching stones at a mark. Broad jumping is a favourite occupation, especially among the monks. And skipping, too, which among the monks, men as well as boys, is a national pastime, and so varied in its scope that it will demand a fuller description later on.

Some boys will stand on their hands, heads down, feet pointing straight in the air, and will try how far they can progress in that unnatural style. Others fashion rough bows and arrows, or slings, shooting at a rock, a branch, or a bird. Others bestride ponies or cattle; or, if the sons of the fortunate rich, ride in a regular way.

One of the games is Wolf and Sheep. The latter form a tail, each child holding the one in front. The wolf has to seize the hindmost, and, when he comes, the queue endeavours to keep facing him so as to prolong his task. As each sheep is caught it is taken out of the tail.

Another game, known as 'Tiger Play, Sheep Play', closely resembles our game of Fox and Geese, as played on a draughtboard. Lines can quickly be marked on the

'The Tibetan children do not lack amusement'

Boy monks dressed for playing

ground with a stick, and small stones used for the pieces.
The stage is square, with twenty-five stations, five by five.
Fourteen sheep and one tiger participate. The game is
a universal favourite.

In the dry cold of the Tibetan uplands the snowfall is
scanty. But in the warmer and moister parts, where it is
plentiful, snowballing affords unending delight. Snow
men are made, and, young and old, all join in the fun, not
excepting the dogs which, long-haired as they are, revel
in snow and ice.

When the young people need a rest, they may sit
down and fashion figures of men, women, and animals out
of clay. These of course come to life, eat, drink, talk, and
so on. The ritual of the priest is imitated; the heroic deeds
of the great kings and ministers of olden days are portrayed.

The girls, true to sex, are less strenuous. They mould
a little home out of clay, complete with the hearth for
cooking; then play at keeping house. They weave flowers
and leaves into hats, or fashion head-dresses out of clay
and dye these in various colours. They sing theatrical
songs. They sing also others from religious sources, and
in this imitate the Lama Ma-ni, those men and women
who tour the country with their pictures, illustrating and
explaining the deeds of the Buddha. In the fields, on the
paths, in the streets you will often see girls and boys,
whirling dizzily round and round after the peculiar
fashion of the actors and actresses in the dramas of this
strange land.

A favourite pastime of children, especially of girls, is
that of 'Big Toe Kick' (te-pe). A sort of shuttle-cock is
formed with a little ball of lead, copper, &c., in a hole in
which feathers are fixed. The girl kicks this up with a
sideways action, using the inside of the foot and ankle, and
keeps on kicking it each time as it comes down, thus pre-
venting it from falling to the ground. The two competitors count the number of times each keeps it up. One
perhaps achieves twenty times, the other twelve, i.e. eight

times less. The winner may then with her first and second finger strike the palm of the loser's hand eight times, or to a similar extent flick the knuckles of the vanquished with her thumb and finger.

Hardy and happy, spending most of the day out of doors, the Tibetan children have abundant pleasure. The spirit is in them, and so they easily evolve games.

XXI

FOOD

WE have already seen what meals the Tibetans of various classes eat. Let me now describe some of the main foods a little more fully.

The staple diet of an ordinary Tibetan is yak's meat, mutton, barley-flour, cheese, and—most of all—tea. With these things a few vegetables and a little fruit, especially among the rich or those who dwell in the lower altitudes. Below an elevation of ten thousand feet fruit and vegetables can be readily grown. Add beer, tobacco, and snuff, and you have satisfied all reasonable needs.

A common method of slaughtering yaks is by suffocating them, the object being to keep the blood in the meat, for this is how Tibetans like it. Death is, however, sometimes hastened by cutting the throat. Some places are set aside for slaughtering. One of these is at a northern entrance to Lhasa near the Ra-mo-che Monastery, both yaks and sheep being killed for the food of the populace. A great many of the butchers here are Tibetan herdsmen. In the Wa-pa-ling quarter of Lhasa there is a colony of Chinese Mohammedan butchers.

Riding one day with Ne-tö Dzong-pön, I saw butchers at work near the village below the great monastery of Dre-pung. A few yaks and some seventy sheep were ready for slaughter, the latter having been brought by nomads from the Northern Plains. This village consists mainly of houses rented for two or three weeks to nomads from the north, who bring cattle and sheep for sale.

The sheep were laid in a row, six or eight at a time, and their four legs tied together. A man cut their throats with a knife, and after him came a woman, who turned their heads over, facing them upwards. The butchers were Tibetans. Slaughtering is prohibited on the eighth, fifteenth, and last day of each month, for these are holy days.

I asked Ku-sho Ne-tö whether the butchers, who thus

over and over again contravened the Buddhist precept against taking the life of any animal, would go to hell. He replied that they certainly would. Some others, however, said that the sin is as it were pooled among the entire community, and, thus pooled, does not amount to very much per head.

There are many, again, who hold that the butchers find it especially hard to avoid sinning, for, as a friend explained to me:

. 'They are carried forward by the power of their own sins, which makes them commit fresh ones of the same kind. In many places butchers will kill yaks and sheep, and hunters will stalk wild animals even on the eighth, fifteenth, and last day of the month. And the greatest sinners will often have the better fortune in this life. If I have a thousand sheep and kill two or three hundred each year, more lambs will be born. If I abstain from killing, there will be but few births and many of my sheep will die. But my sins grow less. For what says the proverb ?

When the time draws near for a sinner to go to hell,
His good fortune bursts forth like a flaming fire.'[1]

The books condemn the taking of life in no uncertain terms. Says the History of Bhutan,[2] after enumerating the good deeds of the third secular ruler of that country:

'Yet there is still one evil custom obtaining in Bhutan, which the Dharma Raja (the spiritual ruler) must have overlooked in the stress of his manifold activities, passing away without having turned his thoughts to it. Subsequent rulers and ministers must either have allowed it to continue out of misplaced regard for some one, or out of ignorance, or out of the pride which is born of power.

'What is this blot on the fair page of meritorious acts? It is said that the taking of life is the worst of all sins. But in Bhutan the custom of taking life for food is prevalent.

'From ancient times in India and Tibet meat and beer were certainly used, but only in very small amounts after being offered

[1]   Dik-chen nyal-wa dro-ren-na,
                 Sö-nam me-tar bar-wa yin.
[2] Lho-hi Chö-jung, folio 95.

EATING MEAT

to the gods. Out of that custom has grown this one of using large quantities. And by the law of Karma this abuse of custom is responsible for the vicissitudes which the Church and Faith have hitherto experienced. If anybody were now to say that meat and beer should be prohibited, he would, I think, encounter violent opposition. Yet there is no knowing what an undaunted and influential person might accomplish, if he could override public opinion. This, however, being outside the scope of my book, is merely mentioned by the way.' [1]

A Hierarch of the Ta-lung Monastery, who lived in or about the fourteenth century, 'attained great fame by his activity and devout conduct. He introduced and enforced a rule prohibiting all trade in meat within the precincts of the monastery'.[2]

This monastery has indeed had an exceptional reputation for strict discipline. To stop the consumption of meat to that extent was no doubt an unusually thorough interpretation of the Buddhist law. For in a cold climate people crave for meat. I stayed for two days at Ta-lung in August. It was cold even then, for it lies at an elevation of fourteen thousand feet above sea-level, at the mouth of a narrow valley. High mountains rise immediately behind it and keep the sun away. In winter it must be piercingly cold; to abstain from meat in such an ice-house is indeed a stern deprivation; if that deprivation was enforced on all, there was strong faith and strong discipline.

There are, of course, very many priests throughout Tibet who of their own free will year in, year out, abstain from meat altogether, but it is difficult to enforce a prohibition on a wide scale. High lamas, who do indulge in meat, are accustomed to perform religious ceremonies for the animals killed in order to ensure that these will be reborn in a higher state, and thus gain by the loss of their lives. The Tibetan saying runs:

> If its flesh be eaten by one of merciful mind;
> It will be led on the road of pure and perfect mercy.[3]

---

[1] Ibid., folio 95.   [2] Tep-ter Ngön-po, vol. viii, folio 104.

[3]   *Sha-di nying-je-chen kyi sa;*
        Nying-je chang-chup lam ne dren.

Whatever sacrifices religious enthusiasm may accomplish, the hard fact remains that in the cold climate of this country it is easy to produce meat, but difficult to produce grain, vegetables, or fruit. The Tibetans have always lived on meat. They are fervent in their religion, but this fervency does not carry them so far as to reject the chief food that Nature provides and their bodily health demands.

And so we find that even in Lhasa itself, since the Dalai Lama's return from India in 1912, the Tibetan Government have established a meat market, where meat is sold under more sanitary conditions than in the ordinary shops. Probably our food inspectors would condemn this market, but for Lhasa it marks a great advance on previous arrangements and meets the requirements of the people. With its air, so dry and cold and rarefied, Tibet possesses a happy immunity from many kinds of germs. Towns and villages, where refuse of all kinds lies month after month in the streets, might reasonably expect occasional visits from typhoid or cholera. But the germs of these cannot live in high Tibet. It is not until he descends to lower lands that the Tibetan learns to his cost that the immunity which he had is his no longer, and, unless he can recast his primitive scheme of life, he is among the first to fall a victim to one of these dread scourges.

Though they may prohibit the eating of meat among themselves, Tibetans do not restrict the white stranger, the non-Buddhist, dwelling within their gates. In accordance with the kindly custom of the East, people bring you presents of food as you travel through their villages. A village headman may bring a dozen eggs. The governor of a district (*dzong-pön*) will give eggs in greater profusion, and add a sheep's carcase. Each time that I entered from Sikkim—usually about June of each year—the Dalai Lama sent me a present which was mainly of food. One such, which may be quoted as a sample, was as follows:

Firstly, the silk scarf of ceremony (*ka-ta*).[1] A cloisonné

[1] Described in Chapter XXIII.

'In Lhasa itself the Tibetan Government have established
a meat market'

At back, left to right, yak-hair bag of barley-flour, yak-hair bag of barley,
yak-skin containing rice. In front, six sheepskin bags of butter

bowl, two skinfuls of Bhutanese rice, five bags of barley-flour, three bags of peas (for our ponies), three carcases of sheep, each wrapped in a sack, and several narrow rolls of material for rough blankets. Each bag, box, or other package was sealed with the seal of the Government treasury, either the ecclesiastical or the secular treasury. The messenger gave the list of presents, itself duly secured with the Treasury seal, to my clerk, Rai Sahib A-chuk Tse-ring, to read out, and then showed him each package with the seal intact. Here, then, were animals offered as food. But if there was one thing more noticeable than another among the Buddhists of Tibet, it was their tolerance towards the customs of other nations, even when these conflicted with their own.

Of the eggs given to us, nine out of every ten were bad. They were always put into one of the zinc baths in the Indian Government staging bungalow, and barely one in ten would sink. It was necessary to be firm with one's servants in dealing with what may be termed the hesitating egg, that would neither float nor sink, but hovered uncertainly between. Their frugal minds were loth to reject any that showed even the faintest glimmering of hope. As for the Tibetans, they prefer their eggs high; when fresh, they find them insipid.

The sheep had been killed the previous October, but the carcases were dry and free from smell; the Tibetan winter had passed over them. There can be but few countries in the world where the householder fills his larder with meat but once a year, and consumes his hoard, healthily and happily, during the ensuing twelve months. But such is the ordinary practice in Tibet. No doubt he supplements it with fresh meat, but none the less he treasures the old. Sometimes the whole carcase is kept, sometimes the meat is cut and dried in strips, the latter being especially useful in travelling. Killed in October, the animals are at their fattest after the good grazing of the summer months. And winter is at hand to freeze the meat and keep it in good condition. The surplus uncon-

sumed at the end of each twelve months goes on from year
to year. It is not uncommon to see mutton five years old.

Soup is a favourite Tibetan dish. It may be served with
minced meat, spices, and thin strips of dough, and is then
known as 'Chinese soup'.[1] If the same dough is cut up
into thin squares and boiled with minced meat, it is
'Tibetan soup'.[2] The third kind is known as 'flour-
soup', and is made of chopped meat, boiled and served
with small pieces of flour rolled into shapes like cowry
shells.

Another favourite dish is made from rice. This is
cooked and into it is poured liquid butter or curds.
Raisins and sugar are mixed in also. But such is available
only to the wealthy, for rice cannot be grown in the cold
uplands of Tibet, and has to be brought over many passes
and plains to the Tibetan household.

Soup may be kept in jars. I have in my possession an
iron soup jar, damascened with silver and gold. It is
several hundred years old, and was probably made in or
near Der-ge in eastern Tibet.

Tibet obtains her supply of salt within her own borders.
The main supply is gathered from the saline deposits
round the lakes in the Northern Plains; a lesser amount
from other parts of the country, including a number of
salt wells on the banks of the Mekong at Tsa-ka-lho.
It is not pure table salt, such as we use, and is somewhat
bitter. But Indians and Tibetans regard it as more
nutritious and wholesome than our salt. They always
give it to animals in preference, and the Gurkhas and
Sikkimese, as well as the Tibetans, prefer it for their own
consumption.

There is a species of hornet in Sikkim, known as *lin-
göm*, which is said to eat wasps and to drink the water of the
Teesta river only, eschewing that from other sources.
The larvae, fried in butter, when prepared by an under-

---

[1] རྒྱ་ཐུག་ (*Gya-tuk*).

[2] བོད་ཐུག་ (*Pö-tuk*).

standing cook, have a slight but pleasant flavour. In Sikkim, indeed, they were esteemed as a great delicacy, and were reserved for the royal household, nobody else being allowed to eat them.

Radishes are largely consumed in Tibet, and turnips by the poorer classes of the community. Green vegetables are grown but sparingly, for the climate is against them. The Chinese and semi-Chinese are the chief growers of such vegetables; they are sold here and there in the Tibetan shops, and eaten mainly by the gentlefolk, somewhat less by prosperous merchants, and least of all by ordinary people. Potatoes are grown and are eaten to some extent by all classes. Those who can afford rice usually take their potatoes and other vegetables with it.

A large amount of wheat is grown in the warmer districts, but the chief Tibetan grain food is barley, which is eaten in the form of barley-flour (*tsam-ba*). The grain is first washed. After this it is fried, rolled in a bag, and winnowed. It is then ready to be ground in a water-mill, if available; otherwise in a hand-mill. There are so many rushing streams which can be easily tapped, that water-mills are plentiful in many parts of Tibet.

The flour is eaten out of a wooden bowl which the Tibetan carries in the fold of his gown. With the barley-flour he mixes tea, butter, and cheese, kneading them together with his fingers. This, with meat, forms his staple food. Butter is one of the main products of Tibet, a country in which cattle so greatly abound. The amount of butter eaten is, to our ideas, enormous.

I have mentioned above that meat is kept for five years. Grain keeps good for at least a hundred years, and possibly for much longer. Given a granary with good ventilation, the cold, dry climate of Tibet does the rest. I visited the Pa-lha village one day with Pa-lhe-se. Though the Pa-lha house, his family mansion, was half destroyed by the fighting in the British Expedition to Lhasa in 1904, yet the granaries could still be seen. There was one room thirty feet long by five broad and twelve feet in height, with five other rooms of about the same size opening out of it, thus: *a*, *b*, *c*, *d*, and *e* are small holes about two and a half feet square; *f* is open, there

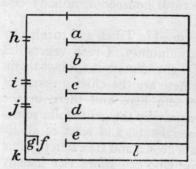

being no wall here; *g* is a hole in the floor to admit ventilation; *h*, *i*, and *j* are holes low down in the outside wall for the same purpose. The floor is of beaten stone, dry and hard. The grain was thrown in loose from the top, and was extracted, when required, through the holes *a*, *b*, *c*, &c., and so through the entrance *f* and the door *k* in the outer wall. *k* was kept locked and sealed, the seal being known as 'the white seal' (*kar-tam*), i.e. that which must be kept pure and intact. The room *l* was used for storing charcoal; its floor was unbeaten and soft.

Each of the six grain-rooms contained eighteen hundred cubic feet of space, that is nearly eleven thousand altogether. It was full of grain during the Expedition of 1904, and indeed there was more grain stored in other rooms. Other large Tibetan houses have similar granaries. The grain keeps good in them, so Pa-lhe-se maintains, for two hundred years. Prosperous farmers store their surplus in the fat years. It can, therefore, be understood that there is a large reserve of food grains in Tibet, which is safe from the danger of a serious famine, except when there is a marked succession of crop failures. In times of scarcity the tenants borrow grain from their landlords.

I was subsequently informed by two members of the Supreme Council, Shap-pes Kung-tang and Sam-trup Po-trang, that the best way of storing grain in Tibet is to make the floor of copper with ventilators underneath. So arranged, grain is said to have been preserved for one thousand years. Round the Yam-dro lake, as they asserted, were a number of places where grain had been kept successfully for several hundred years.

. Maize is grown in the lowest and warmest districts. The Chinese from Szechwan and Yunnan eat rice, for it is to them almost a necessity of life, but Tibetans take it only if their purses permit. It is expensive, as it has to be imported from afar on the backs of animals and men. A large quantity comes from Nepal, an even larger from Bhutan.

In January 1910 I went to Pu-na-ka and made a treaty with Bhutan on behalf of the British Government, a treaty stipulating that Great Britain should not interfere in the internal administration of Bhutan, and that, in its foreign affairs, Bhutan should be guided by the advice of the British Government. Our party returned in February. It was cold in the high mountains; the dark forest of hemlock and fir, and the rhododendron—not only tangled bushes, but trees fifty feet high—barred out the weakly sun of winter. As we trudged through the heavy snow towards one of the passes, the sturdy Bhutanese official, who conducted us, produced as a refresher a spherical mass of fried rice and honey, of the size of a football. This he cut into chunks and distributed to us. A nutritious lump, no doubt, and a not unpleasant flavour. The people of Sikkim carry sticks of sugar cane for a similar purpose and find them refreshing and sustaining on the steep mountain tracks.

Small quantities of barley-flour may be kept in wooden boxes. One in my possession, of dark wood, is flat and circular, thirty inches round the widest circumference. The wealthier classes store thus, and sometimes in cloisonné jars. But for general storage it is kept in sacks, often of yak-hair, rice being kept in yak-skin bags. For daily use the barley-flour is transferred to a small bag (*tsam-kuk*), which may be of coloured cloth, or of white or red leather. The upper classes use silk instead of cloth or leather. The *tsam-kuk* is used everywhere, and figures in a well-known warning against extravagance.

> The good father had a full money bag;
> The bad son uses it as a bag for flour.[1]

[1] Having no money left.

The Tibetans, of Lhasa at any rate, are fond of cakes and biscuits. The Chinese confectioners there are especially good at making them, and the Tibetans eat large quantities of them, more particularly at festivals and picnics, which last throughout the day and necessitate meals in the open air.

Vast is the number of yaks and cross-breeds and ordinary cattle. They abound not only on the Northern Plains and their fringes, not only on the elevated plateaux of western Tibet, but throughout the country. So milk and butter are plentiful and cheap. The consumption of butter is on the most generous scale, and must no doubt help the Tibetan in his fight against the cold climate. The temperature may be below zero, a gale sweeping over the plain. He has no fireplace or chimney in his house, no great facilities for heating water. So he needs fatty products in his food, and takes them.

Though he eats largely of butter, taking it even in his tea, there is still plenty left over. Of cheese he makes large quantities. Still there is more. This surplus goes mainly to the temples. A row of lamps on the altar, each with its little wick floating in butter, is a religious offering as a sacrifice or prayer, perhaps for the soul of a departed relative. These lamps are found everywhere in Tibet; the quantity of butter consumed in them must be immense. In every temple you will find a number of these lamps, wide shallow bowls of silver or copper on elevated stems. When the days of high festival come round, myriads of them are exposed. Nowadays candles are imported into Tibet, but a candle is never burnt on a Tibetan altar.

In other ways also butter is used in the religious services of Tibet, and there is a tendency to mould it into decorative forms. Most of all is this found in the festival known as 'The Offerings of the Fifteenth', which takes place during the night of the fifteenth day of the first Tibetan month. This falls during the last half of February or first half of March. In Lhasa it is a great and interesting ceremony. The large monasteries, the Ministers of State, and others make offerings of butter, eighty or ninety offerings in all. Each is in the form of a triangular wooden frame, forty to sixty feet in height, with a sharp apex. On the frame is stretched a covering of leather, and on this are figures, pictures, &c., all of butter, painted in various colours, and often covered with gold leaf. On each side of the frame is an ascending dragon; in the middle a circular flower or wheel, usually red. Below are figures, in groups and alone. The whole is elaborately and tastefully designed, and the figures are carefully moulded. And all are made of butter.

Over the greater part of Tibet there is not much fruit; it is too cold. There is more in the eastern districts, which lie lower and nearer China. Apricots and walnuts are grown largely in these eastern tracts; those in Lhasa seem to come mostly from Kong-po. Peaches grow in the warmest places and are favourites. Rhubarb grows wild and is of various kinds, some of great height. One species on the Sikkim-Tibet frontier stands gaunt and alone among the rocks, like nothing so much as a sentry at his post. Mushrooms, too, there are of many kinds. The rhubarbs and mushrooms are favourites also.

A variety of mushroom grows at Yum-tang, in the upper part of the La-chung Valley in Sikkim. A day is fixed each year for plucking it, and all turn out then to gather as many as they can. Some have to be reserved for the ruler of Sikkim, and sent to him.

Strawberries and raspberries grow wild, but are not much regarded. Raisins are imported and sold in the Lhasa shops. Fruits, nuts, and the like are laid out for sale in shallow trays and baskets. These are placed both in the shops and outside in the street on trestle tables and empty boxes. A woman will be in charge, or perhaps a small girl.

In the house fruit is usually placed inside china cups, but on the tables of the wealthy it may be found in lacquer bowls, on dishes of jade, or in deep-set trays of enamelled copper, resting one on the top of the other. A pair of the latter in my collection are enamelled white inside. On the outside they are enamelled in various colours, especially blue, showing pictures of fruits, flowers, the eight Auspicious Signs, &c. Such trays may be used both for fruit and for serving picnic lunches. They are of Chinese make. The three Chief Ministers gave me this pair when my son was born. For in Tibet, as in India, the birth of a son means more than in Europe.

Walnuts labour under a disadvantage in Bhutan, for there is in that country a superstition that any one who plants a walnut tree dies as soon as it bears fruit. But if it seeds itself, he is of course free from ill effects. And certainly walnuts in Bhutan are both numerous and excellent. The people of Sikkim have a similar superstition regarding jack-fruit trees. Tibetans of all grades grow and eat walnuts: the women and children are especially fond of them.

Oranges grow bounteously in Sikkim, where they may be bought at the rate of thirty for a penny. But transport of such a fruit is costly, and so in many parts of Tibet they are not seen. In Lhasa they are a rare delicacy, making their appearance chiefly at the New Year festivities in February.

One morning in early February I was riding beyond the Dre-pung Monastery, four miles from Lhasa, when I met a Bhutanese bringing from his country a few loads of oranges, pears, and rice, the first two packed in boxes, the last in cowhide bags. He was taking them to the Bhutanese ambassador in Lhasa,[1] who would present them to the Tibetan authorities.

During the New Year oranges, pears, and other fruit, cakes, one or two bricks of tea, and a big heap of butter are kept by the gentry (*ku-tra*) on tables in their large reception rooms, known as *tsom-chen*, i.e. 'the great assembly'. In another part of the room, where the beer jugs are kept, sugar and wheat and beer are set out. These

[1] *Druk Lo-cha-wa.*

all form a good omen (*tem-dre*) for the year just beginning.
For the first three days at least they must not be consumed; after that it is permitted to do so.

A poor man puts out his omen on the same lines,
though of course in much smaller degree. Having no
'great assembly' room in his cottage or farm, he arranges
the little omen in his chapel.

During my year in Lhasa I was to become well acquainted with the park known as the Park of the Priest
Officials (*Tse-trung ling-ka*), for in it, out in the open, I
gave a theatrical entertainment to my Tibetan friends
lasting for three days. Each summer during the eighth
Tibetan month (September-October) all the priest officials
in Lhasa, numbering about one hundred, entertain themselves in this park. They invite also as guests a few secular
officials, including the Treasurers (*Chang-dzö*) and the
Paymasters (*Po-pön*), who are taken from both the secular
and the ecclesiastical branches of officialdom. No women
come; the priest officials must hold themselves apart from
women.

The party assembles at about nine in the forenoon An
hour later they receive three or four bowls of soup. During
the late afternoon a dinner is given, made up of twenty to
twenty-five dishes. Should there be so many present that
the food prepared for this large dinner will not suffice for
all, then those in the lowest ranks receive each ten bowls
of simpler food. The latter menu is known as the 'Six
Cups and Four Plates'. It provides six bowls of rice
mixed with meat, eggs, dried fish from China, &c., and
to these it adds four plates, shaped like saucers and carrying different kinds of vegetables. Between the two meals
the priests amuse themselves with games of dice (*ba* and
sho), and act plays.

This entertainment is carried on daily for eleven days.
A fund is provided for meeting the cost, but it is insufficient. Two of the priests act as hosts, and pay the
balance. Each year a fresh pair serve in this capacity.

The secular officials (*trung-kor*) stationed in Lhasa feast themselves for seven days. Their fund also has to be supplemented by contributions from individual *trung-kors*. These latter amuse themselves on the same lines as do their priestly colleagues, but for them there is also dancing and singing contributed by the waitresses. The four members of the Supreme Council (*Shap-pe*) are invited for one day to each entertainment.

At the 'Treasurer's Park' (*Chang-dzö Ling-ka*) the gentlefolk of Lhasa, ladies as well as men, are entertained during seven days in the fifth Tibetan month (June-July), and again for ten days in the eighth month (September-October). A few are invited during each day, and the whole community is thus dealt with. Part of the cost is met from Government funds and part is defrayed by the officers in charge of the Lab-rang Treasury (*Lab-rang Chang-dzö*) in Lhasa. There are three such Treasurers, two priests and one layman. Each year in turn one of them pays the balance from his own money.

Their guests may number forty or so each day, and come between ten and twelve in the forenoon. A light meal of soup and vegetables is given at about one o'clock. At five or thereabouts commences the chief feast, long and substantial. It ends two hours later. Then, after a cup or two of tea, all depart to their homes in the gathering dusk.

From the Treasury in the Potala (*Tre-de Chang-dzö*) a similar outpouring of hospitality is expected. And so it is with most of the other public offices in Lhasa. All must entertain yearly, during summer or early autumn, after a prescribed pattern.

The members of the Supreme Council feast the landowners and large merchants living in Lhasa, and their ladies also. Their entertainment continues for seven days. Most guests come for one day only, but specially favoured ones are invited for a second, and even for a third. The cost is defrayed in part from certain governmental receipts, e.g. the sale of marsh grass, but in the main from the pockets of the Councillors themselves.

Nor do the Dalai Lama's Grand Secretaries (*Trung-yik Chem-po*) escape. They, too, must extend hospitality for several days. On one of these they entertain the members of the Supreme Council. One of the Secretaries acts as host and pays the expenses. The following year another takes his turn. The cost is heavy, no doubt, but good profits are made in this post.

An official, when promoted, gives feasts to celebrate the event. In fine, the Tibetans are a hospitable people and enjoy giving and receiving entertainments. All classes give them according to their means and opportunities. Even the peasantry entertain their friends and neighbours occasionally. But their resources are limited, and their work heavy, even during the winter, when weaving, stitching, and other household tasks take up their time. The official New Year in February affords a welcome break, as does the agricultural New Year in December.

When I was in Lhasa the Dalai Lama was taking a little to European food. One October morning an attendant arrived at my house from the palace in the Jewel Park, bearing three or four tomatoes and a few Cape gooseberries (known in India as *tipari*). He was sent to ask me what was the best way to eat them.

One sometimes saw boxes of English sweets being carried up the long trail through Sikkim to the Tibetan plateaux beyond. They keep good for several years in the cold dry air. But Tibetans do not greatly eat sweets. Those who came to Simla and Delhi in 1913 for a diplomatic conference, remaining about nine months, found that, in these warmer climates at least, sweet things were foes to peaceful digestions. They avoided sweet foods and sweet drinks altogether. Their barley-flour and other Tibetan food suited them best.

Other specimen menus for the wealthier classes in Tibet might be quoted. The following are examples of everyday fare.

For breakfast

Barley-flour in balls, meat cooked or raw, eggs, soup

made of barley or wheat (this last in winter as a rule), and vegetables. Soup with macaroni in it is taken only at lunch or dinner.

For lunch

Five or six bowls of soup with macaroni or vermicelli.

Or

Three or four bowls of meat, potatoes and rice, and some vegetables.

Or

Ten or fifteen small meat dumplings (*mo-mo*).

A Tibetan gentleman will often take one of the above three for lunch, but usually with four or five kinds of Chinese vegetables, just a little of each kind. Radishes may be included among these, but not turnips, which are not eaten much by the higher classes in Tibet, except by the children. When eaten, they are taken alone, being regarded as too sweet to be taken with cooked meat. This is a Tibetan lunch, and differs markedly from the expensive Chinese lunches, in which some of the wealthy families indulge. Examples of Chinese lunches, both ordinary and grandiose, have been given above.[1]

If our friend is busy with work, he may not take this meal till five o'clock in the afternoon. In that event he will not have a regular dinner. But otherwise—

For dinner

Two or three bowls of soup with meat either raw or cooked, each bowl holding one and a half to two pints of liquid.

With the vegetable dishes, meat, often fried, is mixed. It is cut up small, so that it can be conveniently eaten with chopsticks.

The food is usually eaten off the small Tibetan tables, two of these being placed together. But some have a larger table, which can be used for meals, as well as for other purposes.

Tea is, of course, drunk at brief intervals throughout

[1] Chapter IX.

the day. With the early morning cup a spoonful of barley-flour may be taken. Some Tibetans believe that, when the stomach is empty, water rises from the liver, and should be pressed down with food and tea. So they call this morsel the 'liver-pressing' (*chin-nön*). Others hold the early morning discomfort to be due to worms rising from the stomach, and find that the hot tea with a pinch of food drives them back again.

The wealthy Tibetan eats his food with a pair of chop-sticks, his poor neighbour with a spoon. The two chopsticks are kept in a wooden case, the outside of which may be painted, or carved, or covered with frog-skin, &c. With them in the case there is a knife which is employed for cutting such meat as is not served in small pieces. An iron vessel, containing a central column heated with char-coal, is sometimes used at meals for keeping warm the meat and vegetables mixed together.

Certain foods are partially or wholly avoided. Fish, being regarded in much the same light as snakes or frogs, are eschewed by many. And there is another reason for this.

I was talking to one of the governors (*dzong-pön*) of Gyangtse district. The conversation turned on pills, of which there are many in Tibet, blessed by high lamas and consequently endowed with magical powers. These are beneficial to the minds and spirits of those who receive them. The small black balls found in some kinds of meat are often termed 'black pills', and these are vastly different in their nature and effect.

'Black pills', said the *dzong-pön*, 'send to hell. These are found in pork, fish, and some fowls and eggs. They are found mostly in pork; in fowls only to a smaller extent. Fowls, by the thousands of worms which they eat, are guilty of the sin of destroying many lives, and so the black flesh forms in them. Pigs to some extent also destroy life, when they nose in the ground. But the chief reason why the black pills form in them is that they must have been guilty of most heinous wickedness in the pre-vious life to have been born as pigs in this life.

'Tibetans do not eat the meat in which such black balls are found, and even try to prevent dogs from eating it, so great is the spiritual harm that results. High lamas avoid these kinds of meat, i.e. pork, fish, fowls, and eggs, altogether, even such as contain no black pills.'

The histories recount examples of holy men who went even farther along the hard pathway of renunciation. A priest in Bhutan, who acted as chaplain to two of the spiritual rulers (Dharma Raja) of that country, 'gave up all solid food, and lived only on milk, flowers, and herbs. He thus obtained the bloom and freshness of countenance, the strength and brilliancy of eye, and the general buoyancy, characteristic of youth'. He was an artist too, being the first to impart to the Bhutanese the art of silk needlework.[1]

An Indian, Vairocana Rakshita, who came to Tibet about the eleventh century, had received 'various secret teachings in the art of living on essences'.[2]

Of a Tibetan lad, Ba-gom, who became a very holy man, we read that during his boyhood 'strife and bloodshed were raging at the time. So his mother thought that it would be safer to let him follow the religious career, as he was the only brother of six sisters'. He was entrusted to a teacher, 'the mother saying that, provided he was not killed, that was quite enough for her'. This young novice became in later life one of the most prominent priests of Tibet, having acquired, among other attainments, the power of sustaining life on small doses of Amrita pills.[3]

[1] Lho-hi Chö-jung, folio 59.   [2] Tep-ter Ngön-po, vol. iv, folio 3.
[3] Ibid., vol. iii, folios 33 and 36.

XXII

DRINKING AND SMOKING

THE chief Tibetan beverage is tea. Indeed, it may be said to be food, as well as drink, for butter is mixed with it, and barley-flour is dipped in the mixture. The men and women of this country consume on an average forty to fifty cupfuls of tea a day, each cup being of the size used by English ladies at afternoon tea. Few drink less than twenty, some as many as eighty cups every day. They often drink a quarter to half of a cup, fill it up,.put the lid on and again drink another mouthful a little later. The cup is always refilled immediately, unless there is going to be a real break in the drinking, either by going out of the house or otherwise.

Even when the peasants go to work in the fields, the teapot or the beer jug accompanies them, carried usually by one of the women. The beer jug, like the teapot, is of earthenware, and often resembles the latter, except that it is larger. As a Tibetan expressed it to me, 'There is no sustained work without tea or beer.'

Of course the component parts of this extensive country vary in tea-drinking as in other respects. Kong-po, for instance, is abstemious. The people of the Tsang province are also abstemious, but make up the deficiency by a largely increased consumption of beer. Tea is expensive in Tsang, beer is cheap, so the menfolk drink more beer. In Lhasa neither the man drinks more tea than the woman, nor the woman than the man, but both equally.

The popularity of this tea, not only in Tibet but in Bhutan also, is attested by the Lho-hi Chö-jung. This Bhutanese history speaks of the visit to Sam-ye of the high lama, who was destined to be the first of the Dharma Rajas, the spiritual rulers of Bhutan. It says:

'Then he visited Sam-ye, where the Chief Tutelary Deity showed him great reverence, edified him with several prophecies of future events, and promised him every aid when they occurred.

And, in particular, he promised to supply tea, that highly esteemed beverage, from the Matsina district of China. As a sign that the promise would be fulfilled, a scent as of white incense [1] filled the air. This must have been the omen which predicted the future popularity of Chinese tea in Bhutan.[2]

Of a truth there is no doubt as to the popularity of this Chinese tea. Not only in Bhutan, but throughout the Himalaya, in Sikkim, Nepal, Lahul, and Ladakh, wherever Tibetans are found, it is their universal delight. Even in Darjeeling, with the far-famed tea of that name at their very doors, the Tibetan population prefer the Chinese tea that has come to them so painfully across their native mountains. It costs more, and they are poor, but they must have it.

And so it was in past generations also. The History of Sikkim tells us that food was cheap there in bygone times. Beef sold for a halfpenny a pound, eggs at three halfpence a dozen, and butter at twopence a pound. 'But for tea and salt everybody had to go up to Pa-ri at least twice a year. Those journeys in those days were no easy matter, since they had to cross all the streams on cane bridges, which were built only twice a year.'

The tea leaves—and twigs—that come from China compressed into the shape of bricks, differ no doubt considerably from the tea leaves that we know in Europe and America. And the method of preparing the tea in Tibet differs so widely from our methods that the actual tea as drunk bears but little relation to the beverage that we know and esteem.

You take a handful of leaves and twigs off a brick, put it into a cauldron with cold or cool water, and add a small quantity of the soda (*pü-to*) that is found as a white powder on the ground here and there, often by the margins of lakes, and mainly on the highlands of the Northern Plains and western Tibet. The soda helps to draw out the colour.

---

[1] Comes from India. Probably a white sap which exudes from the sal tree, and is used by Hindus in the burning of corpses.
[2] Lho-hi Chö-jung, folio 17.

Kitchen utensils. Left, saucepans and teapots ; right centre, wooden
tea churn and dasher ; water bucket on right

Tea shop in Lhasa. Tea bricks on shelf. Sacks, containing bricks, below

Huge cauldrons in which tea is boiled for the monks during the 'Great Prayer' festival in Lhasa

If you cannot by any means obtain it, you may substitute wood ash. Water, soda, and tea leaves are boiled together.

When thoroughly boiled, the mixture is taken out with a ladle and poured through a strainer into a churn (*cha-dong*). The ladle is usually of brass or copper, the strainer of these metals, or of bamboo. Butter and salt are added and the whole churned until it is well mixed. It looks then like *café au lait*. Nomads sometimes add milk to the butter and are thus enabled to economize in the latter, which is one of their chief sale products.

After churning, the tea is poured off into an earthenware pot (*dza-ma*), and thence into a teapot (*ko-til*), which is also usually of earthenware. It is then ready for drinking. Or it may be transferred direct from the churn into the teapot. The tea that remains over in the cauldron, unchurned, is ladled out into the *dza-ma*, to be prepared later on as required.

The tea leaves of India and Ceylon cannot be treated in this way; the result is something bitter and unwholesome. The Tibetan beverage, indeed, resembles soup rather than tea as we know it. It is drunk by ordinary people in the little wooden bowls that every Tibetan carries in his gown. The butter forms a scum on the surface; this you blow aside before drinking. When but little tea is left in the bowl, the Tibetan adds barley-flour to it, and moulds it with his fingers into little balls. To Europeans the Tibetan tea seems an unpleasant concoction, but it is not as unpalatable as it looks, and it is safe to this extent, that the water is thoroughly boiled. Of its nutritive value there can be no doubt.

The butter scum is thrown into the 'grease pot'. Poor people may take it out again, and use it as butter with their tea.

It may well be imagined that the consumption of tea in the monasteries, containing a thousand monks and upwards, is enormous. For the boiling, huge cauldrons are employed. Some are made of copper, some of bell metal, while others are said to be blended of five or six different metals, among which are copper, brass, and iron.

The monks of the large monastery at Gyangtse have sports every autumn. A walk through their camp showed the cauldrons in which the tea was boiled. They were truly capacious and were fixed in the ground. The water for them was drawn from the irrigation channels near the encampment, and was very dirty. Near the cauldrons stood a number of copper teapots, on the rims of which prayers had been carved by the persons who presented them to the monastery. Large as the cauldrons were, those used in the great monasteries near Lhasa are many times larger, as are those used in the festival known as 'The Great Prayer' (*Mön-lam Chem-po*), which is observed during February-March in Lhasa and lasts for about three weeks. Many years ago a monk fell into one of these cauldrons when drawing out the tea—an unpleasant death.

The different kinds of tea consumed in Tibet, and the patient methods of transporting it through this mountainous land, have been described above.[1]

Those who cannot afford to buy tea have perforce to put up with substitutes, seeking something that will darken the water and give it a slightly astringent taste. In Sikkim the Tibetans and Lepchas use the leaves of the maple tree (*Acer caudatum*), known to Tibetans as *Ya-li Shing*, to Nepalese as *Kapashi*. Some ashes are put in a bamboo jar with a small hole in the bottom of it. Cold water is poured on these and leaks through the hole. The water thus soaked in ashes is mixed with the maple leaves, which are then dried. When making the tea from these, salt is added.

Teapots are of earthenware or metal, copper, brass, &c. The general shape is the same throughout Tibet. On the top is a narrow neck, widening out into a large globular body, which in turn draws in to a somewhat small base. The lid is secured by a chain to the handle.

[1] See p. 121.

Among the metal teapots many are of copper. One in my possession had belonged to the Ten-gye-ling Monastery in Lhasa, whose goods were confiscated by the Tibetan Government and sold after its head was convicted of attempting to kill the Dalai Lama by witchcraft. The teapot is of copper with brass bands. Another, an old one from Lhasa, is of brass, quite plain. Another, of copper, is covered with elaborate cloisonné work on the outside. The wealthy often have bands of silver or gold on their teapots.

Among these utensils, as in so many articles of metal ware, the finest ornamentation comes from Der-ge and Bhutan. One from Bhutan represents flowers on its lid, and four of the senses on its neck—a bell for sound, a pot of ointment for smell, a vessel containing food for taste, a mirror for sight. Had touch been added, clothing might have been shown. On the body are four dragons and the Eight Lucky Signs; below these a pair of mythological animals (*shang shang*) with the wings and feet of birds but in other bodily details resembling human beings. Below these is a circlet of leaves. The base is of brass with a silver rim.

A metal teapot with its decorative display is used only on ceremonial occasions, e.g. at the New Year, that time of high festivity. A marriage ceremony, too, may call it into use, as may the entertainment of an important guest, or one who has come from a distant place.

On everyday occasions people, both rich and poor, use earthenware pots, because they keep the tea warmer and it tastes better in them. The well-to-do sometimes have their earthenware teapots lacquered on the outside to improve their appearance.

For a teacup the Tibetan uses his small wooden eating bowl (*por-pa*), which he carries in the ample overlap at the waist of his gown. This will probably be from three to five inches in diameter across the top. Some of the bowls are credited with the power of detecting poison, a mode of attack that cannot safely be disregarded.

I have three such bowls in my collection. They are all cut from one of the excrescences that grow on certain hardwood trees, e.g. maples. Such an excrescence is known as *ba*, which means goitre, for it is like the goitre on the neck of an afflicted neighbour. A kindred goitre grows also on the *sisnu* nettle, the kind whose fibre is so strong. In both cases it is regarded as a gem (*nor-bu*). It shines at night. One is large enough to make a small bowl, and such a bowl has the power of proclaiming the presence of poison. If any one inserts poison, it breaks. Some believe this, but others disbelieve.

Among the cynics there are those who know and use the turquoise remedy. When you find you have swallowed poison, you should swallow also one of the small Tibetan turquoises—the more valuable the better. This drives out the poison. The turquoises that come from India do not have the same effect. The Tibetan variety used to be found in the mountain known as Mount Ha-po, near Sam-ye. It is believed that the Precious Teacher (Padma Sambhava) put them there. He lived on the mountain and at Sam-ye for a long time. A few turquoises are still found there, though it is forbidden nowadays to take them out.

The poison-detecting cups are used by laymen, not by monks. Some have rings round the bottom of the inside, an additional attraction.

Well-to-do people use china cups; those who are wealthy may have cups of jade. Cups of china and jade have stands and lids of brass, silver-gilt, &c. These help to keep the tea warm in the cold Tibetan houses. Jade cups also are believed by some to have the power of detecting poison. In any case it benefits the health to drink out of them.

The water of Lhasa, except that used by the Dalai Lama, which comes from the spring under the Iron Hill, is not good. It is accounted heavy (*jik chem-po*), causing pains in the temples and toothache rather than bowel complaints. Those who are accustomed to it, having lived in Lhasa during their childhood, escape these ill effects, but if they go away for a long time they feel it for a month or two after their return. The water at Pa-ri is notorious, and indeed the water on the Tibetan plains is often hard, discoloured, unattractive; but in the deep, wooded valleys soft and pleasant.

But whether the water be hard or soft, dirty or clean, the Tibetan prefers tea or beer. 'Let us drink beer and be happy!' is a common saying among the manual toilers. The beer is made from barley as a rule, but in some of the lower valleys from buckwheat also, or from a mixture of the two. As made in the Chumbi Valley, the process is somewhat as follows. The barley is washed, put into hot water, and kept over the fire for an hour or two. It is then strained through a bamboo basket, laid out in mats on the ground, and allowed to cool partially. A little yeast is mixed, and it is put into jars covered with cloth, where it ferments for a few days. The longer it is kept thus, the more intoxicating it becomes. The preparation is now complete; the beer can be taken as wanted. It is necessary only to warm it again, put it into a bamboo jar, and pour hot water on it. Then it is ready to drink. A spirit (*a-rak*) is distilled from beer; the people favour it as a warmth-giver when crossing high passes. Men and women drink beer equally, but the use of *a-rak*, warming, but too potent, is less among the women.

I have mentioned above that among the two provinces of central Tibet, Tsang, the western, drinks more generously of beer than Ü, the eastern. Tea and butter are less plentiful in Tsang, while barley is abundant. It may seem strange that butter should be more scarce, for the western province has the greater area of grazing land. But its advantage in this respect is more than annulled by administrative order which prescribes that the land tax due from Tsang to the central Government at Lhasa shall be largely remitted in butter.

It is customary to give beer to actors on the stage, a custom which I was careful to observe in the theatrical entertainment which I gave to my friends in Lhasa. Once every hour or so, the actors partook of this, coming just off the stage to drink it. The stage was merely an open-air space in one of the parks, floored with rough paving and covered by a tent awning.

Some of the Tibetan beer jugs are very handsome. The best come from Der-ge. They are of damascene work, silver and gilt on an iron base; their shape flat or cylindrical. These are used for giving beer at entertainments, and for offerings in the temples on behalf of those who suffer agonies from starvation in one of the hells. Others are used for picnics and on journeys. Some of the types are rare and highly prized, being of a fine craftsmanship that cannot be equalled now. For these are shrunken times, when the influence of Gotama Buddha has passed the half of its allotted span, and, like the half-time moon, diminishes more and more.

In Sikkim, a land of forests, wooden beer jugs find favour; among other varieties from the tree *Bohmeria rugulosa*, whose wood is dark red and heavy with fine medullary rays.

The use of tobacco, especially cigarettes, is nominally prohibited in Tibet. The History of Bhutan, when recounting the laws laid down by the first Dharma Raja and the crimes against which those laws were directed, fulminates against it in no uncertain terms.

'Besides these, there is one evil custom which is the forerunner of the Tempter himself. It is spreading among the general population as well as among the garrison forces and the bodyguards of the Dharma and Deb Rajas. This is the unceasing use of the evil, stinking, poisonous weed named tobacco. The smoke from this drug defiles the sacred objects of worship, the Images, the Books, the Relics. It weakens the Gods above, causes fighting among the Spirits of the Middle Air, and injures the Serpent Spirits below. From this cause arises an endless cycle of epidemics, wars, and famines in the human world. Several prophetic injunctions on this subject have been left by the great Teacher, Padma Sambhava.

'All State officials, Governors of districts, Secretaries, Delegates, and others must make strict inquiries within their own jurisdictions

as to who deal in this drug or smoke it, and must take them to task
for it. If they fail to do so, they themselves will be punished severely.
Those officers who are stationed in the plains on the borders of
India, must prohibit the importation of this article at its very source,
the markets in the plains.' [1]

The prohibition still continues, but it is not found
possible to enforce it on all classes throughout the country.
As with other laws, the observance is stricter in the vicinity
of Lhasa. I asked one of the Dalai Lama's Secretaries why
smoking is prohibited. He replied, 'When people indulged in smoking, there was a serious outbreak of illness. Further inquiry showed that the Spirits of Tibet disliked the smell and caused the illness. So smoking was
forbidden.' Others confirmed this.

Yet many, very many, of the laity smoke the Chinese
pipe with the long stem and diminutive bowl, which is
smoked out in half a dozen whiffs. It is against cigarettes
that the prohibition is strongest. What is in a name?
Indeed, in this name there is much, and it is altogether
bad. For Tibetans pronounce the word 'cigarette' as
shik-re. *Shik* means 'demolish', as of a building; *re* means
'tear', as of a cloth. Truly a word of ill omen, which
denotes that by the use of cigarettes their religion will be
destroyed.

Among the hill peoples of Darjeeling and Kalimpong,
Gurkhas, Tibetans, and Lepchas, cigarette smoking is
lamentably heavy. These are under British-Indian rule,
and there is no restriction. All smoke cigarettes, men and
women, small boys and small girls. But in Sikkim and
Tibet, States under their own rulers, cigarettes are strongly
discouraged. In Sikkim such smoking is on a far smaller
scale; in Tibet, central Tibet at any rate, it is extremely
rare.

Priests are altogether forbidden to smoke, though some
do so in secret. The prohibition, curiously enough, is
stronger among the unreformed Red Hats than among the

---

[1] Lho-hi Chö-jung, folio 107.

more austere Yellows. For it is said that Padma Sambhava forbade smoking, but the Buddha did not.

The herdsmen of some parts smoke the metal pipe (*kang-sa*); in other parts abstain from it. A friend of mine who was Governor of the Nam-ling district north of Shigatse for three years, told me that there were many tents of nomads there, and most of them found solace in their pipes.

It is of a herdsman that the story is told about the religious disputations, which are held during the New Year in Lhasa and are conducted with a certain studied vehemence. Attending one of these, a man from the Northern Plains heard much animated talk about *kang-sa*, a word which also denotes an animate being, i.e. that which becomes full (*kang*) and then decays (*sa*). He came on the morrow, and heard more vehement discussion about *kang-sa*. As it was still in progress on the third day, he could stand it no longer, and, offering his tobacco pipe, he said, 'Sirs! Be at peace; take mine!'

The tobacco is mainly imported from India, and in a lesser degree from China, as well as small quantities from Nepal, Sikkim, and Bhutan. Some of the people, especially in the districts round Lhasa, do not smoke tobacco. They smoke rhubarb instead, and comfort their consciences with the thought that, though tobacco is sinful, rhubarb is not. But the greater part mix tobacco with the rhubarb.

The upper classes do not usually buy the smoking mixture for their pipes in the shops, as it is mixed with sand and dirt. The species of rhubarb which they buy is known as *cho-lo*. After cleaning this and the barley beer that is added to it, they make up their smoking mixture themselves. This *cho-lo* is exported from the districts south of Lhasa over a large part of Tibet. Women do not smoke, except those in Chinese households.

In the form of snuff, tobacco is frequently taken. This was formerly permitted even to monks. During recent years the Dalai Lama has forbidden its use, and some officials have sold their beautiful little Chinese snuff-bottles, often of jade, with a coral stopper and a gold spoon.

But snuff is still taken on a large scale. Many of the monks take it, for the prohibition is not strictly enforced. The women in the towns as a rule avoid it, for they are better dressed than the country women and are keen on the elegancies of life. But the village women, especially those who are elderly, take it, for they do not care about these things. All hold that, when there is a pain in the temples, a common ailment, it may be caused by a small insect in the nose. And this is killed by snuff.

The tobacco for ordinary snuff is ground up locally between two stones; the best medicinal snuff comes from China. Ordinary folk keep their supply in horns of goat or ram; the wealthy ones use snuff bottles from China, delicate little creations, in which the neat artistry of that country finds characteristic expression.

XXIII

CEREMONIAL AND ETIQUETTE

FREE as the life in Tibet seems to be with its large, untenanted areas, yet it is restrained everywhere by rule. In no respect is this more pronounced than in the social conventions that ease and gladden human intercourse. Nothing exposes a Tibetan to greater contempt than the saying, 'He knows not the Way nor the Custom.'[1] From their earliest years the children are taught how to behave. And so it comes that the Tibetan, from prince to peasant, has an innate courtesy in both action and speech. In former days, when their Government was actuated by feelings of suspicion and anger towards Europeans and Americans, this courtesy may have been less marked, and at times interrupted. But that, too, showed the working of rule. For myself, whenever I have competed in the courtesies of conversation with a Tibetan gentleman, I have been almost invariably defeated. They are adepts.

When larger affairs are in progress, due ceremony must be observed. It has always been so. In the History of Sikkim compiled by the late king of that country, Tu-top Nam-gyal, and his queen, Ye-she Dröl-ma, it is recorded that a former king and his son, saying farewell to the Regent of Tibet, were handed the parting scarves of ceremony by the latter's Secretary instead of by the Regent himself. The young prince judged the matter to be of such importance that he made an immediate protest, whereupon the Regent himself gave the scarves. 'Upon their departure', we are told, 'the Regent took this incident deeply to heart, and thought that, if the Chiefs on the borders were to increase in power, there was no certainty that they might not rebel.' And so he set the Black Art to work against the Ruler of Sikkim with the result that, 'The death of this prince and the chain of mishaps to the

[1] Lam Luḳ-sö shing-kyi-ma-re.

other members of the king's family are attributed to those acts of sorcery.'

The first Dharma Raja of Bhutan had great difficulty in establishing his claim against a rival priest. A local magnate tried to establish friendship between them. It was necessary to persuade the Dharma Raja that he was being treated as on an equality, and of this the outward sign is usually found in seats of equal height. So this intermediary invited both to a great feast.

'He laid the seats of the rivals equal in height and overlaid with silks and embroidery to an equal extent. But inside there was much difference, namely, in the materials of the mattresses used. The Dharma Raja came to know this without being told, and exposed the trick by sending his Secretary to examine it. This inspired the De-ba (the intermediary) with fear at the uncommon acumen of the youthful Hierarch, and his unworthy trick having been thus exposed, he was crestfallen, and the attempt at reconciliation failed.' [1]

Had the Dharma Raja sat on the seat which, though of equal height, had inferior material below it, he would have suffered greatly in reputation.

The History of Sikkim, referred to above, shows the importance of granting ceremonial rights to secure the allegiance of unwilling subjects. Speaking of Nepalese dwellers in Sikkim who had rebelled and been defeated, it records that,

'Some were given grand presents and the privilege of having kettle-drums beaten, of bearing banners and flags according to their rank and position, so as to gain their loyalty and friendship. Thus for a time everything was quiet and the land enjoyed peace.'

The ceremony of laying the foundation of a building seems to have been followed in Tibet long ago. It was during the latter half of the eighth century of the Christian era that Sam-ye, the first large Buddhist monastery in Tibet, was built by Padma Sambhava, the great Indian teacher. The Tibetan king, Ti-song De-tsen, 'having put on clothes of white silk and fastened on himself a golden

1 Lho-hi Chö-jung, folio 17.

axe, dug the foundation in the ground. At the distance of one cubit below the ground the earth cracked, revealing white, yellow, and red soil which was perfect when tasted'.[1]

In high ceremonial presents are given lavishly. The gifts received from Tibet by a young king of Sikkim at his coronation form an imposing list. They included a dress, waistband, pouch, and pantaloons, all of silk, an official hat, and red cloth top-boots with silk needlework of divers colours. Bow and arrows, a sword, and a match-lock with a powder pouch. A horse with an ornamental saddle and bridle, silks and blankets, money, bricks of tea, and so forth. And a large white silk scarf.

The third on the roll of Dalai Lamas, though the first to receive that title, travelled in Mongolia and converted many to the Buddhist faith. He was received everywhere with ceremony, and this was accompanied by numberless gifts, horses and sheep, gold, silver, and silk.[2]

One of the central features of Tibetan life is the *ka-ta*, the scarf of ceremony. It is of loosely woven silk, usually white, and at each end is a fringe of silk threads. Varying greatly as it does in size and quality—there are eight gradations of quality—the price ranges from one or two pounds down to one or two pence. For rich and poor, all must use it. So this kind of scarf, made in Szechwan, is exported in vast quantities to Tibet.

When visiting at the house of an acquaintance you give him a *ka-ta* and receive one in return. Friends, who meet by chance anywhere after a prolonged absence from each other, exchange these scarves. At the time of asking a favour, a *ka-ta* accompanies the request and supports it. When returning thanks for a favour received, a *ka-ta* serves to emphasize the feeling of gratitude. A letter or verbal message of congratulation is similarly accompanied. When I was made a C.M.G., my friends in Sikkim

---

[1] Folio 35 of a Tibetan history, ascribed to the fifth Dalai Lama. Its abbreviated title may be rendered *A Feast of Pleasure for the Perfected Youths*.

[2] Biography of Sö-nam Gya-tso, folio 94.

hastened to show their appreciation by presenting me with *ka-tas*.

Even when sending a letter, you cannot simply put it into an envelope and dispatch it. You must enclose something with it, for to send a thing empty is to send bad luck. And you cannot do better than enclose the scarf of ceremony. This need not be so large or of so fine a texture as when presented at an interview, for, as Tibetans say, 'It is but the outer covering.' Still, it betokens purity of motive, and in the letter you may perhaps express the hope that the friendship between you, or between your respective countries, may remain as pure as a knotted silk scarf. The letter will certainly refer to the *ka-ta* in honourable terms, concluding, 'Submitted with a god's robe to support it by so and so on the fifth day of the third month of the Fire-Mouse Year' (or whatever the date may be).

The *ka-ta's* province extends even beyond the bounds of human intercourse. When visiting a chapel and praying to the Buddha or deity there, the Tibetan likes to put a *ka-ta* over the image, throwing it up if the image be a high one.

Indeed, so numerous and so essential are its uses that, wherever they go, wherever they stay, Tibetans always carry a few of these ceremonial scarves with them.

As the *ka-tas* differ from each other, so do the modes of presenting them. The gradations of rank must be scrupulously observed. If the recipient is of much higher position than the giver, he remains seated while the other lays the scarf at his feet: if only a little superior, it is placed on the table in front of him. When both are equal, they stand and place their scarves over each other's wrists. In all cases he who offers the *ka-ta* takes it in both hands. Should the giver be of higher position he lays it over the neck of the other, who bows his head to receive it.

When village elders visit an official on occasions of ceremony, e.g. at the New Year, they bring a scarf, but more often two scarves, each. The officer gives a present of cakes (*kap-se*). These are cooked in mustard oil, but if the recipient be of higher grade, butter is used instead of oil. The official gives one scarf with this present, his servant placing it over the neck of the principal elder as the latter leaves the room.

Among the peoples of India it is an exceptional honour to receive a garland round the neck, but the same rule does not apply to the *ka-ta* of Tibet. And thus the foreigner from India has sometimes been misled, not understanding that, when a *ka-ta* was placed round his neck, he was being marked with a status of inferiority.

If the villagers come to prefer a petition, they bring only one scarf and with it meat, eggs, and money, or any of these. The official waves away the present, but it is pressed on him again. At about the third time of offering he may accept it, if he is going to grant the petition. But, if he refuses the petition, he should also finally refuse the present.

When the Dalai Lama himself was the recipient at a public reception, not even the Chinese Amban or the Tibetan Prime Minister presented his *ka-ta* direct. He handed it to the Lord Chamberlain or Chief Secretary in attendance. At private audiences, but not at public receptions, the Dalai Lama insisted on exchanging *ka-tas* with me on a basis of equality, as described below. When a Minister called thus, he came up bowing his head, laid his *ka-ta* on the little table in front of His Holiness, and received a blessing. The Dalai Lama does not give a scarf in exchange or return the one given, when bestowing his blessing, except in a few cases, e.g. a traveller setting out on a journey, a monk who has passed an examination.

When offering a *ka-ta* to some great or holy personage riding on a journey, it is handed by the visitor, bowing low, to his Secretary, who stands by, shows it to his master, and passes it on to a servant.

Tibetan gentlemen bow to each other as they pass on the road. He who is of inferior rank bows the lowest. They do not usually speak to each other or dismount from their ponies, unless they are real friends. Nor is it the Tibetan custom to take off one's hat on such occasions. In their bowing and other such courtesies everything, being well timed, is graceful and has an air of spontaneity. There is no self-consciousness.

All dismount from their ponies or mules if the Prime Minister or one of the members of the Supreme Council (*Shap-pe*) happens to pass along the road. To officials of somewhat lower position the same respect will be paid by those of inferior rank who are acquainted with them.

When one of the gentry comes down the steps of his house, any servants or lesser folk who happen to be coming up have to go down again to the bottom and move away. Formerly, when the Dalai Lama appeared, people had to run away and hide themselves. But this latter custom His Holiness abolished. He dislikes ceremony, though he endures it patiently, and he dislikes giving trouble.

Tibetan gentlemen address their wives generally as 'Honourable Little Wife' (*Cham Chung La*), and speak of them to other persons in the same terms. Occasionally, but not often, they address them by name. They do not use pet nicknames after the English fashion. A Tibetan of Sikkim may say, 'Ta-shi's mother, please come here', Ta-shi being his son's name. But this custom is not followed in central Tibet.

An invitation to dinner or other entertainment is not issued by the hostess, but by the host. It is not sent by letter, but verbally through a servant. Ordinarily the invitation will be for the following day; but if the guest is of high rank, it should be for the next day but one. The servant brings with him a *ka-ta*, which he holds out or lays on the table. This is returned to him.

In diplomatic intercourse also careful rules must be observed. In 1920, a month after I came to Lhasa, the Tibetan National Assembly wrote a letter to the Viceroy of India, asking him to cancel his order for my return to Sikkim and to instruct me to remain on in Lhasa. The deputation that brought this letter to me for transmission to His Excellency was composed of three Grand Secretaries, two Financial Commissioners, an Abbot from each of the powerful monasteries of Se-ra and Dre-pung, and a high representative from the equally important but more distant monastery at Gan-den. The deputation came thus in force, partly to deliver the letter and partly to urge me strongly to support their request and by some means or other to stay in Lhasa. It is indeed the custom for high officials to bring important letters themselves rather than send them by messengers.

Persons of note, Tibetan and foreign, when travelling in Tibetan lands, are met by the local government officials and the village headmen outside the villages through which they pass as well as on the approach to their final destination. The distances to which these emissaries come bearing their scarves of welcome, depend on the traveller's rank and their own, and on any special intimacy between him and themselves.

For instance, when I used to visit Gyangtse, the land agent of my old friend Pa-lhe-se would ride out nine miles to meet me. The uncle and brother of the present king of Sikkim, though they lived several miles on the farther side of Gyangtse, would come nearly as far, for Sikkim also was in my administrative charge. And near to them would be found the two governors of the Gyangtse fort. Some five miles out the British officer in charge of the Indian detachment waited with an escort of mounted infantry; a little farther on the Tibetan military officers with some of their troops, and last of all the Ken-chung, the chief representative of the Tibetan Government in Gyangtse. And always, from Tibetans, the welcoming scarves.

On the way to Yatung our Trade Registration Clerk, a Tibetan with a slight knowledge of English, would meet me at Cham-pi-tang, a staging bungalow, one day's march before Yatung. On one of my visits he informed me that the caretaker of the bungalow had died seven days previously, and that the work was being done by his

Presents of food from Tibetan Government to author
Butter, eggs, and bags of barley-flour, peas, and rice. On the top dried
carcases of sheep

Author, travelling on horseback, receives *ka-tas* from district officials
and village headmen

widow and son, the latter 'a lad of only thirteen ages'.
Very picturesque were some of the Tibetan notables on
the road. Clad from head to foot in enveloping scarlet
robes, which glinted in the strong Tibetan sunlight,
they assumed an aspect, half fascinating, half sinister,
as though the heads of some quiet but relentless
Inquisition.

In Sikkim and Bhutan one was accompanied by bands,
which might include clarinets, cymbals, trumpets, gongs,
and drums. In Bhutan also by dancers, who walk with you
for the last mile or two, turning round occasionally to dance.
On arrival and departure in some of the Bhutanese districts
the honoured traveller may receive a salute from a leather-
bound cannon, which is carried along, as he rides, and
fired from time to time at his riding mule about twenty
yards away. In my case the Governor of western Bhutan
had lent me a mule—named by his own people 'The Virtuous Fox'—which did not seem to mind at all.

I have already alluded to the curious Tibetan custom
which prescribes that when a peasant, shepherd, petty
trader, or the like meets one of higher social position, he
or she puts out the tongue at him. Possibly it originated
as a sign of awe, of utter submission. It may be repeated
at the end of every sentence. If the difference of rank be
great, the head of the one who gives this salute is bowed
forward and his eyes may protrude, while his replies are
brief and uttered in tones as of breathless fear.

On arrival at intermediate stages presents of food are
brought, to help the traveller on his journey. Rice, barley,
barley-flour, peas, meat, and eggs predominate among
the gifts. At Chung-tang in northern Sikkim the headman
of the village and other villagers came with half a bullock as
a present. The shoulder was laid on one side, the legs on
the other, and the head in the middle with the scarf of ceremony arranged on the horns. Farther north in Sikkim the
governor of a Tibetan district crossed the border to present a Tibetan rug, a sheep, a sack of barley-flour, and
a bottle of milk. Presents of food, sent by the Dalai or

CEREMONIAL AND ETIQUETTE

Ta-shi Lamas or by higher officials, would be, of course,
on a much larger scale.

Whether the presents are many or few, they are accompanied by polite expressions of regard. The little speech
of a leading notable to me in 1912, one of many, typifies
the extreme lengths to which these polite eulogies are
carried.

'You have grasped', he said, 'Tibet, Bhutan, and Sikkim, the three countries, in your hand and have increased
their prosperity. As for Tibet you have done great benefits
to the country and especially to the Dalai Lama, its head.
Other Europeans have set out to see his face, taking
elephants and other presents,[1] but have not succeeded in
seeing him. You, without any such preparations, have not
only seen him but have conversed many times with him
face to face. Bhutan you have put into a very good position. And as for Sikkim you live there and are always increasing its prosperity.'

The veriest novice from Europe soon learns to hear
unmerited praise without a smile, and to reply in the more
restrained, but none the less sincere, courtesies of the
West.

In addition to sending me presents of food, &c., each
year that I came to Tibet from Sikkim, the Dalai and
Ta-shi Lamas used to send letters of welcome couched in
very cordial terms. The Prime Minister used to write and
send presents to my wife. When our boy was seven weeks
old, the king and queen of Sikkim called and brought
presents for him, including a pony. The queen, bending
down and placing her forehead on his, prayed for his long
life and happiness. Both presented him with ceremonial
scarves.

The king of Bhutan, on hearing the news of his birth,
wrote that 'We have been so filled with delight that we
felt as if we had discovered a mine'. In the letter from the

---

[1] A reference to Colman Mataulay, who, receiving permission from the
Chinese Government, prepared to take a Mission to Lhasa, but was prevented
by the Tibetan Government from crossing the Sikkim-Tibetan frontier.

Governor of western Bhutan, the king's uncle, I read
that, 'The birth of your son has given us as great pleasure
as the thunder before summer gives to the flies.'

When giving presents on behalf of his Government to
the representative of another country, an official may
describe them as 'the foundation of the road of harmony'.
The expression sounds somewhat mercenary, but is quite
in order.

On arrival at one's final destination in Tibet, whether
Gyangtse, Shigatse, or Lhasa, presents from the Dalai
Lama or Tibetan Government poured in. They were
chiefly of food, e.g. eggs, rice, butter, carcases of sheep,
and peas for our ponies. Few traits are more deeply ingrained in Tibetans than those of courtesy and hospitality.

XXIV

CEREMONIAL AND ETIQUETTE (*continued*)

THE paying and returning of calls is an integral part in the life of the gentry, and is attended with due ceremony. He of lower rank makes the first call; among equals the visitor calls first on the resident.

As to how far, if at all, the host goes to meet the guest, that depends on their respective ranks. If the latter be greatly superior, the host will go outside the door of the house and even beyond to meet him. If slightly superior, it will be sufficient to go to the door of his room. If the guest's rank be far lower than his own, he barely rises from his seat.

The caller brings his presents with him, or, alternatively, some of them, and a list of the remainder. He may preface the giving of them with some depreciatory remark, such as, 'I have really nothing to offer you this time. But even a flower may be offered to the gods. So please accept these things as a sign of friendship.' The mention of the flower refers to the custom of putting flowers on altars.

Self-depreciation is essential to good manners. Perhaps an Englishman, during a call on a Tibetan gentleman, asks whether Tibet is a large country. The latter will usually reply that it is of middling size. He means that it is large, but it would offend the canon of good taste that he should praise any of his own possessions, even his own country.

The visitor, if of lower position, may be slow to take one of the better, i.e. higher, seats in the room, implying his unworthiness to occupy it. He may be slow, too, to take the light refreshment offered him with the unfailing tea. It is accounted good manners to refuse at first, but the guest expects to be urged further, and will take it at the second or third offer. Europeans and Americans should be patient in such a case; there is no hustle in Tibetan social intercourse. Even the Sikkimese, now accustomed to Western ideas, have been known to err in this, not offering a second time food that has been once refused.

Conversation goes forward in somewhat low tones, for Tibetans of all classes habitually speak thus. One of the labouring classes in Sikkim, when addressing his social superior, may put his hand in front of his mouth, to prevent his breath from reaching the other. The low tones, the bent head, and the obstructing hand combine to make hearing difficult.

Calls are usually paid in the forenoon; unless there is some special reason, it is less courteous to come in the afternoon, for the first half of the day, when the sun is ascending, is more auspicious. In any case tea and light refreshments are offered, whatever the hour may be. And wine is also brought, unless the visitor be a priest of the Yellow Hats or other sect whose tenets forbid it.

As to how soon a call should be returned, that, like so much else, depends on the mutual rank and friendliness of the two. The sooner it is returned, the greater is the honour. When I called on the Prime Minister in Lhasa, he said that he would start on his return call ten minutes after I left. But he was old and infirm, and so I prevailed on him to rest awhile and defer it. But he would wait no longer than an hour.

Visitors to Lhasa or Ta-shi Lhün-po give their presents to the Dalai or Ta-shi-Lama at their first interview. If the visitor is a foreigner with official rank, the lama sends him gifts of food, but does not give the regular return presents, porcelain, jade, cloisonné, &c., until the stranger leaves the town, whether a week or a year later. It will be understood that these two Grand Lamas return no calls.

Visits must always be arranged beforehand. This is done verbally through subordinates or servants. Care is taken that the call, especially the first one, is paid on one of the auspicious dates in the Tibetan calendar. That is of great importance. Tibetans attach such high value to omens and signs, that they are unwilling to commence any important work on an inauspicious date. When I visited Lhasa, the Dalai Lama chose a day of good omen for my arrival, and I picked a good one for my departure.

Farmers, petty traders, and the like, calling on officials, bring small presents with them. The latter do not put these presents or their value into the Government treasuries. The Tibetan system of administration permits them to keep the gifts for themselves. They make return presents to the donors, but of lesser value.

In ending a call due ceremony must be observed. The guest may remark, 'Now it is late; I must petition for leave to depart.' [1] His host will press him to stay on, but, with a few polite remarks on either side, he leaves. On departure his host conducts him to the spot at which he met him. The host says, 'Go in peace' (literally, 'Go slowly'). The guest replies, 'Thank you; remain at peace.'

A visitor who has remained overnight in a friend's house gives on his departure gratuities to the servants, including the bailiff or agent for the property.

A stay of long duration in the town of the other will terminate with further calls and exchange of presents. Officials and other friends ride down the road with the outgoing visitor, maybe for several miles. A tent or booth, furnished with the usual mattress-seats (*böl-den*) and tables may be set up a mile or two from the point of departure, and here the party halts for tea and cakes. In Sikkim also the landlords, village headmen, and others invariably offer light refreshments on the road as one passes through their jurisdictions. Small arbours of bamboo, brightened with the flowers of the countryside, tempt the wayfarer to rest a few minutes, while the local notabilities bring the cakes and biscuits of Sikkim, bananas, and the sweet Sikkim oranges. Tea does not figure here, but beer brewed from one of the millets [2] takes its place.

[1] *Gong-pa shü-go.*
[2] Known as *mön-cha, kodo,* and *marua* in Tibetan, Nepalese, and Hindi respectively.

One such arbour comes back to my memory. It was near Den-tam, only four to five thousand feet above sea-level, on the estate of a Lepcha landlord, named Nam-pu. The bower was set out with leaves and flowers, cannas, roses, and the cherry blossom which flourishes here in November. The hill races are all instinctively artistic, and none more so than the Lepchas. Perhaps their close communion with nature in this very beautiful country guides them.

I told Ne-tuk, my orderly, that I wished to congratulate Nam-pu on his pretty arbour. 'Certainly,' replied Ne-tuk, 'but please first drink the beer which he has provided.' On tendering my congratulations, Nam-pu remarked that the arbour was nothing, and smilingly added a polished compliment. One cannot compete in compliments with these people.

At times of parting, the Tibetan, like the people of some other nations, habitually expresses the wish for future reunions. He may say, 'I must petition that we may meet again from time to time.' And thus we say good-bye to each other on leaving Lhasa, though there is no probability that we shall ever meet again. It sounds a lengthy phrase, but in Tibetan it is shorter, '*Rim-pe je chok-ka shü-go*'. As already mentioned, Tibetan sentences are generally much shorter than their English translations.

And always there are courteous words. On my departure from Lhasa the Tibetan Government sent a colonel a hundred and fifty miles of the journey with me. His last words to me were, 'Tibet owes much to you. Do not forget her.'

Tibetan letter-writing is difficult and intricate on account of the ceremonious terms which have to be employed. Each class and occupation should receive its suitable form of address. I have touched on this subject above, when dealing with the education of the children,[1] so will quote only a few instances here.

[1] See p. 205.

A Minister of the Supreme Council, writing his report to the Dalai Lama, may commence it thus:

'To the feet and golden throne of the excellent Dalai Lama, who is the Protector and Unfailing Refuge of all moving beings including the gods.

'This is submitted by the respectful Councillor . . . bowing down to the ground.'

Then follows the report. It may conclude with a word or two of prayer, such as, 'Protect me now and henceforth', 'Keep this petition in the vast expanse of your mind', &c. Then, with the date, it is ended.

A foreigner, ranking equal with a Minister, might begin with the first sentence above, and continue,

'This is submitted by the respectful one. I offer thanks for that Your Holiness' health is steadfast like the King of Mountains by virtue of the accumulated merits gained in countless ages and by virtue of your good deeds which have increased like the stars in the heavens. Here the respectful one is well, and his affairs are going on as usual.'

The business portion of the letter is then written. And in conclusion more words showing respect, such as:

'Please take what is good and abandon what is bad for your health. It is fitting that the Letters of Command should come to this side like the current of a Divine Stream.[1] Know! Know! Know! Know! Know!

'Sent by   on the eighth day of the fourth month of the Wood-Tiger year, an auspicious date.'

To one who is of equal rank with himself a Tibetan (or foreigner) may commence his letter thus:

'To the feet of the excellent   who is highly accomplished, and compassionate, and learned in a hundred kinds of knowledge.

'I thank you for that your honourable health is like the young moon spreading its bright light, and that your affairs are in a prosperous state. Here I also am well and my affairs as usual.'

---

[1] i.e. 'Please write to me often.'

The accompanying gifts and their condition, whether good or defective, may be mentioned in the communication. In a letter to me the Dalai Lama describes his presents thus: 'An undamaged pair of porcelain flower vases from my private property, blue and white, showing clouds and a pair of dragons facing each other. Also, an undamaged pair of antique cloisonné flower vases with designs of apricot blossoms.'

On occasions of high festival, dances and dramas, sports and games, everything is arranged according to strict etiquette. But this does not interfere unduly with the good spirits of the crowd. The New Year games in Lhasa are controlled by two Masters of Ceremonies.

Though one of the chief methods by which rank is marked is by the height of the seat that a man occupies, yet a Dalai Lama, when young, will frequently sit on a lower level than a high Lama from whom he is learning religion. Even when he was thirty-six years old, there were two very learned Lamas who sat equal with the present Dalai Lama. Such is the respect paid to learning and to the teacher or spiritual guide. The Ta-shi Lama sat a little lower than the Dalai and facing sideways.

The Dalai Lama personally finds ceremony distasteful, and likes nothing better than to escape from it, going off sometimes on a walk accompanied by only one attendant. If a countryman meets him and fails to recognize him, he is all the better pleased.

The story goes that one day—many years ago—he was riding from the Potala towards the Se-ra Monastery, three miles away. At a bridge on the road an old farmer, the worse for drink, met him. Being hustled by some of the retinue and not knowing the god-king of Tibet, he burst out angrily, and concluded his views on the incident as follows: 'You are not the only official in Tibet. I have met many, but none who treated me as badly as this. You might be the Dalai Lama himself, if swagger could make you so.' His Holiness thoroughly enjoyed the joke, and told his people to let the man go without injury.

But though he dislikes ceremony, the Dalai Lama is careful to observe it as religion and policy require. So, too, with other Tibetans. And all appreciate its observance by foreigners who dwell among them.

Speaking of my long visit to Lhasa in 1920 and 1921, a Tibetan friend of mine emphasized the desirability of observing their customs, if Tibetan friendship was to be gained. He said:

'Dr. McGovern had a hostile reception in Lhasa. But your visit was really more critical. You were the first to go there, and remain for a long period, without soldiers. The monks are intolerant of foreigners, and one never knows what they will do. I thought your long stay in Lhasa was full of risk, but your carefulness in observing our customs and respecting our religious susceptibilities gained you goodwill everywhere, and helped to avert the danger.'

On the Indo-Tibetan frontier reports that we had been assassinated were not uncommon.

The usages of courtesy in all its branches stand forth prominently in the teaching of the young Tibetan. Space does not permit me to deal fully with this subject, but perhaps what has been set out above is sufficient to give some idea of it, and to show the important part that it plays in the daily life of the Tibetan people. It permeates their conduct, and helps greatly to shape their character, so that they too, with the men of Winchester, can say, 'Manners Makyth Man'.

XXV

AMUSEMENTS

To the fifth Dalai Lama, the most famous of all the Dalai Lamas, is ascribed a history of Tibet, whose sonorous but lengthy title runs thus: 'The Record of the Sayings of the Chief Ones among the powerful and exalted Kings and Ministers in the Land of Snow, the melodious Songs of the Queen, the Feast of Pleasure for the perfected Youths.' In this history we are told that during the reign of one of the early kings, about the end of the seventh century A.D., there lived in Tibet seven men famous for physical strength.[1] It appears that one could raise a young elephant by his head, another would chase a wild yak at terrific speed on the edge of a precipice, another would ride his pony quickly down a steep descent. Fanciful stories, no doubt, but they show the Tibetan fondness for feats of strength and skill.

Not only such feats, but many kinds of games, sport, and recreation come acceptable to this people. They do not indeed indulge in skating, though ice is plentiful in the 'Land of Snow'. Certainly the ice is rough, coated with dust and sometimes raised into ridges by the wind; and the Tibetan boot is not adapted to skates. But there are many, especially among the lower classes, who shoot game in spite of the Buddhist law against the taking of life.

The Tibetan clerks and servants in the British Trade Agency at Gyangtse used to play polo on their small hard-mouthed ponies with the British officers and Indian soldiers. In Ladakh, a province of western Tibet now incorporated in Kashmir, polo has long been played, though of course on lines far more primitive than those of modern polo.

There are real modernities also. Even to Lhasa the cinema has penetrated. I attended a performance there,

[1] Folio 30.

at the house of the Commander-in-Chief, who himself worked the apparatus. But this is an exotic, just beginning. Tibet has its own range of amusements.

The children's games have been described above.[1] Among adults, horse racing, archery, jumping, skipping, wrestling, putting the weight, dancing, and games of dice are all popular. And so are theatricals.

Being fond, as they are, of the open air, a natural trait in a nomadic people, the Tibetans of the towns indulge largely in picnics during the summer months. Especially is this so among the inhabitants of Lhasa. Delightful groves (*ling-ka*) of willow and poplar, surrounded by walls of stone or sun-dried brick, abound in the vicinity, and hither the people pour, when the young green of spring is at last established after winter's long reign is ended. Round Shigatse and Gyangtse, smaller towns, picnics are less numerous. Whether a *ling-ka* is owned by the Government or by a private individual, any may come and bring their lunch and tea, and spend the day there, pitching a tent if they so desire.

Riding through some of these Lhasa *ling-kas* on the fifth of May, I passed fifteen or sixteen of these parties. The Chinese and Ladakhis and some of the Tibetans were generally ensconced under a white tent roof, sometimes ornamented with the usual blue Tibetan designs. Other Tibetans sat under trees with merely a cloth, some five feet high, stretched upright along one side to keep off the wind.

In a party given by one of the upper or wealthier classes the guests usually arrive about nine in the morning and stay till six or seven. Games of dice are played, and a theatrical troupe may be engaged. The latter will recite one of the well-known plays, relating mostly to the adventures of kings and princes in old-time India or Tibet, and sometimes to ancient events in China. I will deal with these plays in a subsequent work, that the present volume may not be lengthened unduly. Stories of olden

[1] Chapter XX.

View across the Kyi Chu from the Potala

Some of the *ling-kas*, with which the valley is dotted, can be seen

Playing *sho* at a picnic in a Lhasan *ling-ka*

The dice-cup is in the man's hand and the round dice-pad is on the ground below, encircled by cowries as counters

A *ling-ka* near Lhasa with tents of picnicking parties. The trees are willow and poplar

days are recounted by those who know them. There is singing and dancing, especially towards evening; girls are often hired for this. Beer and tea is provided plentifully, and food mostly after the Chinese style.

A party of this kind may last for four or five days, some of the guests returning for a second or third day; others, with whom the host is on intimate terms, for all five days. Tents are pitched in the *ling-ka*; perhaps the host and some of the guests stay there during the nights also, to guard against theft; or, alternatively, all return home for the nights, the care of the tents being left to servants. Picnicking, with its accompaniments, might indeed be termed the national pastime among the townspeople of Tibet.

There is one day in the year on which almost all Lhasa goes on picnic. This is the fifteenth day of the fifth Tibetan month. It is the festival of 'The Incense of the Whole World' (*Dzam-ling Chi-sang*), a time of rejoicing for all the gods. Everybody should offer incense in the morning, and may spend the remainder of the day in one of the *ling-kas* near the river. All put on their best clothes. One notices that the privately owned *ling-kas* are much fuller than those belonging to the Government, because in the latter fires are not allowed to be lighted. Such a restriction is inconvenient when a party comes out for the day, for a brazier must then be brought out with charcoal or yak-dung to keep the tea warm.

Chief among the games of dice in central Tibet are *sho* and *ba*. *Sho* is the national gambling game, played by all Tibetans, high and low, the peasantry included. *Ba* is a Chinese game, played by four persons with dominoes and dice; it involves a good deal of gambling. It requires also considerable skill to play well; thus its devotees are found mainly among the upper classes. *Ba*, and especially *sho*, are favourite games in the *ling-kas*.

Let us consider a picnic among the lower middle classes. Perhaps some fairly well-to-do farmers and two or three petty traders, six or seven persons in all, join in the picnic and subscribe a sum of money equal to a couple of pounds for it. With women and children the party numbers fifteen or twenty. They usually engage an out-side man to cook for them, while the women of the party don their finery and all make holiday.

After breakfasting at seven or eight o'clock in their respective houses, the picnickers repair to the chosen spot, which will be an open, level place with good turf, within a mile or so of their homes. In order to do the thing well, a white cotton tent is pitched, and a black yak-hair tent for the kitchen. Baskets with provisions, a teapot, cups, eating bowls, the hard cushion seats with the coloured woollen sitting rugs (*den*), all are brought along, as well as two or three of the small Tibetan tables which fold up flat and are easily carried. And the family watch-dog, large, black, and long-haired, may come too; he will watch their posses-sions while his human friends are playing.

If the people be of Lhasa, making picnic in one of the *ling-kas* there, the food may be cooked at the caretaker's house. He supplies dry wood from his *ling-ka* and lends tables and seats, receiving a small present in return.

By ten o'clock all are seated in the tent, the women of the party have made ready the cups and plates, and the servants bring in fried rice, rolls of bread, cakes cooked in mustard oil, dried fruits, and cheese. Tea, of course, is provided in plenty. The teapot stands on a brazier that is fed from time to time with yak-dung to keep the favourite drink from cooling.

When the meal is over, a discussion arises as to what game they shall play. Some are for *ba*, others for *sho*. *Ba* is eventually chosen, as being more interesting and less tiring. For in *sho* the dice cup, in the excitement of the game, is brought down on its pad on the ground with such force that, if played for long, the players end by being exhausted. So a smooth cloth is laid on the table and *ba* commences. Some will crack jokes at the expense of those who lose, and the losers will join in the laughter, for they hold it unsportsmanlike to chafe at such losses. It is usual to have these games in the early afternoon, songs and dances later. Meanwhile the small children disport themselves according to their own tastes; a few may be naked, for to them the weather is unduly warm.

After midday beer is brought. Men and women all drink this, and the children also, unless their parents are unusually strict. About two o'clock we may expect a meal with some Chinese dishes, an expensive luxury, to celebrate the occasion. After further jollification the party breaks up at about six o'clock.

Most households in Lhasa have two or three picnics every month, for all love this kind of entertainment. Often they go at midday, men and women, after finishing necessary tasks. Clad in bathing drawers known as 'Water Cotton' (*chu-re*), from the waist to the knees, they enjoy a bathe in the river that flows so near their city. Mixed bathing is not encouraged. After the bathe to sit by the little Tibetan tables and enjoy tea and fruit will not come amiss.

The monks have their own separate parties. They have foot-races, jumping contests, &c. In all these picnics a spirit of kindliness prevails, and it has a softening influence even on the hotheads.

Another favourite game, played at picnics and elsewhere, is one called *shön-be*, in which three players join. Like *ba*, it is played with dominoes, of which each player holds sixteen. *Mik-ma* is more complicated and played less often. In this each of the two players is equipped with one hundred and forty-five lesser, and six larger, stones or beads with flat bases. They are coloured white for one combatant, black for the other, and are placed on a piece of cotton cloth divided into squares.

Gambling has always been rife. Few things are more sacred in Tibet than the relics of a saint, yet the son of Mar-pa, whom the Blue Record describes as 'one of the chief sources of the Buddhist doctrine in Tibet',[1] sold the relics of his saintly father to pay a gambling debt.[2] *Sho* and *ba* and other games testify to the popularity of gambling among high and low to-day.

---

[1] Tep-ter Ngön-po, vol. viii, folio 1.   [2] Ibid., folio 4.

Singing and dancing are fully practised by both women and men. At social festivities they counter each other in alternate verses, as we have seen above.[1] Women sing when walking or working, and sing when drawing water at the well.

Buddhism forbids the taking of life. And so the monks in stricter monasteries are kept indoors during the height of the rainy season, when insect life abounds outside, lest unwittingly they tread on these little ones and destroy them. In many monasteries the confinement lasts for a month, but devout monks stay indoors for three months.

After this period is over, the fraternity hold sports. The boy monks wear short skirts or petticoats of gay colours and all come prepared to enjoy themselves. Some of us attended these games at Gyangtse on the 9th September 1915, the last day of the seventh Tibetan month. They were held near the paper factory there. We went at ten in the forenoon, and were first taken to a tent where we were given tea, cakes, and bowls of macaroni.

The sports opened with a performance of clowns. Then four men, who took the part of a lama, a Chinese, a Nepalese, and an Indian respectively, held a mock competition in jumping, during which they indulged in various antics.

All prelude finished, the real jumping commenced. A spring-board was placed at the top of a banked-up slope. The competitors leapt from it to the ground below. Some of the monks pretended to belong to Bang-gye-shar, the Lhasan name of the Pa-lha family, others to the house of Chang-lo. The two sets exchanged good-humoured chaff and mock cries of victory.

Contests in skipping—or, as the Tibetans call it, 'rope-jumping' (tak-chom)—followed. This is a favourite pastime not only of girls and young women, but of the monks also. As practised by the latter, it is not of the simpler order known in England. Two men held the rope, while the skipper jumped in all attitudes, waving his arms

[1] See p. 173.

'The competitors leapt from the springboard to
the ground below'

Skipping while lying down

or his legs. Sometimes a performer would adopt a half-kneeling posture. Frequently he would lie down, and spring over the rope as he crouched or lay on the ground. Two men, or two boys, would skip together, engaging in a mock fight as they skipped.

Foot-races followed, during which we gave our presents to the participants and returned home. Huge cauldrons were placed here and there for supplying tea to the monks.

During the time of their confinement in the monasteries, indoor amusements are not wanting. One is the game known as Sa-lam Nam-sha, 'The Earth–Heaven Road'. It is played with dice on a sheet mapped to represent the universe. According to the fall of the dice, one climbs to one of the heavens or falls down into one of the hells, or, perchance, for a time wanders in the worlds between.

The smaller monasteries do not have much in the way of amusements; but in large establishments, as are Se-ra, Dre-pung, and Gan-den, the younger monks go off to the parks round Lhasa whenever they can, and play games, favourite among which are quoits and putting the weight.

The last named is known to the Tibetans as 'Round Stone' (Do-kor). Monks and laymen all join in it, especially at the time of the Tibetan or agricultural, as opposed to the Chinese or official, New Year. While the latter falls in February, the former comes about the time of the shortest day. It is the people's New Year and is generally observed in the country districts, where the official New Year is a secondary affair. In Lhasa, Shigatse, and the few other towns of Tibet the official date holds the premier place. Small parties come together and compete in 'round stone'. And during races and other festivities groups here and there are practising it with good-humoured chaff and laughter.

Tibet, say the Tibetan books, is the land of horses. It is natural, therefore, that horse-racing should be a popular pastime. Almost every village, or group of villages, has its race day. All turn out, pitch tents in the ling-kas, and make a merry day of it, picnicking, singing, and dancing. July is a favourite month, when the crops, still green, are in urgent need of rain.

During the proceedings there is a procession round the fields, the set of sacred books known as the *Bum* being carried in procession, and maybe an image of the Buddha as well. This is in effect a prayer that rain may fall for the crops. For in this land, where the things of the spirit are real and true, even horse-racing is bound up with religious worship. And so these races, taking their name from the procession, are known as the 'Crop Circuit'.

The farmers usually ride their own ponies. The race may be half a mile in length, or less, and usually includes the shooting of an arrow at a small target as the competitor gallops past it, and perhaps the firing of a blank charge out of a gun at another target. If a villager, who has no pony, wishes to join in the fun, he may borrow one, but most ride their own.

Competitors are rewarded according to their success. The best receive large *ka-tas* and perhaps some cotton cloth as well. But even the least successful receive a small *ka-ta* each; nobody goes away empty-handed. The *ka-tas* and other prizes are at the cost of the landlord, who also distributes them. But, should the village be one of several on a large estate, his local agent performs this duty on his behalf. There is no betting on the races.

These ceremonies are not all after a set pattern, but vary according to the locality. Sometimes the races take place in the morning, to be followed by picnics in the *ling-kas* during the day, and the Crop Circuit in the evening. There are indeed great differences. As a Tibetan friend remarked to me:

'There are many districts in Tibet, and they vary for better or worse in these celebrations. The first-class ones have horse-races, foot-races, and the Circuit. In the second class there are no foot-races; in the third the Circuit only. And in the worst of all merely a priest reading prayers.'

Archery is another favourite pastime. It is practised by the gentry (*ku-tra*) and by the higher classes of the tenantry. Archery parties are held during the summer, and occasionally in the winter also.

A target is set up in a *ling-ka*. Bows and arrows vary in different parts of Tibet, but are commonly of bamboo. The former are usually five to five and a half feet in length, and the arrows about twenty-five inches with flat iron heads on which poison is smeared both for shooting animals and for fighting foes. But in archery the bow made in China finds favour. It is of polished wood outside and horn inside. And the arrows are, as a rule, without points, square wooden heads with slits in the sides being fitted instead. These whistle as they fly through the air, a pleasing sound. The afternoon is the favourite time for this pastime.

Each competitor puts down his stake, say a *tang-ka*, equal to three or four pence of English money. Should he hit the bull's-eye, he takes perhaps two *tang-kas*, or as may be agreed on. The shooting is not taken too seriously. The host or some of his servants, men or girls, enliven the time with songs. On a special occasion a troupe of actors will be engaged.

Those who eschew alcohol drink tea. But a Tibetan, accustomed to these contests, tells me, 'Beer must be drunk when shooting arrows. Otherwise, the shoulder shakes, and the arrow does not go hot to the target.'

XXVI

THE NEW YEAR GAMES AT LHASA

IF one lives in Tibet and converses freely with Tibetans, one sees and hears many things, which have hitherto found no mention in the books of foreign travellers in this country. Especially is this so regarding the life of Lhasa, which is still almost unknown to the outside world.

And this gap in our knowledge of the Tibetan people, in our capacity to understand them and their feelings, is a large one. For—more than in most countries—the social and political, the cultural and religious activities of Tibet centre in their capital. Here the leading men and women foregather, here are the heads of the Government with some of their cleverest subordinates, shrewd abbots, and others who wield so great an influence in the all-important sphere of religion. And here dwells he who overtops them all in sanctity and power, for he is regarded by his subjects as the Buddha's Vice-Regent on earth.

The good people of Lhasa are fortunate in being able to indulge, more freely than elsewhere, in the national fondness for games and shows and other forms of amusement. In this chapter I should like to say a little about the games which brighten the life of the Holy City during the first month of each year.

The most important festival of the year in Lhasa is that of 'The Great Prayer' (*Mön-lam Chem-po*), often styled simply 'The Prayer'. It commences soon after the New Year, and lasts for about three weeks, during which many religious services are held. The fundamental object of this festival is to shorten the time remaining to the spiritual reign of Gotama Buddha, whose power has passed its zenith, and to hasten the oncoming of the new Buddha, known to Indians as Maitreya, and to Tibetans as 'Love', or 'Conquering Love' (*Gye-wa Cham-pa*).

The religious observances are followed by a few days

of merry-making. From among the higher officials below
the rank of Minister of State (*Shap-pe*) and from those
whose ancestors have been Ministers, are chosen—turn
and turn about—two who supervise these revels. These
are known as *Ya-sö*, 'The Highest Worshippers'. Should
it fall to their turn, they will be taken from even the
younger members of such families. During my year in
Lhasa the two Ya-sö were Do-ring Te-chi, aged twenty-
one, and Tri-mön Se, 'Honourable Son of Tri-mön', who
was still younger. Perhaps it is well that those officials,
whose high birth justifies the hope that they will rise to
exalted positions, should be trained early in organization,
administration, and the art of appearance in public.

On the 1st of March 1921 our party attended the first
of these ceremonies. It is known as 'The Preparation of
the Camp at Lu-gu' (*Lu-gu Gar-drik*). Those who are to
ride in the pony races, and the people generally, attend for
the purpose of listening to instructions from the *Ya-sö* as
to the events of the next few days.

An ornamental tent is pitched on the plain under the
southern face of the Potala hill. To it is added an open
courtyard formed with the sides of tents, a verandah running round on the inside of this enclosure. For the two
'Highest Worshippers' there are thrones inside the tent,
four feet high. At right angles to these, going down into
the open-air enclosure, are two rows of seats, the usual
hard cushions (*böl-den*) placed on the ground. Here sit the
subordinates. Their little tables with cups and bowls are
arranged in front of them; their servants stand behind
them.

Round the thrones are grouped several of the notables
of Lhasa with their wives and children, all smiling and
merry.

Soon after our arrival the Ya-sö enter with their retinue.
The young Presidents themselves are dressed in exceptionally gorgeous robes—probably the best in the family
wardrobes—of Chinese brocade after the Mongol fashion,
in which yellow is the prevailing colour. They are

dressed, in fact, as Mongol princes of olden times. Their office and the race meetings over which they preside, date in their present form from the time of the fifth Dalai Lama, who owed his temporal power to Mongol assistance, and took this opportunity of marking his appreciation of that fact.

Do-ring Te-chi, as the elder, makes a speech to those of the populace who are allowed within the courtyard. He is indeed nervous, but not unduly so. He tells the people that the Great Prayer was instituted by Tsong-ka-pa (who inaugurated the Reformation of Tibetan Buddhism at the beginning of the fifteenth century A.D.); that it was enlarged by the fifth Dalai Lama; that ponies and riders must be properly accoutred, remembering the magnificent standards of the past; that they must not talk as they ride in procession; that all must be strictly sober, and more to the same effect.

The younger Ya-sö then reads the instructions of the fifth Dalai Lama (who reigned from 1641 to 1680 A.D.), two attendants holding up the letter as he reads. These instructions are to the same effect as the Te-chi's speech, which is largely based upon them.

Then the latter delivers a second address recounting the ceremonies that are to follow during the next few days. He tells us that they are of good omen, and that the ponies and men that race are like servants who ride with their master; so these races and processions will be, as it were, an invitation to 'Conquering Love' to come quickly. An event much desired, as is still further emphasized by the 'Invitation to Love' (*Cham-pa Den-dren*) three days hence, when the image of the Coming Buddha will be carried through the city.

The ponies of all the participants are bravely attired, but those of the two Ya-sö are magnificent above all, with saddles and saddle-cloths encrusted with gold work deeply inlaid, and silk trappings on the ponies' heads and tails.

Four ladies, gorgeously dressed in coloured silks and

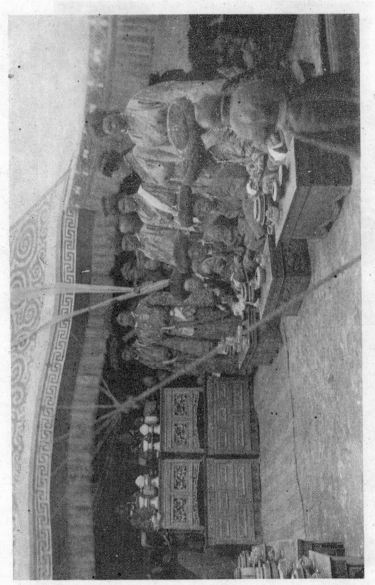

'For the two "Highest Worshippers" there are thrones inside the tent

At right angles to these sit the subordinates'

'Four ladies, gorgeously dressed in coloured silks and head-dresses of turquoise and coral'

The Ya-sös' four Maids of Honour with two assistants

head-dresses of turquoise and coral, offer beer to the Ya-sö.
The latter, taking each a few drops between the thumb
and the third finger, jerk this little offering to the ground.
Thus do they make their oblation to the Spirits, and call
to remembrance the days when the Maids of Honour
offered the flowing bowl to the old kings of Tibet. Refreshment composed of rice, tea, &c., follows. Their stewards
lay these on tables in front of the Ya-sö.

Outside the enclosure 'White Devils' amuse the crowds.
These beggar minstrels pour out a stream of extravagant
language, interlarded with jests which cannot be said to
border on the vulgar, for they are well across the line.

On the following day we attended 'The Account at
Trap-shi'. A part of the plain between Lhasa and the
monastery of Se-ra, two miles to the north, is covered with
white tents ornamented in blue, and a crowd of five or
six thousand persons is assembled to see and enjoy the
show. As we approach, horsemen are dressing themselves
in chain armour, iron breast-plates, and belts made of
small strips of iron and leather. The tent reserved for
our accommodation is immediately to the right of the
Ministers, who preside on this occasion.

It is time for the spectacle (te-mo) to begin. First, we see a
procession of the horsemen. Each noble and each secular
official of high rank furnishes his own contingent. Shap-pes
are expected to send twenty-four horsemen each, De-pöns
('Lords of the Arrows') eighteen, and others a smaller
number, though it will be understood that these figures
are not rigidly applied. Many send nine, which in Tibetan
is a number connoting a countless host. Each rider is
accoutred in a coat and belt of armour, and leather
breeches. His helmet is of iron. Every one carries a spear
(dung), prong-gun, bow and arrows.

Each contingent rides into the cleared space in front of
the Ministers, a rough oval forty yards long by thirty
yards across. Here they are met by four young men, soon
to become secular officials on the civil, i.e. non-military,
side. These examine the leaders of each contingent, and

then advance through half of the distancè intervening
between them and the Shap-pes tent. Removing their
yellow hats and making profound bows, they announce
that everything is in good order, and call out the name of
the owner and the number of his horsemen. Each of the
four budding officials certifiés to the correctness of a
part of the equipment. I ask the Peak Secretary why one
does not certify to the whole, and I am told, 'It would be
too great a tax on one man's memory.'

The horsemen represent the mounted soldiers of the
days of the early Tibetan kings. Over and over again one
finds 'the brave days of old' represented in the spectacles
provided for modern Lhasa, if indeed the epithet modern
can be applied to the Lhasa of 1921, still in the feudal age.

In the times of these horsemen Buddhism had not yet
spread over Tibet with its prohibition against the taking
of life. The Tibetans rode out to raid and fight and
conquer with no great regard for their own lives or the
lives of others. They were brave and hardy fighters, and
so the nation, in spite of its love for Buddhism, looks back
on these ancestors with admiration.

In the centre of the oval space are the prizes, coloured
silks from China and bricks of tea from the same country,
carried three months' journey through the heart of Asia,
And by these are two capacious damascene beer jugs
with handsome gold bands. A little later on these will
provide beer for the competitors.

The affair ends with a procession of all the cavalry,
three to four hundred in number, to Lhasa. The two
young Highest Worshippers ride at their head.

On the fourth of March races and other sports were
held in Lhasa City, in the square near the Temple. We
left our house at half past six in the morning. Just before
we started the firing of a gun proclaimed the start of the
pony race, two and a half miles away. As we were on the
course—the road being the course—we came at a hand
gallop to our destination. It was well that we did so, for
two of the ponies had slipped away before the gun was

fired. For this they were likely to be not only disqualified but fined, as for a criminal offence.

Eighteen degrees of frost, joined to a light north-easterly wind, seemed to underline the earliness of the hour at which our races were held. But, though early, they were not the first event of the day. Between five and six o'clock the procession of the Coming Buddha, 'Conquering Love', had taken place.

It is at first a matter for surprise that so many ceremonies in this icy climate should be held in the early morning, especially during winter. Midday might be at least moderately warm. But, like so many other happenings in Tibet, this is a question of good or bad omen. The early morning, when the sun is mounting straight upwards, is the auspicious hour. For an ascent, whether of the sun or of other things, is auspicious, while a descent is the reverse. The procession of the Coming Buddha a little before sunrise is an invitation to him to come quickly, and to appear, as the sun is about to appear, in his might.

During the Prayer Festival on the fifteenth day of the first month, the Dalai Lama holds a religious service and preaches a sermon publicly in one of the squares near the Temple. This, too, is held very early in the morning. In fact, as I am told, it is customary to hold religious services and to preach during the early hours, for the mind is fresh and clear then, but clouds over during the day. Another adds that early morning is the best time for the long pony race and foot race, as it is cool and fresh then for both ponies and men. And, indeed, it is so on a March morning on the heights of Tibet!

We are accommodated in an upper room of a house by the square, a little to the right of the Dalai Lama and on the same level. So we have an excellent view of each event. Very soon after we arrive the ponies commence to arrive also. They start from near the Dre-pung Monastery, four miles away, pass through our square, and go on to finish at one of the *lin -kas* to the east of Lhasa, a distance of five or six miles. Few seem to view the end of the race; it is here in the square, at two-thirds of the distance, that the spectators are assembled.

However, a Government delegate of good rank goes to the finish at Tel Pung Gang ('Dust Heap Ridge') and records the arrivals there. He also hands out for each pony a small piece of wood bearing a number that shows the order in which the pony finished. A groom, or other servant of the owner, carries this in his upraised hand back to the square in Lhasa, where we viewed the race.

Another peculiarity of the race is that the ponies run without riders. Occasionally they stop, or attempt to diverge up a side street, but receive no encouragement from the crowd, who urge them forward to their goal. A pony belonging to Tsa-rong Shap-pe, the Commander-in-Chief, is the first to pass the Dalai Lama; another of Tsa-rong's ponies is second. The ponies are trained beforehand to gallop along this course. Grooms also ride behind each pony or set of ponies from the same stable, to urge them on, and to make sure that they do not go astray. The grooms ride in relays, three or four being required to cover the whole course.

Yet another peculiarity is that entries are compulsory. Tibetans term it a tax or forced service (tre), 'for', they say, 'there is no profit, but only loss, in the race'. Those who hold official rank in Lhasa, from the Ministers downwards, have each to enter a prescribed number of ponies in accordance with their rank. The Government itself enters a large number of ponies.

Occasionally some of the Government men drive a competitor's pony off the course. This is done quietly, so that their offence does not come to the Dalai Lama's ears. In the races at Gyangtse attacks of this kind have been more frequent and open.

The pony race is followed by a foot race over the same course. The first competitor to arrive creates much merriment in the crowd by his unrestrained pleasure at being first. He bows three times to the Dalai Lama, and then

with a caper of delight runs on at a good steady pace.
The later arrivals run stolidly by, without bowing to the
Presence. Belated ponies of the former event continue to
arrive among the competitors in the foot race, and are
driven on by the populace and by the *She-ngos'* assistants
with their long willow rods.

It must be explained here that the fifth Dalai Lama,
during the seventeenth century, introduced the present
system of adminstration in Tibet. Among other innova-
tions he transferred the civil and criminal jurisdiction of
Lhasa City during each year's Prayer Festival from the
hands of the regular judiciary, and entrusted it to the
Dre-pung Monastery, his own monastery. Accordingly,
each year two Dre-pung monks, known as *She-ngo*, are
chosen for this important work. The regular police of
Lhasa, such as they are, depart for the time, and the
She-ngo appoint their own. This system led, as was inevitable, to many abuses, but the present Dalai Lama has
removed these, or at any rate the worst of them.

The race goes on. A little dog, running up the street
with the solemn air of a competitor, provokes a roar of
laughter from the crowd. So does a woman, who, when
crossing the street, falls down with her baby on her back,
and is unable to recover herself without assistance. It is
a merry crowd, easily moved to laughter. It is also very
closely packed, for fresh arrivals from behind push it
forward, only to be driven back by the long rods of the
'scullery men' (*tap-yok*), if they advance beyond the line
allowed.

After the races are ended, there follows a competition
in lifting a heavy stone. Only one man succeeds in this;
he shifts it cleverly on to his back, and carries it for about
a hundred yards.

Wrestlers now appear. They are recruited from the
ranks of the Sim-chung-nga, who are themselves recruited
from central Tibet. And who are these Sim-chung-nga,
these 'Little Soldiers', as the name means? They represent the old-time infantry of Tibet—as the horsemen of

the Lu-gu Camp Preparation represent the mounted arm
—and ordinarily they are dressed in chain armour and
carry flint-lock guns.

These Sim-chung-ngas are divided into a right and a
left flank. In this wrestling competition representatives
from the right flank contest with those from the left.
All are as near to nakedness as decency permits. It is a
case of 'Catch as catch can', and the bout frequently commences by the contestants throwing barley-flour in each
other's eyes. Each carries a handful for use, if occasion
serves. There are sixteen competitors from each flank;
some look hardy and muscular, but many seem weedy.
As soon as one throws the other to the ground, attendants
run forward, throw the wrestlers' clothes over them, and
hustle them out of the arena, though often not before the
conqueror has punched his adversary with his fists in
order to emphasize the victory.

The successful wrestlers are rewarded with pieces of
silk and large *ka-tas*; the losers with small *ka-tas* only.
Sim-chung-ngas, who are of higher rank and might perhaps be termed non-commissioned officers, act as um-
pires. During the New Year festival these arrange their
hair after the style adopted by the lower grade of secular
officials (*trung-kor*). So they are known as 'One month
trung-kor'.

The first to arrive in the foot race, and the grooms of
the leading ponies in the pony race, also receive pieces of
coloured silk as prizes. These are known as 'Name
Numbers' (*tsen-trang*). All competitors receive *ka-tas*.

The races are emblems of speed, the weight-lifting and
the wrestling are emblems of strength. And so all go forth
as good omens, accompanying the invitation to the next
Buddha, 'Conquering Love', to come in his power, and to
come quickly. Sports and games in Tibet are seldom
without a religious background.

On the day following these sports in the heart of Lhasa
we are invited to another kind of racing. It is popularly
known as 'The Gallop behind the Fort' (*Dzong-gyap*

Tents and spectators at 'The Gallop behind the Fort'

Cakes for sale under umbrellas in right and centre foreground

Gun and arrow shooting competition at Gyangtse

Competitors with their prong guns

Sham-be), being held at some distance behind the Potala, whose origin as a fort is indicated in this and other names. Near by stands the great Lha-lu mansion with its park, accounted as one of the chief beauties of Lhasa.

There are several tents on the plain, coloured prettily in blue and white according to the usual designs. And as happens also at the spectacles at Lu-gu and at Trap-shi, there are many restaurant booths, formed of gaily-coloured umbrellas, several of them bright red, under which the presiding genius stores her cakes and biscuits, as well as her oranges from Sikkim and Bhutan. A crowd of several thousand people is assembled, the women in their gala dresses, and all in the best of humour. At present there is no trace of drunkenness, but the Peak Secretary has no hesitation in assuring me that by the evening there will in this respect be a great change. And so it is, for, meeting the returning parties in the late afternoon, Kennedy finds many who are drunk, though none who are ill-humoured or quarrelsome.

We are given a tent to the right of the large one occupied by the Ministers and *Kungs*. Our place is the one which the Chinese Amban used to occupy when he attended these sports.

The horsemen, representing the old-time cavalry (*ta-pa*) of Tibet, are arrayed in Mongol hats (*sok-sha*) and robes which are gorgeous, though cumbersome. The ponies, too, are gaily caparisoned. Each rider, undismayed by his pony's trappings and his own exuberant clothing, indeed exulting in them, starts galloping down a narrow track, like a shallow ditch, with his flint-lock gun and his bow and arrows slung over his shoulders. Pulling forward his gun, he fires it from a few feet distance at a disk, a good way down the course. The disk is about one foot in diameter, with a red centre and a white rim. This is suspended five feet from the ground by a yak-hair rope, strung on poles. Hastily the rider now pushes back his long, clumsy gun with its prongs of horn, and, during the few seconds that his galloping pony allows him, pulls forward his bow and arrows, adjusts one of the latter, and shoots it as he passes within a few feet of another similar target some eighty yards from the first. Those who do well are allowed to go by without remark. But those who fail are greeted with laughter by the crowd, and jeers of 'A-le! Den-dre', 'Bah! That kind'.

When a detachment has finished, it comes before the Ministers. One of the Government Treasurers gives a *ka-ta* to each member who has succeeded with either gun or bow, his name being read out by a lesser official. There are also in attendance four or five other officers of lower rank, who commenced their official careers as Dance Boys, performing at the Dalai Lama's New Year Reception.[1] Now that they are grown up they hold minor posts under the Government. One of these, who is still a Dance Boy, stands in front of the competitors, holding a silver cup full of beer that has been brewed from barley. After receiving his *ka-ta*, each man dips the thumb and third finger of his right hand in the beer, and jerks a drop or two on the ground as an oblation to 'The Three Chief Rare Ones', the Buddha, the Priesthood, and the Sacred Books, the Supreme Buddhist Triad.

The scarf-giving officials and the competitors who have succeeded with both weapons now cross to the other side of the Shap-pes' tent. Here each receives a second *ka-ta*, one being for the gunfire, the other for the arrow. The horsemen, still dismounted, then retire a few paces, and give the old Mongol salute. Each raises his right arm to the height of his shoulder, sends it on a horizontal sweep backward, and then brings it forward and downward, nearly to his knee. We see thus again the Mongol influence in these games, established in their present form during the reign of the fifth Dalai Lama, to whom the Mongol chieftain, Gusri Khan, gave the secular sovereignty over Tibet. Having completed their salute, the competitors move off, and a fresh contingent takes the field.

[1] See p. 213.

While the Masters of Ceremonies, the Ya-sö, represent
Mongol princes, the horsemen themselves are said to
represent those of the time of King Ke-sar, of the pre-
Buddhist days, when skill and bravery in war were among
the chief attributes of kings and their subjects. Different
people have different opinions as to where was Ling, the
country over which Ke-sar ruled. The Peak Secretary
puts it in the Mang-kam of these days, a province in
eastern Tibet.

When the competitors reach their master's home in the
country, the difference between success and failure is not
ignored in the day's feasting that follows. Those who
have done well receive money presents of ten to twenty
tang-kas (half a crown to five shillings) each, pieces of silk,
and tea. Those who have failed receive little or nothing;
their food is doled out to them in markedly poor vessels,
and they are jeered at by their fellows. Anybody who lets
his bow or gun fall to the ground during any of the events,
has to stand a drink of beer all round, a penalty imposed
by his fellow-competitors.

During the forenoon the horsemen of the right flank
compete; during the afternoon those of the left. Do-ring's
troop is the first among the right flank to display their
skill, for an ancestor of this House, the celebrated Do-ring
Pandita, was the first layman to hold the proud position
of Regent during the minority of a Dalai Lama. This was
during the time of the seventh Dalai, and so the Do-ring
troop still performs before even those of the Ministers.
After him the contingents of the Ka-lön Lama, and Tsa-
rong, two of the Ministers, show their prowess.

Similarly of the left flank Sam-trup Po-trang's troop is
the first to perform, for his family, descended from the
father of the seventh Dalai Lama, is the oldest of the
'Father Estate' (Yap-shi) families, i.e. those descended
from the father of a Dalai Lama. After him Kün-sang-tse
and Tri-mön, the two remaining Ministers, send out their
men. It was Gusri Khan, the Mongol chief, who built
and occupied the Sam-trup Po-trang mansion in Lhasa.

Having conquered Tibet, it was perhaps natural that he should call it Sam-trup Po-trang, i. e., 'The Palace of the Fulfilled Purpose'.

After lunch the general merriment increases. Songs break out among the crowds, and even some of the competitors, who make good shots, wave their arms and give vent to shouts of triumph.

To the right of the Ministers' tent—in which Kungs, Dza-sas, and Te-chis are also seated—at right angles to it, sit lesser officials in the open. With them are placed the teachers and students in the Finance Office (*Tsi-kang*), where boys are trained for the secular (as opposed to the ecclesiastical) branch of the Civil Service.

The events of the afternoon are similar to those of the morning. We leave between three and four o'clock, and are followed as usual by a crowd.

On the next day, a Sunday, an archery competition was held, known as 'Heaven's Arrows'. We did not attend it. On the following day the Dalai Lama, who came in state to reside at the Potala Palace before the festival commenced, returned by the same route and in the same manner to the Jewel Park, his country seat. His Holiness does not witness the games excepting only the races and sports in Lhasa itself.

The games and spectacles, which finish and follow the Great Prayer Festival, are now ended. And—most important of all to those who see beyond the veil—the invitation has gone forth to the Buddha of Love to come in the fullness of his power. So, as the good people of Lhasa disperse to their homes, and those from districts far and near disperse to theirs, you will hear many repeat the refrain:

> Lhasa's Prayer is ended;
> Love is now invited.

XXVII

THE LAST RITES

THERE are several aspects of Tibetan daily life, with which
I should have liked to deal in the present volume, both
on the secular side and on the religious. But to do so
would lengthen this book beyond the patience of my
readers, and these aspects must therefore stand over for
future treatment.

The present little work, however, has dealt with birth
and marriage, and—as far as space permits—with other
features of the daily round in that great mountain land.
And so something must be said of life's end and of the
observances, necessarily religious, which are associated
with it.

When the time comes for him to die, the Tibetan does
not feel that he will live no more in this world, but merely
that another link in the long chain of his lives has been
completed. If he is religious or wealthy, a priest is summoned. The latter will tell him not to let his mind cling
to his property and other worldly concerns, nor even to his
wife or children. For now he must leave behind his body,
which is but 'a temporary lodging'. And when leaving it
—his chief possession—wife, children, and property are
left as a matter of course. Let him therefore turn his
thoughts to the Three Chief Rare Ones, to his guardian
deity, and most of all to his 'Root Lama', the one in whom
he reposes especial faith. Let him visualize the Root Lama
as resting on him, a connecting link between his poor self
and the merciful Lord Buddha. The latter is pictured as
drawing beings with a hook up to better worlds. And so
the saying is handed down:

> Though the Lord Buddha has a hook for drawing,
> Yet the mind-owner [1] needs a ring for holding.

---

[1] One who has a mind, i.e. a human being or animal.

Unless a man has faith in his religion—and the meditation on his Root Lama is a sign of this faith—even the Buddha, by himself, can do nothing.

To a dying king of Sikkim, stabbed at the mineral baths of Ra-lang, a monastery in south-western Sikkim, the lama preaches 'the text on the recognition of the Bar-do [1] state', i.e. the period which intervenes between death and rebirth. Thus will he understand how to conquer the dangers and difficulties that will confront him on the road. Such also is the practice throughout Tibet, but more often this text is read after the death.

The books record that a funeral ritual was introduced into Tibet during the reign of one of the earliest kings, Tri-kum Tsan-po, from Shang-shung.[2] Be that as it may, the rituals are now well defined.

When death has come, a priest is sent for as soon as possible. He conducts a service in the house of the deceased for about half an hour, and then sits in meditation for perhaps half an hour more. His duty is—by his prayers—to cause a hole to form in the top of the deceased's skull, so that the latter's mind, or consciousness (nam-she),[3] may escape through it.

An astrologer (tsi-pa) must also be consulted to ascertain for how long the body should be kept in the house before being sent to the 'assembled tombs' (tur-trö), so called, though, as a rule, no burying takes place. He will decide, too, what sacred pictures should be painted. And monks are summoned to hold religious services until the corpse goes to the place of disposal.

Corpses in Tibet are treated in one of five ways. Among these is burial, but it is confined to babies and those who have died of small-pox or other infectious disease.

Cremation is reserved for priests of note. Wood is scarce in the Tibetan uplands, and the use of yak-dung

---

[1] Usually so transcribed, but in Lhasan speech pronounced *Par-to*.
[2] Fifth Dalai Lama's History, *The Feast of Pleasure for the Perfected Youths*, folio 11.
[3] རྣམ་ཤེས་

is considered unfitting in these last services to the dead.
Vultures and ravens, on the other hand, are plentiful.
And religion, as in Leviticus, has stepped in to sanction
and support Nature's limitations. It would be considered
sacrilegious to cremate the body of a layman, however high
his rank. It might bring calamity on the countryside, illness attacking the people, hailstorms attacking the crops.

In the biography of Gan-den Trup-pa, the teacher and
saint who originated the line of Dalai Lamas and died four
hundred and fifty years ago, we read of the will that he
left. In this will

'It was said that there are various reasons for which his bones
will be required, and therefore they should be offered to the God of
Fire. The dead body was accordingly wrapped in cloth, besprinkled
with sweet scents, and placed in the chapel of the goddess Dröl-ma
("The Deliverer"), until the silver vessel should be ready.' [1]

Images made from the ashes, as well as other relics and
'precious books', were placed in the silver vessel. A rainbow appeared in the sky, and a rain of flowers fell from
above.

Reference has already been made to the large monastery
known as 'The Tiger's Prophecy' (Ta-lung). After the
cremation of a famous hierarch of this monastery images
of him were fashioned from his ashes.[2] At cremations of
learned or saintly lamas miracles are often recorded. At
one such the sacred pills, which come from the bones of
the Buddha and some high lamas, fell like rain from
the sky.[3]

At another, 'images of various gods came out of the
body. His eyes were placed inside some gold images at
Chi-bu, his heart at Che-ka, his tongue at Bu-gu-do. Four
conch shells turned to the right (i.e. turned the reverse
way and therefore of exceptional sanctity) also issued from
his corpse'.[4]

[1] Folio 59 of the book entitled 'The Rosary of Gems, which tells the wonder-
ful and excellent history of the omniscient Lord Gan-den Trup-pa Pal Sang-po'.
[2] Tep-ter Ngön-po, vol. viii, folio 72.   [3] Ibid., folio 93.
[4] Ibid., vol. v, folio 17.

Sö-nam Gya-tso, the third in the line of Tsong-Ka-pa's successors, who spread Tibetan Buddhism in Mongolia, abolished the custom—which had hitherto prevailed throughout part of that country—of burning or burying the living wife with the dead husband.

Addressing a large gathering, he said,

'Hitherto ye have committed sinful acts and lived on flesh and blood, and lived in darkness, but henceforth ye, Chinese, Tibetans, and Horpas, must abide by the laws of the ten virtues. Especially do I speak to the Mongols in Cha-kar. In the past, when one of you died, his wife, servant, horse and cattle were burnt alive and sacrificed. Henceforth ye shall not sacrifice lives. If you do, a fine of horses and cattle will be imposed and offered to the priests for the performance of the necessary services. Ye shall not sacrifice any lives after a death.' [1]

In former days when a high lama was cremated, a chö-ten would be built to house his remains. His bones were placed in it. Sometimes they were ground into powder mixed with clay and thus worked into a paste. This might be in the form of a thick disk. On it were stamped images of the Buddha, of Jam-pe-yang the God of Wisdom, of the Goddess Dröl-ma, or of other. Instead of one large disk, this paste of bones and clay would sometimes be in many small pieces, perhaps a thousand, each stamped with the image of the Buddha, or of a deity, or with a sacred inscription such as Om A Hum.[2] This incantation cleanses from sin the person who arranges and pays for these relics. With them were placed miniature chö-tens (tsa-tsa) fashioned from the same ingredients. Occasionally also the bones were placed in the chö-ten unmixed with clay and unstamped.

According to modern custom, in central Tibet, at any rate, such relics are not deposited in the ordinary chö-tens that stand out of doors. They may rest, however, in an earthen vessel, covered with silver and shaped like a chö-ten, to be kept in his monastery. An image of the

---

[1] Biography of Sö-nam Gya-tso, folio 95.
[2] The vowels in this incantation are long; the letter m is but half pronounced.

lama is modelled from the bones, and kept in the vessel. Small printed rolls, charms and the like, are also put in. The *chö-ten* itself stands for the lama's mind, and thus are represented the Body, Speech, and Mind of the holy man.

And the *tsa-tsa* are nowadays made entirely from clay. There is in Lhasa a nunnery known as 'The Nest' (*Tsang-Kung*). Its inmates devote much of their time to the fashioning of these little memorials.

It occasionally happens that an image, thus fashioned from the bones of a very holy lama, comes into the possession of a private person. Carried in a charm-box on the chest, it is believed to guard against death from gun or sword.

Ku-sho Pa-lhe-se has one of this kind, four or five inches high, said to be made from the bones of a former Ta-shi Lama, Tem-pe Nyi-ma. The brother of the present Ta-shi Lama gave it to him. Such images are rare and are given away with caution, for fear lest the recipient, feeling himself immune against bullets, may become bolder to take the lives of others. Thereby the holy image would bring sin rather than merit. A few grains, when taken from the base of an image of this kind and mixed with water, will effect a cure of coughs and colds.

The dead bodies of the poor are sometimes consigned to rivers and streams. Robbers often accord similar treatment to the bodies of those whom they murder. Babies, beggars, and lepers frequently find water-burial in eastern Tibet: in the central province babies are buried underground in small boxes.

Indeed, in the districts round Lhasa, more closely governed than those far away, water-burial is prohibited. The reason for the prohibition is partly to check the robbers, but mainly to prevent the defilement of the rivers, for many people drink the water from them. If the authorities come to hear of a corpse in a river or stream, the landlord is fined, unless the inquiry succeeds in discovering the guilty person. And so it comes that, partly to prevent identification, and partly to make it sink, a dead body is usually dismembered before it is thrown into the water.

The commonest form of disposal is one by which the corpse is broken up in some wide, empty space and given to the vultures. This method has much to recommend it in a country like Tibet. Burial is difficult, for the ground is frozen hard during the winter. Cremation is difficult, for there is no coal, and but little firewood. Casting into rivers pollutes the drinking supply.

Several places are set apart for this purpose on the plain and side valleys round Lhasa. Sixteen miles from Lhasa is the monastery known as 'The Rock of Purity' (*Tra Yer-pa*), where the great Indian teacher, Atisha, lived nine hundred years ago. While I was staying there, I noticed three fires burning on a neighbouring mound. They came from one of the varieties of juniper, which is largely used as incense. Just below these fumes of incense was the platform where the corpses of the Tra Yer-pa monks were cut up. It was a flattened piece of ground, somewhat larger than a man's body, floored with slabs of slate. A small slab stood vertically in the ground; to it the dead monk's head was secured, while pieces of the flesh were chopped off the corpse and given to the birds.

If the deceased is of the gentry, the corpse is carried to one of these disposal grounds (*tur-trö*) by the *tom-den*.[1] The limbs are doubled up and tied with cords. Thus bent, the body is carried in a white blanket, and a ceremonial scarf or two, the last tribute of respect, may be placed on the top. The *tom-den* are a class by themselves, carrying on their prescribed occupations from father to son. They are not much higher in social position than the Ra-gyap-pas, the beggar-scavengers of Lhasa, but they do not live in a quarter by themselves as the Ra-gyap-pas do.

Should the deceased be of the lower or middle class, the corpse is carried by Ra-gyap-pas or other beggars even

<hr>

1 སྤུར་སྡུན་

Vultures and a solitary raven awaiting the end

'A flattened piece of ground, somewhat larger than a man's body'

farther down the scale. For the Ra-gyap-pas rank above some. There are other corpse-carriers, beggars, whose status—and fee—are the lowest of all.

No relative accompanies the corpse to the ground. 'Because they weep too much', a Tibetan friend explains. But the upper classes and all who can afford the expense engage a monk, that he may go to the ground one day before the corpse and pray to the spirit (*lha*) of the cemetery to comfort the mind (*sem*) of the deceased, when it sees its body being cut up and torn from it. The flesh is cut off with a knife, and the bones are pounded with heavy stones, while a monk, armed with a stick, keeps the hungry vultures at a workable distance. The flesh is first thrown to the birds. The pounded bones, mixed with some baked flour, are given later.

A learned priest, known as the Guide (*lam-tön*), is also engaged. He accompanies the corpse to the ground, but sits apart from the place where the body is cut up. It is his duty to show the way to the disembodied one. Such a priest will belong to the sect—Yellow Hat, Red Hat, or other—in which the deceased has felt the strongest belief. 'When these two helpers cannot be engaged,' says a landed proprietor, who holds the position of *Dzong-pön*, 'the deceased undoubtedly has a harder time.' Now and again, but very seldom, a high lama may receive a vision of the *Bar-do* stage before his death.

The ice lies thick on the streams meandering through the Lhasa plain as you ride across it on a sunny winter morning, and lies still thicker as you enter the darkening valley which comes down by the great Se-ra Monastery. Near the junction on your left you may see a large stone slab, even now surrounded by vultures, for here is one of the places where corpses are broken up and distributed.

The Tibetans, following the Hindus, believe that the human body is composed of four elements, namely, earth, fire, water, and air, and that on death it should return to its origin. Burial gives the body to earth, cremation to fire, the rivers to water. Feeding the birds gives the body to

the air. The fifth method, embalming, is reserved for a
few: it will be described presently.

A young king of Sikkim died in December 1914. I
was at that time on my way back from a visit to Nepal,
but was able to reach Gangtok, the capital of Sikkim, in
time for the funeral. We British residents in this beautiful
little country attended at a chosen spot on the march of
the *cortège*, to offer our last tributes of respect.

Unlike Lhasa and Tibet generally, Western influence
had already made itself somewhat felt at this funeral. For
Sikkim is a State under the protection of the British Government. A few Europeans live there and many visit it.
And so the procession was preceded not only by men
bearing sacred pictures (*tang-ka*), and by priests, but also
by the dead man's ponies and by his orderlies carrying
rifles reversed. A coffin was borne on bamboo poles under
a canopy covered with silk hangings. My wife and I had
sent a wreath to the palace that morning; it was carried
on the top of the canopy.

When the coffin reached us we each offered a scarf of
ceremony to Barmiak, the Councillor of State who accompanied the procession. He placed it by the canopy, telling
the spirit of the deceased who had presented it to him.
The detachment of the 113th Indian infantry, then
stationed at Gangtok, furnished a Guard of Honour.

Bhutan and Sikkim enjoy a warmer climate than Tibet.
They enjoy also the abundant rainfall that drenches the
mountain sides of the eastern Himalaya and promotes the
growth of vigorous forests. The necessary fuel being thus
available, cremation is general in these countries.

The laws enacted by the Rulers of Bhutan have something
to say on the subject of funeral rites. In the History[1] we read:

'There is a custom of slaying many animals [2] for the performance
of funeral ceremonies. Now this is good neither for the living nor
for the dead. It is therefore enacted that henceforth during the
cremation rite the priests who preside should receive white food

---

[1] Lho-hi Chö-jung, folio 112.   [2] e.g. cattle and pigs.

only.[1] If this be done, the State's fee, which used to consist of the head of an animal and one of its quarters, may be commuted for the payment of half a *tang-ka*.[2] The head priest's fee may be commuted for a roll of cloth.[3]

'But if the person concerned cannot afford the white food meals, he must in any case give the share due to the deceased as well as to the State and the head priest. For the other priests in lieu of the meat which they should have received he may offer four handfuls of rice, or the same value in cloth if preferred.

'If it is absolutely necessary to kill an animal for the purpose, he may kill one and one only.'

We see here the constant fight that is waged by the more ardent spirits in the priesthood of Tibetan lands to restrain the taking of life. The fight is difficult, for a cold climate cries for animal food. And animals are plentiful, while vegetables are scarce. Still, much can be done with milk, butter, and cheese.

There is worldly wisdom, too, in this law. For, if the monasteries enforced it, the presents thus collected would remove the need of giving them the large measure of State aid which they must otherwise receive.

It is prescribed also that the funeral ceremony must be performed where the death occurred, and not in any other place. The cremation must be done within not less than one day in summer and two days in winter. Should the priests delay, the ceremony must be performed at the monastery, and not at the home of the deceased.

The law which I have quoted refers to the food set aside for the dead man. This, in Bhutan, is always necessary, until the funeral ceremony has been completed. Oil with rice or other grain may be set on a plate as provisions for his journey to the next world. These are poured on the corpse while it is burnt.

So says the Bhutanese History. But in central Tibet it is only lamas who are cremated, and food is not set before the deceased, whether he be priest or layman.

---

[1] Cheese, butter, rice, vegetables, &c.

[2] A *tang-ka* is worth about three pence now, but was probably worth more in those days.   [3] Worth perhaps eight to ten shillings.

In an earlier chapter [1] we have seen that a rich person may spend a large sum in the hope of securing thereby a better rebirth for husband or other relative. The ceremonies performed at funerals are intended to purify the deceased from all evil *karma*, or, as we should say, to cleanse him from his sins. And on the death of a king or other rich man presents may be distributed. An instance of a king's gifts to his subjects is recorded in the History of Sikkim compiled by King To-tup Nam-gyal and his queen. Money, cloth, and salt were apportioned to the subjects on a set scale, and especially to the priests.

I have enumerated the four ordinary methods of treatment applied to the bodies of the dead. The fifth, and last, must be briefly described.

Embalming has long been practised in Tibet, though it is not common. Mr. Teichman, who travelled in eastern Tibet, relates that he 'never came across a mummied lama' there.[2] But the histories record instances of embalming from time to time, and I have myself seen two or three mummies in central Tibet.

In the Blue Record can be read the life-story of a Tibetan priest, named 'The Eagle Clan Yogi Adept', who lived about the tenth century A.D. He was embalmed when he died, and preserved in an urn of gold and silver.[3] The body of another noted priest was, at his own request, embalmed—instead of being cremated—and placed within a silver *chö-ten* facing eastwards.[4] When Sö-nam Gya-tso, the Dalai Lama who introduced Tibetan Buddhism among the Mongols, died,

'In memory of his body his portrait was painted on cloth, in memory of his speech one copy of the Kan-gyur was printed in gold letters, and in memory of his mind a silver tomb thirteen cubits in length was built by the people.' [5]

[1] See p. 85.
[2] *Travels in Eastern Tibet*, by Eric Teichman (Cambridge University Press), p. 84.
[3] Tep-ter Ngön-po, vol. ix, folio 4.   [4] Ibid., vol. viii, folio 57.
[5] Folio 105 of the book entitled 'The Biography of the Reverend Omniscient Sö-nam Gya-tso, like a Chariot in the Ocean'.

A Dharma Raja of Bhutan, who disturbed the embalmed body of his earliest predecessor, fell into various calamities, and these were ascribed to the disturbance and consequent displeasure of the guardian deities.[1]

The early kings of Tibet were embalmed and placed in tombs. History records that the last tomb was built for the son of King Lang-dar-ma.[2] And this may well be so, for Lang-dar-ma was himself the last king who ruled over the whole country.

Nowadays embalming is reserved for very high lamas and the members of the two or three noble families that can trace their descent for a thousand years and more right back to the days of these early kings, themselves regarded as Incarnations of the Buddha. 'Such embalming stamps a man as divine (kön-chok),' says a Tibetan friend, 'for the sacred fire (chö-me) is offered to him henceforth'.

The body of a lama, so embalmed, is, like the relics of cremated lamas, placed inside a clay vessel, shaped like a chö-ten, and covered with silver. There are many of these in or near Lhasa. From the time of the fifth, most of the Dalai Lamas have mausolea in the Potala. These are covered with gold.

Twenty miles north of Lhasa beyond a mountain range lies the Pem-po Valley. Dry though Tibet is, when we visited this valley in August we found it, ten miles wide in places, as green as any plain could be. It has an ancient history, and is mentioned on the obelisk, which stands at the foot of the Potala.

We stayed in the old monastery known as 'Elephant Plain' (Lang Tang), and were accommodated in the original building, known as the Root Monastery, which was erected during the twelfth century of our era.

The following morning, before starting for our next camp, we visited the old original chapel of "Elephant Plain'. A heavy door in the wall of the Assembly Hall was unlocked and pushed open. The original wooden pillars, said to be of poplar (ja-pa), that support the roof, were

[1] Lho-hi Chö-jung, folio 62.   [2] Fifth Dalai Lama's History, folio 46.

still standing in the chapel, helped by an extra pillar or two, for the roof is heavy.

On the farther wall was the mummy of an Indian teacher of religion, who lived over a thousand years ago. His name was 'Holy Buddha' (*Tam-pa Sang-gye*). He is a highly revered figure in Tibetan annals and is mentioned at length in the Blue Record as receiving instruction from early Indian teachers, and evolving a new doctrine named 'The Pain Neutralizer', designed to uplift those who, from evil actions in past lives, were in pain, or poverty or other state of woe. Tradition avers that he lived for a very long time.

A wooden frame covered the lower part of the body. The mummy-like wrappings protruded from it, the old, old cloth still showing faintly the check which divided it into squares, with sides of about three-fourths of an inch in length.

The tombs in which embalmed bodies rest are known as 'Red Tombs' (*mar-tung*). Those containing the ashes are known as 'Body Tombs' (*ku-tung*). But here we saw the mummy itself.

For embalming purposes, salt, known as 'corpse salt', is rubbed in. 'This draws out', says my informant, 'the body juices. The body dries up and is built out again with clay, being fashioned and painted after the likeness of the deceased.'

There is another Red Tomb at Lhün-trup Dzong, north of the Pem-po Valley, thirty miles from Lhasa. We passed near it on our way to 'Tiger's Prophecy' (Ta-lung) and 'Uplifted Horn' (Re-ting), the great monasteries— till then unvisited by white men—whose high priests governed as kings in the old days before the Dalai Lamas.

The year before our visit a miracle had happened. The people were rebuilding the *Dzong*, then almost in ruins. Close to it was a *chö-ten*, enclosing the embalmed body of the mother of him who had rebuilt Ta-lung Monastery when destroyed by fire. So the priest summoned the local deity after the manner of Oracles and told him that they were going to repair the *chö-ten* also. But the answer came, 'Leave it alone'.

Soon afterwards the house, in which the *chö-ten* was kept, fell down. The *chö-ten* itself was broken, the corpse was uncovered and went tumbling down the hill-side, four hundred feet, rolling over and over. When the people went to look at it, they were astonished to find that not only was the corpse uninjured, except for a cut near one of the ankles, but that the flesh on the body was as fresh as during the lady's lifetime. They found, too, that it was pure flesh, and not built up with clay, as is the regular practice. The body was carried up the hill again and is encased now in a fresh *chö-ten*. All believe this story with the single-minded devotion to their religion that characterizes the Tibetan. They believe also that when the body was placed in the *chö-ten*, the cut would gradually heal up, as the lady was 'like a manifestation of the Buddha'.

The religion of the Lepchas of Sikkim resembles in many ways the pre-Buddhist faith of Tibet, known as *Pön*. As to their funeral ceremonies the History of Sikkim says:

'When a person dies and a funeral ceremony has to be performed, it is done thus: They sacrifice a bull or cow, a fowl or pig, and believe that this is the present of the deceased to the spirits of his ancestors. For this purpose they slay a pig, and, having pierced the entire length of its body with a sharpened bamboo stake, the *Pön-pön* recites some prayers or incantations called *Pön* for three days and nights.'

The Lepchas believe that their spirits are taken after death through subterranean passages to the local deities of Kinchinjunga [1]—the highest mountain in Sikkim and the third highest in the world—as well as to those of other mountains. Different sub-tribes among the Lepchas have different subterranean passages.

But Buddhism, after the Tibetan pattern, is firm set in Sikkim. And therefore many Lepchas nowadays resort to Buddhist rites. As in Tibet throughout the centuries,

---

[1] The pronunciation usual among Europeans. The correct pronunciation is *Kang Chen Dzö Nga*, 'The Five Treasuries of Great Snow'.

and as in Mongolia since Sö-nam Gya-tso conducted his campaign of conversion and reform, so in Sikkim also Buddhism is steadily pushing out the older faith. One of my Lepcha servants died, leaving no children, brothers or sisters, but a widow only. The other Lepchas in my employ at once subscribed one rupee each for a lama to perform the funeral ceremonies.

In Tibet there is a funeral hymn, ascribed, as are so many other writings, to King Song-tsen Gam-po. It portrays the sorrows of old age, the pains of death, the four kinds of funeral, the terrors of the Judgement, and ends on a note of repentance. It is too long to quote in full, but I should like to give the three concluding verses. My translation is no doubt a bald one, but it expresses the Tibetan original with fair accuracy.

> Gone is all the wealth he gathered, snapped
>   up by whoever can;
> But the sins he gathered in the taking of
>   that wealth remain.
> So by dreadful myrmidons he 's led before the
>   Lord of Death.
> Come thou down, most precious Lama, come and
>   thy protection give!
> From life's endless round
>   deliver, highest, mightiest Chen-re-si!
>
> Falling down th' abyss into the three great
>   Regions of the Damned,
> Feeling nothing fixed, but driven like a
>   feather by the wind,
> Powerless along the cliffside path that
>   down the *Bar-do* runs.
> Come thou down, most precious Lama, &c.
>
> Youth with rising powers has passed
>   regardless of the Holy Faith;
> Now in life's declining years I put
>   aside all slothfulness.
> Grant that I may thus go forward steadfast
>   while this life shall last.

Come thou down, most precious Lama, come and
        thy protection give!
From life's endless round deliver,
        highest, mightiest Chen-re-si! [1]
Om ma-ni pe-me hum hri.

Death and the Judgement of the dead, these are there.
But they do not end all. As I have said in the beginning
of this chapter, they are to the Tibetan but links in the
chain of his lives. Meanwhile he must pass through the
'Between the Two' (*Bar-do*), the state between death and
rebirth. And so it is for the lama to show him the way
through: that is looked on as the chief object of the funeral
rites.

It may be that he will have to pass on to a lower world,
even to one of the hells, of which there are several, both
hot and cold. These, the first insistent danger, must be
avoided, if possible, by a good life, a life in accordance
with religion, and by the prayers and offerings of relatives
after his death.

The hope of the ordinary Tibetan, man or woman, is to
return soon to this earth with opportunities for following
a religious life. And to return as a man, for woman is the
'lower birth'. Very common among all Tibetans of both
sexes is the prayer:

> Grant that I may be reborn in a man's body;
> And that I may meet the Holy Religion.

He cannot yet dare to hope for 'Sorrow Passed Away',[2]
the heights of the Buddhas and Bodhisattvas far beyond
his ken. Birth and death and birth again. For him the
Wheel of Life goes on and on.

Meanwhile, he hopes to be in the world, but not of the
world. Riches and honour make up the little happiness;
they do but bring anxiety; one can lose one or the other.

---

[1] In the Tibetan original each of the first four lines has nine syllables and the
fifth line has ten. But Tibetan, being more condensed than English, can hardly
be rendered without extra length.

[2] *Nya-ngen-de*, the Tibetan term for Nirvana.

Who has greater cares than a king? The war may go against him; sickness and poverty may afflict his subjects.

And so his eyes turn towards the far-distant goal, to be gained by slow degrees, the goal of Buddhahood, the Great Happiness. In the Round of Existence there is no peace.

> The round of lives is like a needle's point;
> Can you be happy, when transfixed thereon?
> Who loves the little happiness, can ne'er
> Gain the Great Happiness, that ends it all.

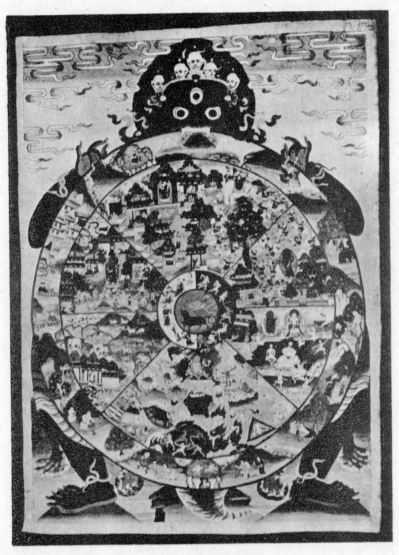

The Wheel of Life

APPENDIX I

The Unit of Land Taxation

THE rental of land, whether paid by the tenant to the landlord, or by the landlord to the Government, is based on the *kang*. Each *kang* is an area of land, to sow which a certain quantity of seed is required. This seed-quantity is apparently the same throughout each estate, but varies in different estates, and averages about 40 *ke*.[1] In those parts of an estate where the soil is good, seed is sown more closely than in poor soil. So in the former the *kang* will be smaller in area, in the latter larger.

But in different districts the *kang* may vary greatly. It is small in the poor soil of Pa-ri, large in the more fertile lands round Gyangtse; an indication that the Gyangtse *kang* contains four or five times the seed capacity of its namesake at Pa-ri.

Each *kang* throughout an estate pays the same amount of cash, grain, and supply of transport and porters. Therefore in each estate the taxation of the cultivator depends not on his general prosperity as was the old custom in Sikkim. Nor on the number of members in his household, as was the former system in Bhutan. Nor yet on the area of his land, which latter consideration fixes the main taxation of the cultivator in India at the present day. But solely on the amount of seed which is required for the sowing of his land. Of two families, one may be better off than the other, owning more ponies, mules, yaks, &c., but if their lands are such as to take the same amount of seed, their taxation will be the same. The Tibetan system, in its method though not in its amount of taxation, approximates to that introduced into Sikkim during the closing years of the nineteenth century.

[1] A measure containing about thirty-three lb. of barley or peas and seventeen lb. of barley-flour.

APPENDIX II

The Ser-chok Estate

THIS estate, which was leased by the Tibetan Government for some years to Ku-sho Pa-lhe-se, has its head-quarters at Gyangtse.

Pa-lhe-se, being absent on duty with me, employed an agent (*Chan-dzö*) to look after it. In lieu of pay the *Chan-dzö* received a piece of land worth £90 a year.

Under the *Chan-dzö* were:

(*a*) The *Lang*, whose income was largely derived from presents given to him by the tenants, worth in the aggregate perhaps £15 yearly. He had to collect the rents, and occasionally to settle disputes among the tenantry, but the bulk of these were decided by the *Chan-dzö*, and important cases by the landlord himself.

(*b*) The *Tso-pön*. He received a plot of land worth £11 a year, and presents from the tenants under him, averaging £4 a year. His work was the provision of free transport, both porters and animals (ponies, donkeys, yaks, &c.), to authorized Government travellers, the collection of such rents as the *Lang* did not realize, and the settlement of petty disputes.

(*c*) The headmen (*Gem-pos*), of whom there were ten under the *Lang* with five or six hundred households of tenants in the aggregate. The rent of these was paid mostly to the Dzong-pön, but they were included in the Ser-chok estate and Pa-lhe-se was responsible for the settlement of disputes.

Apart from these there were sixteen pieces of home lands scattered here and there in the estate, and containing about a hundred farms. These belonged to the landlord. He managed them through one headman with sixteen assistants. The produce of such farms belonged to the landlord. Those who cultivated them for the landlord received in lieu of wages separate rent-free grants of land.

The estate also owned scattered lands in other districts. These paid the landlord mainly in grain, and to a smaller extent in butter, wool, carcases of sheep, and money.

The estate paid revenue to the Tibetan Government and to the

chief monastery at Gyangtse (Pal-kor Chö-de) approximately as
follows:

I. *Government revenue paid by tenants through the Lang to the
    Dzong.*

This was paid chiefly in sheep's carcases, of which about five
hundred were given; as well as in butter and wool. And about two
hundred pounds in money.

Also transport by animals and men (*tau* and *ula*).

II. *Government revenue paid by home lands of landlord.*
    Cash, equal to about two hundred pounds sterling.
    60 *ke* of barley-flour.
    550 *ke* of barley.

The landlord had also to supply one complete copy of the Kan-
gyur every three years, written by hand, to the Government. For
this he employed sixteen writers and one superintendent. These
also made the covers for the sacred volumes, the wood for the purpose being sent by Pa-ri Dzong and the Kam-pu Valley, near Pa-ri.

III. *Revenue paid by home lands to Pal-kor Chö-de Monastery.*
     This is met as far as possible from IV below.
     15,000 *ke* of barley.
     2,000 *kel* [1] of butter.
       200 carcases of sheep.
        50 boxes of tea.
     Mustard oil for burning in lamps.
     Firewood.

IV. *Landlord's income.*
    From the home lands and the land in other districts.
    20,000 *ke* of barley.
     1,000 *kel* of butter.
       500 *kel* of wool.
       500 carcases of sheep.
    Cash, and rents from some tenants for lands let out on rent, might
        total £250.
    Rents from grazing-grounds and profits from cattle let out on
        the 'No birth, no death' contract,[2] might total £100.
    Profits on 1,500 sheep and 200 goats, for which a fee of one *sho*
        each has to be paid yearly to the Government.

---

    [1] A weight of about 6 or 7 lb.   [2] See p. 25.

It will be understood that the above figures are only approximate. Out of his profits the landlord has to maintain a large number of servants for work on the estate at a cost of about £600. Certain offerings to other monasteries and priests are morally incumbent on him, and these will absorb about £150. But on the other side of the account he gains further profit by employing the tenants' *tau* and *ula* on his own affairs, whether trading transactions or domestic necessities.

The tenants' rents on the Ser-chok estate are somewhat lower than those on the Drong-tse estate, because the former originally belonged to a monastery, while the latter was always the property of a layman. In Sikkim also I noticed the same tendency. The rents on monastic estates were usually lower than the rents on those owned by the laity.

BIBLIOGRAPHY

BELOW is given an explanatory list of those books that seem best to illustrate the secular life of the Tibetans. This, it is hoped, will be more helpful than a long uncharted list of books, varying in scope, interest, and trustworthiness.

BELL, SIR CHARLES, *Tibet Past and Present*. (Clarendon Press, 1924.) Second Impression 1926. Cheap Edition 1927.

Gives a *résumé* of early Tibetan history, a full narrative of modern political events, and an account of Tibet's relations with China, Japan, Russia, Mongolia, and Nepal. Affords sidelights on Tibetan customs, especially those of the leaders of society.

—— *Grammar of Colloquial Tibetan*. Second Edition. (Bengal Secretariat Book Depot, Writers Buildings, Calcutta, 1919.)

Describes the language spoken in central Tibet, and the customs in conversation. Gives a little further information showing how dates are reckoned, money and goods counted up, &c.

COMBE, G. A., *A Tibetan on Tibet*. (Fisher Unwin, 1926.)

An eastern Tibetan describes his journey in Tibet, and gives a variety of information.

DAS, S. C., *Journey to Lhasa and Central Tibet*. (Murray, 1902.)

The author, a Bengali, spoke Tibetan. He travelled in disguise, but gives much information, generally accurate.

—— 'Early History of Tibet' (*Journal of the Asiatic Society of Bengal*, 1881, pp. 211–45).

Compiled from Tibetan historical works.

DAVID-NEEL, ALEXANDRA, *My Journey to Lhasa*. (Heinemann, 1927.)

The authoress, a Frenchwoman, speaks Tibetan and has much knowledge of Buddhism. Travelling, however, disguised as a beggar, her opportunities were limited.

FRANCKE, A. H., *A History of Western Tibet*. (Partridge, 1907.)

A scholarly, trustworthy book.

HEDIN, SVEN, *Trans-Himalaya*. (Macmillan, 1909.)

A long work, mainly geographical, travel, and adventure. Vividly written and illustrated.

HUC, *Travels in Tartary, Tibet, and China*. (Kegan Paul, 1898.) Translated into English by W. Hazlitt.

Shows life in Tibet in 1846, as it appeared to two French Lazarist missionaries. A classic among books of travel; most delightful to read. The writer is over-credulous at times, but the information is usually accurate.

KAWAGUCHI, EKAI, *Three Years in Tibet*. (Theosophical Publishing Society, London, 1909.)

The Tibetans as seen through Japanese spectacles. The author is, perhaps, too stern a critic, but, being an Oriental scholar and a Buddhist, who has resided in Tibet, has a great grasp of the subject.

MARKHAM, SIR CLEMENTS, *Bogle and Manning*. (Trübner, 1879.)

Tibet and Lhasa as they appeared to the first English visitors during the end of the eighteenth and the early years of the nineteenth century.

O'CONNOR, CAPT. (now Sir) W. F., *Folk Tales from Tibet*. (Hurst and Blackett, 1906.)

A charming selection of Tibetan fables, fairy tales, &c., illustrated in colour by a Tibetan artist.

RIN-CHEN LHA-MO, *We Tibetans*. (Seeley Service, 1926.)

The only book on Tibet by a Tibetan woman. Describes the daily life, food, houses, dress, priests, women, children, &c., emphasizing the Tibetan point of view as regards some of those features which have been attacked by Western writers.

ROCKHILL, W. W., *The Land of the Lamas*. (Longmans, Green, 1891.)

A journey through eastern Tibet. The scholarly American author wrote with understanding, and seldom erred.

—— *The Dalai Lamas of Lhasa*. (Oriental Printing Office, Leyden, 1910.)

Gives the history of these from about A.D. 1400 to the present day. Carefully compiled.

—— *Notes on the Ethnology of Tibet*. (Based on the collection in the National Museum, U.S.A., 1895.)

Categorical descriptions, accompanied by accurate illustrations, of Tibetan dress, houses, religious and secular implements, &c.

TEICHMAN, E., *Travels of a Consular Officer in Eastern Tibet*. (Cambridge University Press, 1922.)

Narrates the fighting in eastern Tibet between the Chinese and Tibetans from 1905 to 1917, and the political conditions in that country. Accurate and clear.

WADDELL, L. A., *Lhasa and its Mysteries*. (John Murray, 1905.)

Describes the British military expedition to Lhasa in 1904, showing the Tibetans at war.

WESSELS, C., *Early Jesuit Travellers in Central Asia*. (Martinus Nijhoff, The Hague, 1924.)

An account of the travels of some of the early European explorers. Tells us a little about the Tibetans of those days.

INDEX

A-chuk Tse-ring, 221.

Aconite, 23, 24.

Actors, peasants often become, 61; beer given to, 242.

Adultery, laws against, in Bhutan, 195.

Agricultural Department created, 58.

Almora, 113.

Altar described, 71, 108.

Amban, Chinese, x, 281.

Am-do, 45, 46, 143; pilgrims from 123; Am-do-was in Lhasa, 142.

Amrita pills, living on, 234.

Arbours, wayside, in Sikkim, 258, 259.

Archery, 75, 81, 96, 271, 284.

Archimedes, mentioned in Tibetan book, 209.

Army, enmity between, and priesthood, 144.

Astrologers, 210, 286.

Atisha, 15, 36, 164, 290.

Auspicious days, 179, 180, 183, 184, 210, 257; auspicious hours, 277; eight auspicious signs, 228, 239.

Ba and *sho*, games of, 170, 171, 229, 265, 266.

Babies, how buried, 289.

Baby carried in a box when travelling, 197.

Bang-gye-shar house, 69, 93, 268.

Barbers, Chinese, 129.

Bar-do state, 286, 291, 299.

Bargaining, method of, 111, 112.

Barley, 26, 30, 34, 51; when reaped, 39; threshing of, in Chumbi Valley, 41; in Sikkim, 42.

Barley-beer, 96, 173.

Barley-flour, 223, 225.

Barmiak Lama, 292.

Ba-tang, women of, wear one plait, 147.

Beer, how made, 241; offered to the gods, 181; drunk in Tsang, 235; given to actors, 241, 242; drunk at picnics and archery, 265, 267, 271;

offered to Ya-sö, 275; at 'Gallop behind the Fort', 282; beer jugs, 242, 276; 'begging beer' ceremony, 179, 183, 184.

Beggars, 132-9; professional and hereditary, in Tibet, 132; form of address used by, 134, 135; on the Sacred Way in Lhasa, 135; shelters for, outside Lhasa, 137; in Northern India, 208; beggar who claimed to have risen from the dead, 138; beggar fiddlers, 136, 275.

Bell, Mr. (now Sir Charles), makes land settlement of the Kalimpong district, 211; goes to Bhutan to negotiate treaty, 56, 225; at Gyangtse during harvest, 41; met by officials when travelling, 252, 254; congratulated on birth of son, 254, 255; receives *ka-tas* on being made C.M.G., 248, 249; at funeral of Maharaja of Sikkim, 292; meets Do-ring Ku-sho, 91; lunches with Do-ring Ku-sho, 98-101; visits Drong-tse, 76; Dalai Lama's presents to, 220; visits Dor-je Pa-mo, 166; in Lhasa, 31, 45, 123; exchanges *ka-tas* with the Dalai Lama, 250; lunches with Ku-sho Ne-tö, 60; sees Sacred Dagger, 92; visits Lha-lu house, 78; dines with Commander-in-Chief in Lhasa, 157; receives deputation urging him to remain in Lhasa, 251, 252; at New Year festivities in Lhasa, 272-84; gives theatrical entertainment in Lhasa, 171, 229, 241; stays at Talung monastery, 219; visits Re-ting monastery, 26, 40, 53, 126; Tibetan view of Bell Mission, 262.

Bhutan, 5, 32; brigands in, 145; castles in, 50; crops and fruit in, 32; funeral rites in, 292, 293; history of, 55; houses in, 50; laws against adultery in, 195; Maharaja of, 126, 254; late Maharaja of, 57, 145;

Poison, cups that detect, 239, 240.
Polo, 263.
Polyandry, 29, 159, 192–4.
Polygamy, 192.
Pom-da-tsang, 130.
Pön religion, 10, 12, 184, 186, 297.
Ponies, 53, 98; from Sīnīng, 122, 123.
Porters, loads distributed among, by
garter, 160.
Potala, 135, 281; built, 12; rebuilt, 16;
hail not allowed to fall on, 44.
Prayer flags, 51, 133, 134, 137.
Prayer wheels, 77, 136.
Prayers, children's, 202; fastened to
yaks, 23.
Praying-room at Drong-tse, 75.
Presents, exchanged, 248; how de-
scribed, 261; petitioners', 250; to
travellers, 253, 254; when calling,
257, 258.
Priest who gave up all solid food, 234.
Priest-kings, early, 15.
Priests, administrative posts given to,
64; check on upper classes, 109;
dress of, 21; duties of, at death-beds,
285, 286; education of, as boys,
199; embalmed, 294; hair shaved,
198; married, 189, 190, 191; smok-
ing forbidden among, 243.
Prime Minister, 82.
Pronunciation of Tibetan words, viii,
x.
Prophetesses, 169.
Proverbs, 4, 38, 211, 212.
Pün-kang family, 66, 81.
Putting the weight, 269.

Queen, early, 161.

Rab-den Lepcha, 168.
Races, popularity of, 269, 270; during
Great Prayer Festival, 276–80.
Ra-gyap-pas, 137, 138, 290.
Rain, services to produce, 37; story
of Uncle Töm-pa and, 37, 38.
Rainfall, 7.
Ra-ka-shar family, 66, 84; incarna-
tions in, 90; rik of, 95.
Ral-pa-chan, King, 13, 14.
Ra-lang monastery, 286.
Ra-lung monastery, 182, 183.

Ra-mo-che Prayer Festival, 161.
Rank, how indicated when sitting,
261.
Reading, teaching of, 204.
Rebirth, ceremony to secure good,
85, 294.
Red Hat sect, 13; marriage allowed
in, 190; smoking forbidden to, 244.
Religion, importance of, to Tibetans,
26, 210.
Religious disputations, 244.
— services, when held, 164.
Rent, how fixed, 36; how paid, 83,
128.
Re-ting monastery, 52, 189, 296;
'Holder of the Keys' at, 26; 'Holder
of the Keys' goes to Mongolia to
trade, 126; peasant graziers near,
26; ro-lang (standing corpse) at,
138; reaping near, 40; trade of, 126;
visit to, 126.
Revenue in coin and kind, 83.
Rhubarb smoked, 244.
Rice, where grown, 32; imported, 118,
225; rats attack, 48; fried with
honey, 225.
Rik, 95.
Rin-chen-ling, private nunnery at,
108.
Ring worn on left thumb by men, 153.
Rivers, 6.
Rockhill, W. W., on use of boots as
medium of exchange, 128; on posi-
tion of women, 156; on polyandry,
192, 193.
Rong, 2.
Roofs, flat, 50, 51.
Rosaries, 154, 155.
Rouge pads, 149.
Rugs, Tibetan, 129; factory for
making, 117.
Russia, influence of, in Tibet, 17;
silk from, 130.

St. Andrew's Colonial Homes, 113.
Saints who left no physical body behind, 133.
Sa-kya monastery, 15.
Salt, 110, 116, 125, 128; imported
from Nepal, 118; where obtained,
3, 222; salt lakes, 3.